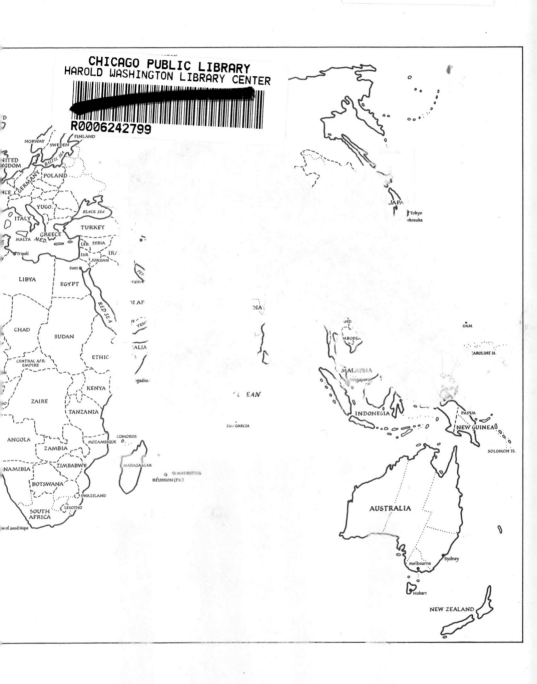

FIRST LINE OF DEFENSE

FIRST LINE OF DEFENSE

The U.S. Navy Since 1945

Paul B. Ryan

HOOVER INSTITUTION PRESS
Stanford University, Stanford, California

PHOTO CREDITS

All photographs with the exception of numbers 2 and 3 are courtesy of
the U.S. Navy. Photographs 2 and 3 are courtesy of the U.S. Naval
Historical Center.

Hoover Press Publication 237

Designed by Elizabeth Gehman

Contents

Tables and Figures

Foreword

When Pericles observed that the art of seamanship "allows one no spare time for anything else," he hit squarely on the dilemma facing professional seamen in democratic states from the birthplace of democracy, his own classical Athens, down to the United States of Paul Ryan's period of study, our own time. Naval officers have always become admirals primarily because of their artistry as ship commanders and not because of political, diplomatic, or even strategic acumen. This is as it should be, for navies demand an expertise gained only by long experience at sea.

Thus, when the U.S. Navy faced the complex political, diplomatic, and strategic demands of the cold war world after 1945, its leaders—weaned on preparing for and executing a fairly traditional naval war against Germany and especially Japan—were ill prepared for the challenge. And yet, the professional statesmen and generals were no better off. So, what I regard as the "world wars generation" had to educate itself about the new realities and to do it while on the job. Mistakes were inevitable, made as they were out of ignorance—ignorance of alternative policies and methods, of the limits of technology, and of precedents, which is to say, history.

Had America's naval (and political and military) leaders been schooled in the sweep of world history and strategy since the age of Pericles or even since 1776 rather than on the short episodes of this country's own brief and discontinuous wars, they would have been mentally prepared to understand the efforts by Soviet Russia to fill the political vacuums left by the collapse of Nazi Germany and imperial Japan as well as of British and French hegemony. The final education, however, took place in the 35 years or so after 1945, a process ably chronicled for the first time in this book.

The Navy had always maintained that it was the first line of defense, which indeed it had been—with no small help from the British—all the way from the 1790s to 1945, and which it has since continued to be (except for the brief interlude of the manned strategic bomber, about 1945–1960). The measure of this line, however, has always eluded precise definition, particularly in the post-1945 era of immense sociopolitical and technological complexities. For lack of anything more tangible, the yardstick has remained the ships themselves (with their guns, missiles, and airplanes). The trouble has arisen over the proper roles and missions of this expensive hardware, a debate carefully presented here by Captain Ryan.

Historical parallels are always dangerous, simply because history never repeats itself precisely, and yet historical examples must be invoked if American leaders are to break away from a nagging feeling of being isolated from the past, of a hopeless ignorance and lack of guidelines. Knowledge of what naval (and national) leaders of major powers did in earlier times will assist the present leadership to develop a much needed sense of perspective as policymakers and as managers on a level with the civilians who resumed their pre−World War II control after 1945.

The closest parallel with the third of a century covered in this fine book is the international and naval balance and races of the third-century preceding World War I, roughly 1880−1914.

Great Britain had since 1815 been using its Navy both to deter major war in Europe and to police the sea-lanes of the world on which its prosperity and indeed its democracy rested. The agent of its deterrence (a passive presence) was its battleship fleet; that of its policing (an active role), its gunboats. The former, glamorous and obvious, demanded the major share of the defense budget and the closest civilian control. The latter, unseen and unheralded, was administered at the distant tactical level by naval officers in remote seas. In the 1880s Germany began to challenge this supremacy, ultimately with battleships but only marginally with gunboats and colonial troops. The resulting bitter disputes in Britain between First Lord Churchill and Admiral Fisher far exceeded in intensity, for example, the similar struggle between Defense Secretary McNamara and Admiral Anderson, treated herein.

As Captain Ryan's story unfolds, a striking parallel emerges between the above case and America's passive deterrent force of the *Polaris* submarine missile fleet and the active policing role of the aircraft carriers and amphibious units. The great difficulty has been in learning to manage both under a single system of administration and control, the one demanding tight strictures of the "Supermac" type to avoid a nuclear holocaust, the other requiring tactical flexibility in the very real limited wars that the Navy has been fighting around the world since 1945. Of course, the roles often overlap and always defy simple solutions, but throughout the gnashing of teeth the Navy has remained the first line, and the public is being educated, however imperfectly.

Identifying our enemies and appraising their intentions has become the business of nearly everybody—the Departments of State and Defense, the Congress, the National Security Council, the Joint Chiefs, the CIA, think tanks, universities, and pundits—while the military has had to focus primarily on our enemies' actual capabilities. In the case of the Soviet enemy, however, these investigators would do well to ask whether Russia's Mahan (as Ryan calls him), Admiral Gorshkov, can overcome the inherent problems and weaknesses also faced by his continental predecessors who tried and failed to build and wield superior navies within authoritarian, army-dominated dictatorships: Colbert under Louis XIV, Napoleon's admirals, Tirpitz under Kaiser Wilhelm II, Makarov under Tsar Nicholas II, Raeder under Hitler, and Yamamoto under Tojo.

The Navy and its managers must, ultimately, serve the elected and appointed officials of our republic, and both must continue to patiently educate the other in their respective areas of expertise. What the Navy of this maritime nation is helping to defend also, of course, is the capitalist system of free enterprise, which includes not only the shipbuilding and shipping industries but the future of their technology and of American technology in general.

Midway through the period studied by Captain Ryan emerged what may well prove to be the Achilles heel of American prosperity and of the viability of the U.S. Navy as it moves toward the twenty-first century, namely, the dependence on oil. Every likelihood exists that our dependence on the internal combustion engine may well bring us down. A technological breakthrough to an alternative source of energy and propulsion, on the other hand, could well erase the Arab threat, restore the American economy, and enable the U.S. Navy to carry out its increasing number of missions more easily in the next century.

Bold thinking and experimentation to achieve such an end were not the rule in the tight management and control of either Defense Department leaders or the Navy in the period examined by Captain Ryan, although boldness did occur in other realms—successfully in the development of the Polaris missile system under Admirals Rickover and Raborn and much less so in the human relations activities of Admiral Zumwalt. Failures of innovation must not discourage civilian, business, and naval leaders from looking for fresh alternatives.

America is superior to the Soviet Union precisely because of its ability to develop and realize new ideas and techniques and to decide which methods of the past to use and which to discard. Attaining the proper mix will not be easy, as this book shows all too well, but its rewards are immense: preserving our very enviable way of life.

CLARK G. REYNOLDS

Preface

The purpose of this book is to present the changing nature of American sea power since the end of World War II and to trace the reasons for this change. My account does not deal solely with fleet operations, but takes note of influences that include national politics, a social revolution, and particularly, a ruinous war in Indochina primarily directed from the White House.

Some readers will note that I have omitted certain naval episodes. The primary reason is that in a relatively short overview of 35 years an appraiser must necessarily be selective. Nevertheless I have tried to portray a historical pattern of domestic events against a background of global developments that, collectively, left the United States in 1980 with a greatly reduced Navy facing a growing Soviet maritime force in some respects superior. As one who wore the naval uniform for over three decades, I make no apologies for approaching this issue from the viewpoint of an insider.

If this work helps to present the role of U.S. sea power on which American national security depends and the necessity for an enlightened people to understand this role, then the author will feel that his labors have not been in vain.

For their generous aid, I am indebted to the many experts who are listed in the Acknowledgments. Any shortcomings, of course, are the responsibility of the author. Finally, the conclusions expressed herein are not to be interpreted as representative of the Navy Department or of the Hoover Institution.

Acknowledgments

I am grateful to the staff of the U.S. Naval War College, particularly for providing research material from its archives.

Professor Thomas A. Bailey, Stanford University; Professor Frederick Hartmann, the U.S. Naval War College; Professor Stephen Jurika, the Naval Postgraduate School; and Dr. Carl A. Amme reviewed the manuscript and, without assuming responsibility, offered valuable comments, some of which were accepted.

My appreciation extends to Admiral Robert B. Carney, Admiral Arleigh A. Burke, Admiral Jerauld Wright, Admiral George W. Anderson, Admiral U. S. Grant Sharp, Vice Admiral Edwin B. Hooper, and Admiral James L. Holloway, III, all retired officers, and to Lieutenant General Victor H. Krulak, USMC (Ret.) for their kindness in allowing lengthy interviews. I was also fortunate in having extended conversations with Vice Admiral James B. Stockdale, USN, and Captain Richard Stratton, USN. Both are naval aviators who were shot down in Vietnam and spent over six years there as prisoners of war.

General information on naval matters was generously provided by Admiral Worth H. Bagley, USN (Ret.); Professor Paolo Coletta, U.S. Naval Academy; Admiral Ralph W. Cousins, USN (Ret.); Vice Admiral William J. Crowe, USN; Admiral Robert L. Dennison, USN (Ret.); Admiral H. D. Felt, USN (Ret.); Rear Admiral S. B. Frankel, USN (Ret.); Rear Admiral N. C. Gillette, USN (Ret.); Vice Admiral John T. Hayward, USN (Ret.); Rear Admiral C. A. Hill, USN (Ret.); Colonel Robert D. Heinl, USMC (Ret.); Admiral John J. Hyland, USN (Ret.); Captain Lionel Krisel, USN (Ret.); Vice Admiral Gerald E. Miller, USN (Ret.); Rear Admiral George H. Miller, USN (Ret.); Rear Admiral Henry L. Miller, USN (Ret.); Admiral Horacio Rivero, USN (Ret.); Admiral James S. Russell; Dr. Paul R. Schratz; Vice Admiral James B. Stockdale, USN (Ret.); Dr. Frank N. Trager of the National Security Information Center, New York City; and Captain F. K. B. Wheeler, USN (Ret.).

The historians, archivists, and librarians of the U.S. Naval Historical Center, Washington, D.C., were most helpful and special thanks are extended to Dr. Dean C. Allard, Barbara Gilmore, Barbara Lynch, Dr. William James Morgan, and J.

E. Vajda. Curator Henry A. Vadnais, Agnes Hoover, and Charles R. Haberlein were highly cooperative in providing photographs. Frances L. Carey of the Naval War College Library was most helpful. Dr. John T. Mason, Director of Oral History, U.S. Naval Institute, was of special assistance.

Technical information and other data were readily supplied by the Naval Chief of Information, Rear Admiral David M. Cooney, and Robert A. Carlisle and Anna Urband of his staff; and Hilja Kukk, Linda Thomas, and Catherine Foster of the Hoover Institution.

I am especially grateful to Betty J. Herring, who not only typed the manuscript but made valuable editing suggestions.

My thanks go also to publications manager Phyllis Cairns, editor John Ziemer, and book designer Elizabeth Gehman, all of the Hoover Institution Press, for their ever ready assistance.

1. Fleet Admiral Chester W. Nimitz, the new Chief of Naval Operations in December 1945, with his predecessor, Fleet Admiral Ernest J. King.

2. Secretary of the Navy James V. Forrestal at the Naval Air Station, Pensacola, Florida, December 1946.

3. President Eisenhower, General Paul Ely, Chairman of the French Joint Chiefs of Staff, and Admiral Arthur W. Radford, USN, Chairman of the Joint Chiefs of Staff, at a White House meeting in late March 1954 to discuss U.S. aid to the French in Indochina.

4. Admiral Thomas B. Hayward, Chief of Naval Operations.

5. Admiral Hyman G. Rickover.

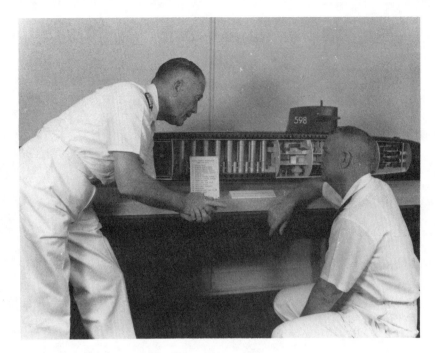

6. Rear Admiral William F. Raborn (left) discusses the operation of the *Polaris* submarine-launched ballistic missile with Admiral Arleigh A. Burke. The cutaway model represents the first nuclear, ballistic submarine *George Washington*

7. Admiral Arleigh A. Burke   8. Vice Admiral William F. Raborn

9. South China Sea, August 1969; Admiral John J. Hyland, Commander-in-Chief Pacific Fleet, and Rear Admiral Ray M. Isaman cross the flight deck of the *Oriskany*.

10. Commander (later Vice Admiral) James B. from Captain Bartholomew J. Connolly III Stockdale subsequently was shot down and cap oners of war, he was awarded the Medal of

13. Admiral Elmo R. Zumwalt, fers with Rear Admiral Robert S. Vietnam, during a helicopter flight

12. Defense Secretary Robert S. McNamara and General Earle G. Wheeler, Chairman of the Joint Chiefs of Staff, at a debriefing of naval pilots on board the *Oriskany* off Vietnam, October 1966. Vice Admiral John J. Hyland, Commander Seventh Fleet, is pictured in center, second row.

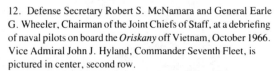

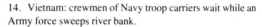

11. At sea . . . a starboard-quarter stern view of the destroyer USS *Elliott*, DD-967, under way.

Stockdale receives the Distinguished Flying Cross in August 1965 on board the carrier *Oriskany*.
tured. For his heroic leadership of American pris-
Honor.

Jr., Chief of Naval Operations, con-
Salzer, Commander Naval Forces,
in Indochina.

14. Vietnam: crewmen of Navy troop carriers wait while an Army force sweeps river bank.

15. Secretary of the Navy W. Graham Claytor at the launching of the nuclear-powered, guided missile cruiser *Arkansas*, Newport News, Virginia, on October 21, 1978.

16. Secretary of the Navy Edward Hidalgo. As Assistant Secretary of the Navy in 1967–1979, he had successfully resolved a bitter legal battle between contractors and the Navy Department over costs and payments.

17. Admiral U. S. Grant Sharp (*left*), Commander-in-Chief Pacific Fleet, shown here at Naha, Okinawa, with Major General John M. Masters, USMC, in November 1963.

18. Defense Secretary Harold Brown has lunch on board the nuclear attack submarine *Narwhal* at Groton, Connecticut, in April 1977.

HARPOON LAUNCH VERSATILITY

SHIP LAUNCH

SUB LAUNCH

19. The Navy's Harpoon missile can be launched from all types of vessels and planes against enemy shipping. It is radar-guided and has a range of over 50 miles.

20. A naval helicopter lifts a load of supplies from the replenishment oiler USS *Wabash* to a nearby ship off the Philippines in August 1974.

21. The nuclear carrier *Eisenhower* under way in the Gulf of Mexico in November 1978.

22. An artist's conception of the sea-control ship, a small carrier of 40,000 tons, designed for the protection of shipping. It would handle conventional and VSTOL (Vertical Short Take-Off, Landing) aircraft.

23. The USS *Iwo Jima*, an amphibious assault ship, under way in the Atlantic in company with an amphibious transport. Landing by "vertical envelopment" using helicopters instead of boats was first initiated by the Marine Corps in 1948.

24. Marines in jeeps ascend by elevator to the flight deck of the amphibious assault ship *Guadalcanal* during a practice assault in 1978.

25. The dawn of the submarine missile age. The submarine *Tunny* with a Regulus I guided missile ready for launch off Point Mugu, California, August 1954.

26. The first *Trident* submarine, the *Ohio*, shown here on a building pier at the Electric Boat Company Yard, Groton, Connecticut, in early 1978. The *Ohio* class boats displace 18,700 tons, are 560 feet long, and are equipped with 24 *Trident* ballistic missiles. The *Ohio* was scheduled for delivery in late 1980.

27. Admiral of the Fleet of the Soviet Union, Sergei Georgi-yevich Gorshkov, Commander-in-Chief of the Soviet Navy and First Deputy Minister of Defense.

28. A Soviet *Yankee* class nuclear, ballistic-missile submarine. The circles amidships are launching tubes for missiles. This type has a surface speed of 25 knots, but can cruise at 30 knots while submerged.

29. The Soviet aircraft carrier *Kiev* under way in the Mediterranean. This 35,000 ton ship can operate ten Forger aircraft and 25 helicopters. The *Kiev* appeared in 1976 and presaged a Soviet carrier navy.

30. The Soviet long-range strike bomber, the Backfire, photographed in July 1978.

31. The Soviet Navy shows that it has mastered the technique of underway replenishment. Here a *Kresta II* class guided-missile cruiser (*top*) and a *Krivak* class guided-missile destroyer refuel west of the Azores in June 1977.

32. A Soviet *Gulf II* class ballistic-missile submarine off Denmark in 1978 is escorted by the U.S. frigate, *Pharris*. The *Pharris* detected the submarine on sonar at a range of 27 miles.

33. A-3 Skywarrior aircraft readied for catapult launch on board the USS *John F. Kennedy*.

34. South China Sea: aviator heads for debriefing after his aircraft's recovery on board the USS *Hancock*.

35. OVERLEAF: A nuclear task group. Three nuclear-powered ships photographed while cruising in the Mediterranean in 1964: the carrier *Enterprise* flanked by the cruiser *Long Beach* (*top*) and destroyer *Bainbridge* (*bottom*).

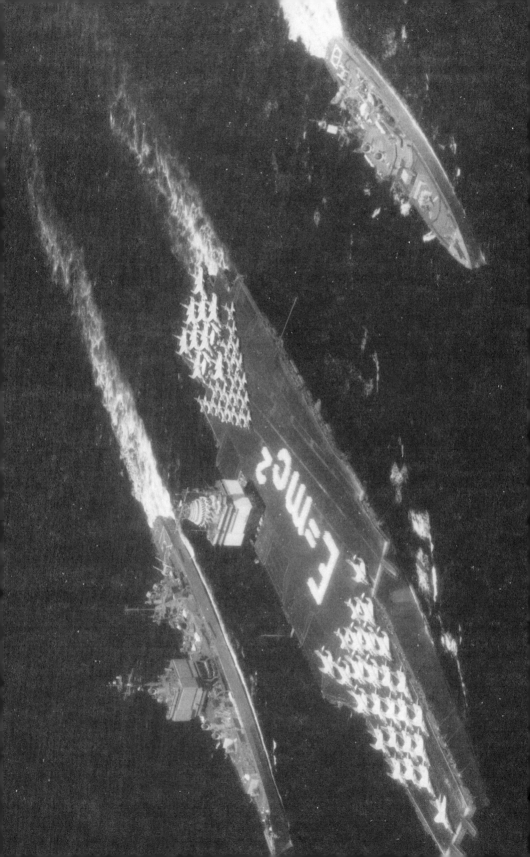

Introduction

SOME THOUGHTS ON NATIONAL DEFENSE AND SEA POWER

Rudiments of Sea Power and Diplomacy

MOST AMERICAN VOTERS understand the role of the Navy in the realm of foreign policy. If the average citizen cannot formally define the term sea power, he senses that when trouble erupts overseas the chances are U.S. warships will appear at the scene to protect U.S. lives and property.

The simple truth is that from the days of ancient Greece navies have been called on to play two roles, sometimes separately, sometimes simultaneously: (1) to support foreign policy and (2) to wage war on a scale commensurate with a nation's political goals. During the Vietnam war, the U.S. Seventh Fleet was in continual combat; at the same time, the Sixth Fleet maintained a naval presence in the Mediterranean and, on occasion without firing a shot, provided the military muscle to persuade certain nations to adopt a posture favorable to the United States, while giving heart to weaker allies or neutrals.

Without a formidable fleet and the will to use it, diplomacy becomes impotent, as the United States first learned when President George Washington was nearing the end of his second term. In order to protect U.S. merchant ships from capture while transiting the Strait of Gibraltar, the infant republic was obliged to pay enormous tribute to the Arab rulers of Algiers, Tripoli, and Tunis.

These humiliating pacts with Arab despots foreshadowed events in the Mediterranean and Persian Gulf areas almost two centures later when once again, as American lives and property were threatened, U.S. naval battle groups were alerted in the Mediterranean and the Indian Ocean. Present day naval officers may recall that in 1815, after two decades of terrorizing U.S. ships and sailors, the dey of Algiers was brought to terms only after Commodore Stephen Decatur's Mediterranean squadron sank his flagship and threatened a blockade. The intrepid Decatur then sailed for Tunis and Tripoli and imposed similar terms. No more tribute was paid, and the Arab rulers were forced to indemnify the United States for damages to American shipping. Decatur's intrepid exploits proved that without sufficient naval power the United States could not enjoy the degree of respect essential for the proper treatment for its citizens and national interests.

Geography and the Navy's Mission

Unlike Russia, a massive continental power potentially self-sufficient in most of its material needs, America's geographical position has forced it to become a sea-minded nation. For all its common borders with Canada and Mexico, the United States is virtually dependent on the world's sea-lanes for its existence as an industrial power. Without the flow of thousands of tons of vital materials in maritime trade, the American economy would collapse and with it national security. Conversely, without the unimpeded use of the world's sea-lanes, U.S. goods and commodities could not be exported to earn the profits that pay for U.S. imports.

FIGURE 1
USSR/U.S. DEPENDENCE ON IMPORTS OF
STRATEGIC MATERIAL

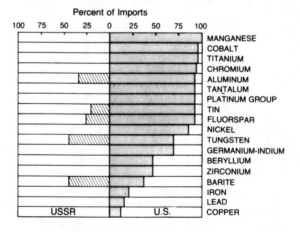

Source: Report of Secretary of Defense to the Congress, Fiscal Year 1978 Budget, Fiscal Year 1979 Authorization Request, and Fiscal Years 1978–1982 Defense Program, January 17, 1977, p. 7.

The vast stretches of the Atlantic and Pacific always have protected the United States from invasion—unless we count the short-lived British raid on Washington in 1814. In keeping danger at arm's length, Americans have sought to fight their wars across the oceans on foreign soil. With the same thought in mind, the United States has forged military alliances and stationed thousands of fighting men overseas. Not immediately apparent to the casual observer is a stark fact: the success of these alliances rests on the ability of the Navy to support these allies and U.S. overseas forces with a maritime logistics pipeline protected by U.S. warships.

FIGURE 2

WORLD TENSION SPOTS, 1945–1975

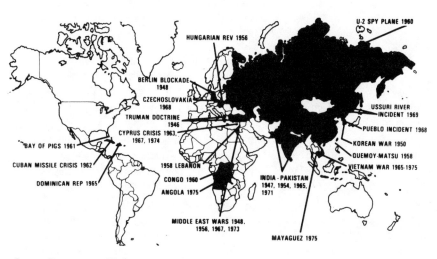

Source: Department of Defense.

National Strategic Policy and the Navy

National strategic policy is basically a reflection of the security goals desired by the U.S. public in its relations with the rest of the world. The people make these goals known through the voting booth, public opinion polls, and the media. To achieve these goals, the White House, aided by the State Department and other government agencies, translates the people's desires into specific plans and policies. Long-range U.S. interests, economic programs, foreign aid projects, and defense budgets are among the principal considerations in the formulation of strategic policy.

For example, at the end of World War II, Americans were shocked to discover that relations with their wartime ally Russia had withered to a level where if the two nations were not at war, neither were they at peace. Soviet domination of Eastern Europe and its imposition of a communist regime in North Korea generated deep distrust among many Americans who cheerfully supported the expenditure of billions of dollars to counter the spread of communist aggression. The Marshall Plan, the United Nations Relief and Rehabilitation Administration (UNRRA), and the permanent stationing of powerful fleets in the Mediterranean and the Far East all testify to the national strategic policy readily adopted by the U.S. people in 1946. Some thirty years later basic American distrust of Soviet intentions continued to justify the cost of maintaining the U.S. Sixth and Seventh fleets thousands of miles from home waters to support U.S. security aims.

"To Provide and Maintain a Navy"

The Congress is empowered by the Constitution "to provide and maintain a Navy" and to make laws necessary to implement this power. By law the business of the Navy is to organize, train, and equip a maritime force for prompt deployment for sustained combat at sea. Other tasks include naval reconnaissance, antisubmarine warfare (ASW), and the protection of shipping.

On an even higher level of combat, the Navy, since the 1960s, has operated 41 strategic missile submarines as part of the nation's nuclear deterrent force. These 41 strategic submarines were not part of the Navy's conventional forces and represented a force of last resort at the instant command of the president.

Traditionally, the U.S. Navy has emphasized its ability to exercise sea control of threatened areas ("freedom of the seas") and to project power into enemy-dominated areas. In a milder form, power projection may take the form of establishing a naval presence, sometimes interpreted as "showing the flag" or (usually by critics) as "gunboat diplomacy."

As the legislative voice of the people, the Congress expresses the public will through the annual naval budget and laws affecting the organization of the armed forces. Over the years the Congress and the president have clashed occasionally over naval programs. These controversies can be traced to different perceptions of the external threat to national security, the need to economize in government, or the relative combat effectiveness of various classes of ships. An arresting example combining all these issues was the bitter debate in the 1970s over a new nuclear carrier in which in the end the carrier proponents carried the day, undoubtedly because Americans finally realized that the United States had become dangerously dependent on Middle Eastern oil and had lost valuable time in strengthening its naval power in the Indian Ocean.

The extent to which the president, the Congress, the Pentagon, and the National Security Council formulate strategic policy and the Navy's role depends ultimately on the public. Crises sharpen the public's appreciation of naval power and the functions of the fleet. Conversely, once the danger passes, Americans tend to be lulled into a false feeling of security that may dim their understanding of dangers that may lie ahead.

In the long run, the public's understanding of potential dangers determines national strategic policy and hence the missions assigned to the Navy. Difficulties arise when the public and the Congress are slow to sense—or when the Navy fails to persuade them—that the sea service lacks the ships and weaponry to match its responsibilities. Thus U.S. sea power will be only as strong as an informed public's perception of the Navy's role in national security.

One

THE TRANSITION TO A POSTWAR NAVY

All the world knows that the United States will
not tolerate the disorder and destruction of war
being let loose again upon the world.

JAMES V. FORRESTAL
Secretary of the Navy, September 19, 1945

Forrestal and Postwar Naval Missions

WORLD WAR II ENDED, officially at least, on September 2, 1945, when, on the deck of the battleship *Missouri* moored in Tokyo Bay, the Japanese signed the document of surrender.

At the high tide of victory the Navy boasted three million men, some twelve hundred ships, and 219,000 aircraft. Steaming with the fleet were scores of aircraft carriers, hundreds of destroyers, and dozens of cruisers. In Washington some economic planners spoke optimistically of reducing the U.S. armada to some four hundred ships, but this hope was soon dashed by nakedly aggressive Soviet moves in Europe and the Middle East. As the iron curtain descended from the Baltic to the Adriatic, Navy Secretary James V. Forrestal and Fleet Admiral Chester W. Nimitz, who had become chief of naval operations (CNO) on December 15, 1945, advised President Truman to retain a Navy and Marine Corps of sufficient strength to block the surge of Soviet or Communist Chinese advances in the West and the Far East.

Forrestal, a former Wall Street financier (Dillon, Read and Company), was brilliant, hard driving, and work addicted. During World War I he had served as a naval aviator. In June 1940 he had joined President Roosevelt's White House staff and was appointed shortly thereafter as under secretary of the navy. In this post he brought fiscal discipline and order to the Navy's mushrooming logistics program. Later, in 1944, when he was named secretary of the navy, Forrestal revealed superb analytic talents in assessing probable postwar political developments and the role to be played by the U.S. Navy.

As a clear-eyed realist, Forrestal had little patience with those government planners who failed to heed his warnings that the Soviets were determined to grab territory by military means, or if possible, through native communist proxies. In his view, an opinion that he shared with Admiral Ernest J. King, the wartime commander-in-chief, the world was entering a period of extreme tension, much of it generated by Moscow. In light of this grim forecast, Forrestal reasoned that U.S. postwar strategy and naval policy would impose four missions on the Navy: (1) to support a U.S. peacekeeping commitment to the recently established United Nations; (2) to maintain a navy superior to the Soviet fleet; (3) to protect U.S. interests abroad and to prevent an attack on the United States; and (4) to support the Army and Air Force in joint combat operations. The missions envisioned by Forrestal became realities in the troubled years ahead.

To carry out these tasks the service could count on an enormous arms inventory, if not the personnel, needed to man the fleet effectively. The tough-minded secretary, testifying before a congressional panel, left no doubt that be was baffled by those who saw little need to provide the funds for a big navy. "If this country," he declared, "in the present state of the world, goes back to bed, we don't deserve to survive."[1] Clearly Forrestal had in mind the American predilection on the morning after a victorious war to demobilize the armed forces, return to the palmy days of peace, and ignore Europe and the rest of the world.

But strife and turmoil in Greece, Turkey, Palestine, China, Malaysia, and the Philippines (to name but some of the trouble spots) convinced the Truman administration that, like it or not, the United States was regarded by its friends as a policeman for the world. To support this unexpected national mission during the "cold war," the Sixth Fleet in the Mediterranean and the Seventh Fleet in the Far East became for the next two decades impressive national symbols in the stormy era paradoxically called the *Pax Americana*. Unlike the years after World War I, when disillusioned Americans returned to their traditional ways of nonentanglement with Europe, the U.S. public in 1946, as revealed in public opinion polls, collectively realized that the Soviet Union was not to be trusted and that Russian aggression, unless checked, would result in a communist world.[2]

Thus did Moscow, by its brutal international behavior, shock Americans into the conviction that Soviet aggression had virtually forced them to adopt the counterstrategy of containment of communist-dominated lands. Parenthetically, if the U.S. public had not initially deluded itself in 1945 that the shooting war was over and clamored for a swift demobilization of the armed forces, the cold war might have been delayed indefinitely and U.S. naval strategy substantially changed.

Forrestal's determination to preserve U.S. naval strength did not square with President Truman's understandable aim to avoid an economic recession in the wake of wartime prosperity. Not surprisingly, the administration slashed the armed forces budget at a time when ship deployments to the Far East and the Mediterranean were on the rise. To introduce cost-control frugality in the Navy Department after an era of free spending, Forrestal centralized naval financial affairs in the new office of fiscal director. Eventually this office evolved into that of the assistant secretary of the navy for financial management.

Forrestal's motive was praiseworthy, but in retrospect it could be argued that civilian officials, rather than professional officers, gradually assumed control of procurement of ships and weaponry. As we shall see, those who controlled the purse strings eventually gained virtual authority to set the roles and missions of the Navy. But in the late 1940s, no one could foresee that the trend toward fiscal control by appointed civil officials would progressively reduce the Navy's ability to control the structure of the fleet.

Naval Suasion in the Cold War

The carrier task force concept perfected during the war proved to be ideal during the cold war for establishing a naval presence in situations involving U.S. interests. As the core element of the Sixth and Seventh fleets, the carriers and their support ships could project naval power almost anywhere on the world's oceans. Moreover, carrier planes launched far at sea were capable of striking countless inland targets, except for those deep in Asia. American warships, accompanied by their replenishment vessels, needed no foreign bases, although, as a consequence of the war, the Navy enjoyed access for the time being at least to ports scattered over the globe.

As an imposing instrument for enforcing U.S. foreign policy, the Navy had no equal, whether the action involved the sudden arrival of the battleship *Missouri* off Turkey in March 1946 to cool Soviet intimidation of that nation or the positioning of a Seventh Fleet patrol force in the Formosa Strait as a signal to Communist China to keep its hands off Taiwan.

In depicting the postwar Navy as a maritime juggernaut that exerted a compelling psychological power on the international scene, a naval analyst has pointed out that the Sixth Fleet foreclosed a number of military options otherwise open to Russian leaders. American ships by their very presence exerted a "latent suasion" that deterred possible Soviet moves.[3]

During the decades of the cold war, the two fleets continued to demonstrate those characteristics unique to a powerful Navy; that is, each fleet performed political functions by virtue of its mobility, its flexibility in using measured force, and its wide radius of action. The U.S. Navy, with no maritime adversaries to oppose it, contained communism by ruling the seas. The unanswered question was: Would Soviet Russia be sufficiently impressed by U.S. maritime might to watch silently while the United States assisted its allies in Europe and the Far East by mammoth economic and military aid programs, or would Moscow decide to embark on a gigantic military buildup to counter the naval power of its number one adversary? In short, how long would the carrier task force retain its superiority as the technology of weaponry continued to accelerate?

Unifying the Military

While the Navy was grappling with political crises in European and Asian waters, a controversy that profoundly affected the respective roles of the services erupted in Washington. The move toward unification of the armed forces, spearheaded by such senior Army officers as General George C. Marshall, the Army chief of staff, was probably inevitable. After World War II many Americans perceived that consolidation would result in greater economy and efficiency. To begin with, President Truman, a student of military history and a longtime admirer of Marshall, favored the merger. Many politicians, facing election in the 1948 campaign and anxious to scale down the vast outlay of dollars for defense, saw in unification a means to eliminate duplication in procurement of arms and supplies, thus achieving substantial savings.

As the principal Navy spokesman, Admiral Nimitz endorsed a single secretary of the armed forces but envisioned (mistakenly as it turned out) separate services directed operationally by professional fighting men.[4] No one was more experienced in tri-service operations than this quietly brilliant strategist upon whose judgment the course of the Pacific war had rested.

Finally, the Army Air Forces, intent on equal status in the defense organization, argued that strategic air power (that is, long-range aircraft armed with the atomic bomb) was now the major element of American arms.

The fight over unification seemingly ended when an apparently workable arrangement was hammered out in the National Security Act of 1947. In essence, the Congress created a federation, not a union, of the three services. When the widely respected Forrestal was selected by Truman to be the first secretary of defense, the appointment was roundly applauded.[5]

Naval Resistance to Unification

The Navy's resistance to unification despite the formidable consensus for merger stemmed from fundamental differences among the services over strategy. Besides dissenting from the Air Force's view of strategic bombing, many naval officers reasoned that the Army, obsessed with the belief that land warfare was the ultimate answer to victory, viewed the Navy essentially as a transport service for ferrying troops to overseas combat zones. Correctly or not, many naval supporters suspected that under unification, a land-minded supreme chief of staff or a civilian defense secretary might inject himself into naval operational matters with disastrous consequences. Moreover, the Navy reasoned that it would be outvoted by the Army and Air Force (itself once part of the Army) in controversies over roles, missions, and budgets.

Other questions rankled senior naval officers. Would the Navy be dependent on a nonnaval procurement agency for its ships, aircraft, and weaponry, all peculiar to sea warfare? Accustomed to a wartime atmosphere in which the sea forces asked for and obtained the best (and possibly the most expensive) weapons and equipment that money could buy, the Navy found painful the notion of centralization of authority in a single Cabinet official.

Many naval officers were unwilling to give up a command system that had been the key to victory in a complex war. They pointed out that the Navy had fought the war with a surprisingly small headquarters staff and with a minimum of administrative drag. For example, if the fleet wanted a new weapons system, the Navy Department almost always supplied it swiftly without questioning its cost or the possibility of cheaper weapons.

During World War II, senior line officers—not civilian officials—under the dual-hatted Admiral King (who was both CNO and commander-in-chief) supervised materiel programs designed to render timely support of the forces afloat. The system worked because President Roosevelt, by executive order, had placed the technical bureaus (such as Ordnance and Ships) under King's authority in all matters pertaining to fleet effectiveness. There was constant communication between the fleet commanders and the Navy Department, which was extremely responsive to the needs of the fighting forces. The catch was that this efficient procurement system was hinged to a wartime budget, in effect, an open-ended checking account that understandably ended abruptly with the coming of peace. Thus with its officer corps expressing open dissatisfaction, the Navy was reluctantly brought into a tri-service association, if not union, with the Army and Air Force.

Forrestal plunged into his job with characteristic diligence. Working sixteen hours a day and exhausting teams of stenographers with his rapid-fire dictation, he quickly recognized that unless he were given more authority in his job, his efforts to run the department would be largely wasted. Specifically, he lacked the legislative power and the staff to carry out his mandate for establishing ''general policies and programs.'' For example, under the National Security Act, the three service secretaries retained their Cabinet seats and the power to manage their domains. Moreover, the Joint Chiefs of Staff (JCS) possessed the authority to develop strategic plans and to create unified commands composed of Army, Air, and Navy components.

Dissatisfied with a post that, for all its lofty title, lacked sufficient clout in the Pentagon, Forrestal pressed for an expansion of his powers in his 1948 annual report to President Truman. Results came swiftly. In 1949 the Congress drastically modified the 1947 act. The traditional Cabinet rank of the service secretaries was abolished. As a consequence, the services no longer enjoyed the status of executive agencies but were downgraded to single military departments. More important, the revised law created an Office of the Secretary of Defense with three assistant secretaries and granted the defense secretary increased power over the defense budget.

So began a slow but inexorable move toward civilian monitoring of military operations and weapons procurement. Gradually, the power to oversee service-originated plans and programs was transformed into the power to control them. As matters turned out, the structure of the fleet and ultimately the roles and missions of the Navy did not prove immune to such supervision.

The Carrier Task Force or the B-36

America's noisy victory celebrations over the Japanese surrender had no sooner died than the Navy found its aircraft carriers labeled obsolescent by a high-ranking Army Air Forces officer. In November 1945, Lieutenant General James Doolittle jolted the Navy in his testimony before a Senate panel on a proposed merger of the services.[6] The carrier, he announced, had passed the peak of its usefulness, presumably because it could be sunk by aircraft. Apparently Doolittle was not impressed by the carriers' high rate of survival in World War II.

According to the doughty Doolittle, the answer to America's future security lay in long-range bombers.[7] "When we get aircraft with sufficient range [to bomb the enemy to rubble] we will not need carriers," he declared. Doolittle evidently had in mind giant aircraft, even bigger than the B-29s of World War II, equipped with nuclear bombs and capable of penetrating deep into enemy territory anywhere in the world.

Doolittle's jab at the Navy foreshadowed the corrosive B-36 controversy of 1949. At the time the Air Force (formerly the Army Air Corps) proposed that U.S. strategy be based on "atomic blitz" warfare and that long-range strategic bombing be an exclusive function of that service. To prove that carrier aircraft could deliver nuclear bombs, Commanders John T. Hayward and Frederick L. Ashworth led a successful drive to show that heavy aircraft could be fitted with and deliver atomic bombs from carriers. By 1948 the Navy had in fact demonstrated that its operational carriers could accomplish this feat. In other words, the Air Force no longer could claim a unique, nuclear capability.[8]

Defense Secretary Forrestal, in delineating the roles of the two services in strategic air warfare, decreed that the Air Force would have the principal role in strategic bombing, but the Navy (with its nuclear-bomb-equipped carrier aircraft) would be called on for similar missions as the situation demanded. Although Forrestal and his colleagues could not foresee it, the carrier proved to be a much more usable weapons system than Air Force bombers for waging the limited wars of the decades immediately ahead.[9]

One critic was Admiral Arthur W. Radford, commander-in-chief of the Pacific Fleet, who claimed that those who believed the Air Force concept of a cheap and easy victory should war come were deceiving themselves. Contending that American strategy should not be based on total "strategic" bombing as a course of action, Radford reasoned that to spend millions on huge land-based aircraft designed for high-level "carpet bombing" was militarily ineffective, morally wrong, and politically disastrous. On the other hand, the naval carrier task force, with its inherent mobility and flexibility, could deliver precision attacks on designated targets and achieve far more effective results. A veteran of the carrier war in the Pacific, Radford was recognized as one of the Navy's foremost strategists, and his testimony carried considerable weight.[10]

Lofty strategic rationales aside, the Navy worried about its very existence in an era when the false belief was current that (1) the United States needed only a monopoly in nuclear weapons to be militarily dominant and (2) the Air Force was the sole service to carry out nuclear missions.

The B-36 uproar subsided after lengthy hearings conducted by shrewd and capable Congressman Carl Vinson of Georgia, chairman of the Armed Services Committee.

Louis Johnson's Heavy-Handed Tactics

Broken by overwork, Forrestal resigned his post in March 1949 and entered the Bethesda Naval Hospital for treatment. His life ended tragically when he fell through an open window, an exhausted victim of dedicated service. In his stead President Truman named Louis A. Johnson.

Tall, burly, outspoken, Johnson was a West Virginia lawyer, Democratic party stalwart, and a former assistant secretary of war (1937–1940). Determined to end service dissent and reduce the defense budget, Johnson lost no time in asserting his control over organizational and fiscal matters.

Significantly, as a sub-Cabinet officer in the late 1930s, Johnson had helped to spur the production of the B-17, a mainstay of American heavy bombing squadrons in World War II. If anything, he was more disposed in 1949 to accept the Air Force claim that its concept of strategic bombing would prevail in future wars and that conventional naval forces could be de-emphasized.

At the time the Navy had completed the design of a so-called supercarrier, the *United States*, capable of handling aircraft armed with five-ton nuclear bombs. When the keel was laid at Newport News, Virginia, Johnson, without consulting

Navy Secretary John L. Sullivan, ordered that construction be stopped. The defense secretary's ham-handed action prompted Sullivan to resign in protest against Johnson's attempt to stifle the development of a powerful new weapons system.

No sooner had the initial uproar subsided than Johnson committed the politically unpardonable sin of intruding on the jealously guarded domain of Congressman Carl Vinson, longtime chairman of the defunct Naval Affairs Committee and its more inclusive successor, the Armed Services Committee. In mid-April 1949 Johnson told a group of newsmen that plans were under way to transfer Marine aviation to the Air Force. A week later in New York City he compounded this error by making essentially the same statement. Clearly adding to the Marine Corps' growing alarm, Army Secretary Kenneth Royal informed a Senate panel that he advocated making the Marines part of the Army.

When news of these controversial ideas reached Vinson, the "Admiral," a term referring to his tight control of naval issues before the Congress, reacted swiftly. On April 28, 1949, after calling Johnson to a private meeting in his office, Vinson laid down the law. Henceforth, any proposed action relating to changes in the organization of the armed forces were to be referred to the Congress beforehand. Vinson then forced the chastened Johnson to send him a letter pledging that he would follow this procedure in the future.[11]

By reining in Johnson (and presumably President Truman), Vinson had reminded the executive branch that Congress also played a major role in shaping national defense policy. Rather than alienating the powerful Vinson, Johnson quickly repudiated his rashly uttered words.

The "Revolt" of the Admirals

The Navy's festering discontent at what it considered unfair treatment from Johnson and his supporters erupted in October 1949 during hearings before Vinson's Armed Services Committee. Ostensibly the witnesses were called to give testimony on unification and strategy. In fact, the sessions turned into a contentious forum for senior officers to air their complaints against sister services.

General of the Army Omar Bradley took aim on the short life expectancy of the Marine Corps by prophesying an end to future amphibious operations (with the Inchon landings less than a year away). The Marine Corps commandant, General Clifton B. Cates, countered by his assertion that the Marines faced possible elimination of their amphibious warfare role if bare-bones budgets crippled the major function of the corps.

Naval proponents, notably Admiral Louis Denfeld, the CNO, charged that the Unification Act was not being implemented as the Congress intended. A major complaint turned on the Navy's contention that unification did not mean that the

Army and Air Force (by representing a majority among the three chiefs of staff) should control the Navy's future. In other words a two-to-one vote by the JCS should not be allowed to determine issues of prime relevance to the Navy, such as choice of ship types, the status of the naval or Marine air arm, or the amount of budget funds allotted to each service.

Behind Denfeld's objections to the workings of unification lay his apprehension that the nation's security could be jeopardized if the Navy's future were left to the judgment of a civilian defense secretary and a nonnaval JCS majority. For his frank testimony, Denfeld was asked to resign as CNO by the new secretary of the navy, Francis P. Matthews; the admiral promptly retired rather than continue on active duty. According to Matthews, Denfeld had failed to maintain a ''harmonious relationship'' with his superiors in working toward unification. Matthews believed that he was justified in his action because Denfeld had not kept him fully informed of daily developments on the Navy and unification. Denfeld ''tells me nothing,'' Matthews complained privately to Admiral Nimitz, a conclusion with which the latter had to agree.[12]

Subsequently, the committee issued a report stating that Denfeld's dismissal was a ''keen disappointment.'' Admiral Denfeld officially left the Pentagon on October 28, 1949, as hundreds of officers, enlisted men and women, and civil servants gave him an affectionate cheer. The new CNO, Admiral Forrest P. Sherman, was hurriedly flown from his Sixth Fleet flagship in the Mediterranean to Washington to assume the heavy task of restoring the Navy's battered morale.

When the smoke cleared away, reflective observers concluded that the emotional debate had obscured the real issue: how to determine the proper roles of the defense secretary and the Congress in establishing missions for each of the services in a world in which both the United States and the Soviet Union could wage nuclear war. Events in the next three decades were to demonstrate that this issue still remained the paramount question.

As events turned out, in August 1950 Truman, upset with Matthews's naiveté in publicly suggesting a preventive (nuclear) war against the Soviet Union, sent him to Ireland as U.S. ambassador. Shortly thereafter, the president replaced the irascible Johnson as defense secretary by naming General of the Army George C. Marshall to that post. Even the Navy obtained its supercarrier when the *Forrestal* was commissioned in 1954.

The Kremlin Plays the Korean Card

When in 1949 Admiral Radford identified Russia as the ''one potential enemy of the United States'' and urged that the United States plan accordingly, he spoke with more prescience than he knew.[13] On June 25, 1950, North Korean forces, trained and equipped by the Soviets, suddenly invaded South Korea. Only a year before, the United States had withdrawn all its troops from the Korean peninsula except for a few advisors. Overnight the Land of the Morning Calm became a battlefield. Yet it was only one segment of a protracted and worldwide conflict between Soviet Russia, working through its proxies, and the United States.

One may well ask why Josef Stalin approved North Korea's plan for invasion. One explanation can be traced to the 1949 Mutual Defense Act in which Congress authorized U.S. arms and technical assistance for NATO nations. Possibly to divert U.S. weapons and equipment away from Western Europe, the Kremlin acquiesced in the North Koreans' desire to strike south across the 38th parallel. But Khrushchev writes that Stalin had his doubts and agreed to the invasion only after Mao Tse-tung (Mao Zedong) approved of it. [14]

Sixteen members of the United Nations eventually became involved in Korea, but the United States bore the major burden of combat. Interestingly, precedents set by Washington decision makers in this strangely fought war surfaced again in the 1960s. Once more, American policymakers adopted a fatally flawed strategy of gradualism in waging war against a small Asian nation.

Two

LIMITED WARS
AND CENTRALIZED CONTROL

Korea: Rehearsal for Vietnam

FOR SOME THREE YEARS U.S. forces including the Seventh Fleet and Marine Corps units fought an essentially limited land and air war to stop the North Koreans and Chinese communist armies from gobbling up South Korea. The cost was 54,000 U.S. fighting men killed and 103,000 wounded, plus $20 billion (in 1950s dollars).[1] Privately many in the military, particularly those senior officers who had fought in World War II, viewed the Korean experience as setting three fatal precedents: (1) the assumption by Washington that it could win limited political goals by placing restraints on its military forces; (2) the perception by potential enemies that U.S. reluctance "to go all out" was a signal to engage in future aggressions under the same ground rules; and (3) the readiness of the president to engage in a major war without the expressed backing of the U.S. people.

The *Washington Post* took an opposite view, declaring that President Truman had fought for and achieved his limited objective without damaging "our dominion of world strategy" and in fact had improved that dominion.[2] Crusty Admiral J. J. "Jocko" Clark, a carrier admiral in World War II and commander of the Seventh Fleet in the last year of the Korean War, scoffed at limited war, asserting that "you shouldn't be in a war if you don't want to win it."[3] Thus Washington, reluctant to strike at China (which had entered the war in the autumn of 1950) because to do so would broaden the war, was forced into a less than all-out war.

As this military stalemate wound down, U.S. carrier pilots understandably were puzzled that their high-risk sorties over North Korea were being continued, not to gain a victory, but to make the enemy bleed enough to force him to the truce table. For the carrier aviators the experience was a searing introduction to limited warfare.[4]

Significant lessons in theater strategy emerging from the conflict were tragically ignored. For one thing, American strategists failed to learn that air attacks to interdict source-targets and transport systems would not succeed against an enemy who believed that he could outwait the United States unless the Navy and Air Force mounted sustained, continuous air attacks, both night and day. Intermittent strikes allowed the enemy to regroup, bring up new supplies and more men, and continue the war. Finally, said the critics, it was clear that to win a war U.S. forces should never fight on the enemy's terms or be forced to fight with only one hand. Over a decade later these chickens came home to roost in the jungles of Indochina.

In 1957, only five years before President Kennedy committed 15,000 troops to Southeast Asia, two naval combat officers, Malcolm W. Cagle and Frank A. Manson, wrote a much-praised history of naval operations in the Korean conflict. Prophetically, Cagle and Manson noted the grave portent of this first limited war to be fought by the U.S. Navy. They rejected the tendency in military circles to dismiss the Korean War as so ''artificial, anachronistic, unorthodox and hedged with restrictions'' that any study of it was unprofitable.[5] In the book's foreword Admiral Arleigh A. Burke, then CNO, observed that because major nations shrank from wreaking nuclear destruction on one another, the probability of limited war had increased. Burke urged that the authors' distillation of the war's lessons receive careful study.[6]

Burke's warnings were largely ignored, perhaps because administration leaders found their attention focused on brushfires in Egypt, Hungary, the Caribbean, and the Orient. As a result, the military lessons of Korea were lost in a flood of position papers and studies on current issues.

Admiral Radford and the Indochina Crisis

On a trip to the Far East in December 1952, President-elect Eisenhower was most favorably impressed with Admiral Radford, then the commander-in-chief of the Pacific forces.[7] Radford's grasp of global politics, his distinguished war record, and his all-round capabilities were strong reasons why in August 1953 the president named him chairman of the JCS to succeed General of the Army Omar Bradley. The new chairman found himself almost immediately embroiled in the problems of French Indochina.

The U.S. Navy first sailed close to the shoals of Vietnam early in 1950 when President Truman approved an initial $15 million in aid to the newly formed states of Indochina (Vietnam, Laos, and Cambodia). He did this in the belief that the guerrilla forces of Ho Chi Minh, supported by Russia and Communist China, were determined to spread communism over Southeast Asia (the domino theory).[8] In March of the same year, two U.S. destroyers, *Stickell* and *Anderson*, arrived at

Saigon with the Seventh Fleet commander, Vice Admiral Russell S. Berkey, flying his flag, in *Stickell*. As a symbol of the might of the U.S. naval presence in the western Pacific, 60 aircraft from the carrier *Boxer* flew over the city in tight formation. Thus began a gradual buildup of military assistance to French forces bogged down in their seemingly endless rice-paddy war.[9]

Radford, in his memoirs, throws considerable light on the Navy's near involvement in the battle for Dien Bien Phu, an episode that highlighted Washington's ambivalent attitude toward the defense of Southeast Asian states against communist aggression. The administration was willing to send military aid (some $3 billion by 1953) to the French, but was dead set against sending U.S. combat forces; the U.S. death toll in Korea was too recent a memory.

In March 1954, at the height of the French war against the communist Viet Minh, thirteen thousand French soldiers were trapped in a small valley some eight miles from the Laotian-Vietnamese border. Besieged by fifty thousand enemy troops armed with Chinese-supplied heavy weapons, the plight of the garrison seemed hopeless.

To resolve the Indochina crisis, representatives of nineteen nations were summoned to Geneva in April 1954. Conscious that if Dien Bien Phu fell, Ho Chi Minh could conceivably win a diplomatic triumph at the conference, President Eisenhower called on his military chiefs for a plan of action.

Back in Washington, Radford informed Eisenhower and Secretary of State John Foster Dulles that U.S. carriers in the area had been placed on twelve hours' notice for possible action in support of the French. The CNO, Admiral Robert B. Carney, in a dispatch to Vice Admiral William K. Phillips, commander of the strike force, made clear that although there was no plan for intervention, Washington officials were aware of "the grave consequences that could result from loss of Indochina to the Communists."[10] In brief, the Navy made all preparations for a carrier air strike should the president so decide.

Radford recounts that on April 3, 1954, he and Dulles met with members of the Congress, who stipulated that if the United States intervened, it should do so only as a member of an international coalition.[11] But British Foreign Minister Anthony Eden explained that Commonwealth politics dictated England's refusal to participate. Dulles, according to Radford, attributed British reluctance to their fear of Chinese intervention that would lead to World War III.

Writing in 1972 just before his death, Admiral Radford asserted that if Washington's efforts to build a coalition of allied forces to support the French had been successful, the United States might have avoided the terrible war in Vietnam. But with U.S. public opinion unprepared for unilateral intervention and with the British unwilling to internationalize the war, the White House felt compelled to hold back.[12]

Counseling caution, the JCS warned that limited—that is, piecemeal—U.S. involvement in French Indochina would increase the risk of a general war, bringing with it an expanded draft and a call-up of guard and reserve units. Radford emphasized that he and his colleagues wished to avoid becoming deeply involved in a militarily unimportant area of Southeast Asia. Admiral Carney declared that any temporary tactical advantage gained by U.S. naval intervention should be weighed against the possible military and political consequences, that is, Chinese intervention and a major war. In fact, as Admiral Radford put it, "The plan to save Dien Bien Phu by an air strike never reached the operational stage."[13]

On May 7, 1954, the stricken French force was overwhelmed by Viet Minh troops, a development that prompted the Eisenhower administration to accelerate its fence-building moves to contain communism in the Far East. The result was twofold: the establishment of the Southeast Asia Treaty Organization (SEATO)[14] and a stepped-up aid program for South Vietnam.[15] Both actions ensured the U.S. Navy a major part in Washington's plan for the defense of South Vietnam.

The French and Viet Minh signed the Geneva Accords on July 20, 1954. The agreements, in a manner similar to the Korean truce, divided Vietnam at the 17th parallel into two separate states, with North Vietnam retaining seventeen million people. The ten million souls in South Vietnam were to vote in 1956 on their political future. The election was never held. The accords stipulated that until the movement of troops on both sides was completed, civilians on either side of the 17th parallel could migrate to the other. This provision immediately generated a major transportation problem for the Navy.

The Navy's humanitarian sealift, known as the Passage to Freedom, stemmed from the decision of thousands of residents in communist North Vietnam, many of them Roman Catholics, to flee to the south. At the request of the French government, President Eisenhower directed Admiral Carney to organize a ferry service from the north to Saigon and other ports. Of some 800,000 transported south, about 311,000 sailed in U.S. naval ships. Thousands of other refugees put to sea in small boats. In an operation to be repeated in the 1970s when Vietnam's "boat people" were being turned away by certain Asian nations, the ships of the Pacific Fleet rescued many from certain death by starvation or drowning in stormy seas.

Sadly, the Navy's memorable feat ensured only temporary freedom from communist rule for the refugees from the north. When the Americans evacuated Saigon in 1975, once again the luckless Vietnamese were faced with a choice of living under an iron-fisted regime or taking to the sea in unseaworthy craft. Many chose the latter.

Peking Tests the Seventh Fleet

The fall of Dien Bien Phu tempted the Chinese communists to strike more boldly at the U.S. and British presence in Southeast Asia. On July 7, 1954, a U.S. naval reconnaissance aircraft over the Formosa Strait was jumped by Chinese communist planes but escaped unharmed.[16] Two weeks later, a British Cathay civilian transport plane flying from Bangkok to Hong Kong with eighteen passengers on board was shot down by Chinese communist fighters. Responding to the pilot's Mayday, Seventh Fleet ships and aircraft, together with British and U.S. Air Force planes, located nine survivors, one of whom died. On July 26, 1954, two Chinese communist fighter pilots made the mistake of attacking a U.S. naval Skyraider.[17] The Skyraider pilot turned and shot down one assailant. Other naval planes joined the fray and destroyed the second attacker. As the tension mounted, the importance of protecting Taiwan as a naval and air base for U.S. forces assumed major proportions. To forestall further aggressive action by the Chinese communists, Eisenhower took the unusual action of asking the Congress to empower him to use force to defend Chiang Kai-shek's domain. The result was the Formosa Resolution of January 1955, which proclaimed:[18]

> That the President of the United States be and he hereby is authorized to employ the Armed Forces of the United States as he deems necessary for the specific purpose of securing and protecting Formosa and the Pescadores against armed attack, this authority to include the securing and protection of such related positions and territories of that area now in friendly hands.[19]

As noted later, the Formosa Resolution served as an ill-starred precedent in 1964, when a compliant Congress passed the Tonkin Gulf Resolution, thus presenting President Lyndon Johnson with virtually blanket authority to expand the war in Vietnam.

Defending Taiwan

To protect this island bastion against invasion attempts, the Seventh Fleet established a patrol force, a clear signal that any attempt to cross the Formosa Strait would be costly. An opportunity arose in early 1955 for the Navy to demonstrate its absolute sea control in the China Sea. At that time the Tachen Islands, situated off the Chinese mainland, were held by the Nationalists. The tactical value of this real estate to Chiang was small, but the islands provided a base from which to land spies on the mainland by fishing boat. On January 10, 1955, communist aircraft began intensive bombing of the islands prompting the Taiwan government, perhaps persuaded by U.S. military advisors, to decide on evacuation. Quickly Vice Admiral Alfred M. Pride, the low-keyed, salty New Englander who commanded the Seventh Fleet, positioned his ships within air and artillery striking distance of the islands. The communists' attacks ceased immediately.[20] Eight days later when the Republic of China requested U.S. assistance in evacuating thousands of souls from the besieged islands, Admiral Pride's ships were ready.[21]

True to Pride's reputation for running a "quiet bridge," this rescue operation was no Dunkirk but an orderly, deliberate evacuation.[22] Five carriers and their planes provided air cover and, incidentally, let the Red Chinese radarscopes display the fearsome extent of U.S. air power. A surface action force of cruisers and destroyers patrolled offshore as the amphibious ships and their landing craft moved in toward the beaches. In all, the Seventh Fleet evacuated 27,000 military and civilians in an 85-hour period. The amphibious ships loaded 8,600 tons of equipment, 166 heavy guns, and some one hundred vehicles. All ships were fueled and provisioned by underway replenishment from mobile logistic ships.

The Tachen operation was such an impressive display of American sea power that many newsmen from the U.S. and foreign press converged on the fleet flagship to observe the event firsthand. *Time* magazine carried a cover story, "Admiral Pride of the Seventh Fleet," underlining the willingness and capability of the United States to employ its Navy in the rescue of its weaker Pacific allies.[23] The Tachen affair undoubtedly aroused apprehension and anger in Peking and in the Kremlin, as the Politburo pondered ways and means of overcoming the U.S. maritime might that allowed Eisenhower to wage the cold war so effectively.

The incidents off the China coast continued. In August 1958 the successful entrenchment of Nationalist forces on the island of Quemoy off the Chinese mainland provoked the communists to seal off that tiny outpost by a continuous artillery barrage. At once the CNO, Admiral Burke, with the approval of the president, ordered the Seventh Fleet commander to concentrate his forces in the vicinity of Taiwan. The carrier *Essex* with its escorts sailed from the Mediterranean through the Suez Canal for the China Sea. An amphibious task group with Marines steamed from Singapore to join the fleet. This visible show of might evidently convinced the communist leaders of American resolve, and the bombardments were reduced to alternate days, a face-saving device that allowed the Chinese Nationalists to ship in supplies on nonfiring days.

In sum, during the 1950s the U.S. Navy carried out its mission in the Far East by virtue of its ability to move ships swiftly and to tailor its task forces to the situation at hand. Because of the Navy's success in supporting U.S. diplomatic goals with relatively minor expenditure of resources, Washington policymakers, with the tacit assent of the public, optimistically believed that the Seventh Fleet could control brushfires in Asia indefinitely. Only in later years did it become evident that the sharp cutback in ships, coupled with a serious lack of trained personnel, meant an inevitable decline in the Navy's capability.

Meanwhile, as a consequence of the accords reached in far-off Geneva, the U.S. government agreed to train a Vietnamese force of some 100,000 men for the security of South Vietnam.[24] Unknowingly, Eisenhower had taken one more step into the Indochinese morass. No one in Washington foresaw that a shooting war was in the offing and that ship obsolescence would accelerate rapidly because of combat operations. Congressional and naval leaders in the late 1950s reasonably assumed that an orderly shipbuilding program would continue into the distant future, a belief that all too soon proved an illusion.

The Price of Extended Deployments

The frenetic tempo of naval operations during the Eisenhower era inevitably exacted a certain toll on the readiness and morale of the fleet. Serving as the spearhead for the Eisenhower-Dulles policy for containing communism in the Far East and in the Mediterranean, naval ships and their overworked crews (including Marine amphibious units) were deployed to foreign stations far too long. The average cruise to the western Pacific (Westpac) lasted eight or nine months, and more frequently than not, the period was extended because of minor aggressions and other emergencies.

Four carriers, together with destroyers, cruisers, and support ships, were continually on station in the Far East, imposing long overseas tours on the men and causing setbacks in training and refitting periods. A concerned Admiral Donald B. Duncan, the acting CNO in 1954, described the situation to Admiral Radford:

> The deployment of 4 CVA [attack carriers] to the Far Eastern Command is the most difficult commitment to maintain. It has now been extended for over two years. To continue it: ships have been switched from ocean to ocean, sometimes temporarily, at other times permanently; carrier Air Groups from one Fleet have been married to carriers of the other Fleet and the entire unit pressed through an abbreviated training period which has proved unsuitable to prepare the ship for its intended duty.[25]

Although Admiral Duncan stressed the erosion in combat training of the carrier crews and air wings, he might well have added that all ships of the fleet and their men were suffering, respectively and in varying degree, from maintenance problems and operational fatigue.

What prompted naval leaders like Radford and Duncan to continue to carry out a killing fleet employment schedule with a minimum of protest? One answer lay in the "can do" spirit developed to a high pitch in World War II in the Navy and Marine Corps. Perhaps too, Admiral Duncan hoped to impress his political superiors with the need for more carriers. In any event, Duncan's warning to the JCS chairman proved fruitless. Radford and his colleagues understood only too well the deleterious effect of long deployments on men and materiel. Nevertheless, the JCS also knew that U.S. foreign policy could not be carried out unless sufficient naval muscle was at hand. Moreover, the naval tradition of always being ready for action continued to motivate officers and crews alike to remain at their battle stations and carry on with the tasks at hand.

Back at the White House, at a time when the U.S. military services were being overextended in foreign lands, President Eisenhower set in motion events that paved the way for diminished control of armed forces operations by the professionals, a development that reached full flower during the Kennedy and Johnson administrations.

The Fragmentation of Naval Command

On April 30, 1953, President Eisenhower, in a move to strengthen the power of the defense secretary, notified the Congress that the defense establishment was ''in need of immediate improvement.''[26] To ensure undisputed civilian control, the president proclaimed that ''no function'' in any agency of the Defense Department should be performed independently of the ''direction, authority, and control of the Secretary of Defense.'' Thereupon, Eisenhower issued a presidential directive empowering the secretary to designate a military department as his ''executive agent'' and issue operational directives to the field forces. In effect, as the deputy commander-in-chief, the secretary was authorized to control directly operations of the unified commands in the Pacific and elsewhere.[27]

Under perceptive Defense Secretary Thomas Gates, these changes brought no revolutionary changes in the Navy because the CNO, acting as the secretary's designated executive agent, retained the direction and control of fleet operations. As Admiral Burke recounted, he was always able to alert his fleet commanders to potential emergencies so that ships might be positioned in advance of trouble. At the same time he kept the president, the defense secretary, and the JCS informed of his actions. The fleet operations during the Tachen evacuation, the Suez crisis of 1956, and the Lebanon landings in 1958 were classic examples of how the new system, though deemed faulty in concept by senior naval officers, could be made to work—at least, under Admiral Burke's direction.

Major administrative changes at the Pentagon also entered the picture. Eisenhower's 1953 reorganization plan had increased the number of assistant defense secretaries from three to nine. In addition, the Navy Department's so-called bilinear organization came under presidential criticism. As the department operated, the navy secretary managed nonmilitary matters while the CNO remained in charge of military affairs. As a retired army general, Eisenhower was accustomed to a single channel of command but was persuaded, initially at least, by the Navy to retain the bilinear system that had proved its worth in two wars.[28] As the Navy soon learned, this arrangement was short-lived.

To keep the controversy in perspective, we should recognize that senior civilian officials in the Pentagon leaned toward the belief that if the defense secretary allowed the military to dominate decisions relating to costly military programs, especially procurement, the country's economic stability would be shaken. However, the military argued that if the defense secretary did not accord sufficient weight to the views of the JCS, then the nation could conceivably find itself in strategic difficulties.

Still dissatisfied with central command arrangements, in 1958 Eisenhower recommended further startling changes in the Defense Department. These modifications set the stage for a future secretary of defense to assume virtually total control of military operations, with hazardous consequences for the Navy's role in the Vietnam war and possibly on into the 1970s. The president's action was undoubtedly prompted by a report prepared by a board of organizational experts, none of whom was a naval officer.[29] Interestingly enough, the director of this unofficial project, which was financed by the Rockefeller Brothers Fund, was a Harvard professor named Henry Kissinger.

The board found that the secretary was so burdened "with the negative tasks of trying to arbitrate and control inter-service disputes that he cannot play his full part in the initiation and development of military policy."[30] The tone of the document came through in words such as consolidation, amalgamation, real unity, unified control, and integrated procedures, all of which implied that the Army, Navy, and Air Force would be more effective if the proposed powers were given to the defense secretary. However, as one flag officer later observed, it all depended on how the incumbent defense secretary exercised the extraordinary authority granted him. With the judicious Gates (himself a World War II naval officer) in charge of the Defense Department, Eisenhower and the Congress correctly anticipated that no radical measures would take place.[31]

Isolating the Chief of Naval Operations

As finally enacted into law the Defense Reorganization Act of 1958 effectively isolated the CNO from the Navy's *operational* chain of command. Henceforth, the unified commands, including the commanders-in-chief of the Pacific and the Atlantic, reported to the president through his de facto deputy, the defense secretary. Thus Eisenhower initiated conditions by which a defense secretary could issue orders through the chairman of the JCS to the operating forces. Indeed, the secretary, on occasion, could and did communicate operational instructions directly to field commanders, bypassing the chain of command and, understandably, angering the military professionals. Slowly and inexorably, the status of the CNO as an operational commander weakened.

The full effect of the Eisenhower-sponsored changes did not become apparent until Robert S. McNamara arrived at the Pentagon and pressed the Navy Department to reorganize further. After a prolonged but unsuccessful rearguard action to prevent a "layering" of the defense secretary's technical analysts between the navy secretary and his professional staff, the Navy reluctantly adopted a single-line command structure that, in the opinion of many of its senior officers, significantly diluted the authority of the CNO and his staff.[32] In the Navy's collective mind was a suspicion that the new command system would retard the development of programs in ships, aircraft, and armaments and generate major problems for the future.

In 1961 the energetic McNamara attained complete charge of military operations. At the Pentagon the chief of naval operations no longer was charged with
fleet operations. In fact, his title had become a misnomer. Under the new system
the CNO and the commandant of the Marine Corps found themselves serving as
administrators for the navy secretary (who was no longer a Cabinet officer) in
carrying out policies regarding organization, logistics, personnel matters, training, and nonoperational affairs. In matters of strategy, the CNO and the commandant sat as members of the JCS and were advisors to the defense secretary on
policy matters, contingencies, and long-range plans. The net result was a civilian
filtering of JCS military recommendations, which were then conveyed to the
president by the defense secretary.

Gone were the Eisenhower days when the members of the JCS were invited
individually to the White House for a talk with the commander-in-chief. Admiral
Burke, in a talk with the author in 1979, expressed regret that this custom had gone
by the board, particularly in the Carter administration. Chief executives after
Eisenhower relied more on the counsel of their civilian defense secretaries and
treated lightly the legal status of the chiefs of staff as military advisors to the
president. Many officers thought that this tendency, inadvertent or not, was but
one more step by successive administrations to accord less urgency to national
defense at a time when pressing social and economic problems clamored for
attention and time.

The Conglomerate Syndrome and the Pentagon

Admiral Burke, who headed the Navy for six years (1955–1961), was a bluff,
affable officer, quick to cut to the heart of complex problems. A graduate of the
Naval Academy in 1923, he later earned a master's degree in chemical engineering
from the University of Michigan. As a destroyer squadron commander in World
War II, he was the epitome of the inspirational combat leader. His remarkable war
record was matched by his strategic planning skills in the peacetime Navy. After
retiring from active service in 1961, he achieved further distinction in industry by
his unerring ability to diagnose organizational weaknesses in big corporations.

At mid-century America was characterized by conglomerate fever. The symp-
toms were evident in major firms, which acquired many smaller companies in
hopes of expanding profits. As Admiral Burke observed, senior corporate executives frequently tried, unsuccessfully, to manage these satellite companies from
headquarters hundreds of miles away. As a career officer, he had learned that large
organizations or commands operate effectively only if subgroups are assigned
general goals (*what* to do), but without detailed instructions on procedures (*how* to
do it). Burke was surprised that many top business leaders were unfamiliar with a

basic military command principle: the commander at the scene of action has a much better grasp of the tactical situation than has an admiral (or a defense secretary) sitting in his far distant headquarters.

So it was in the Defense Department where centralized, bureaucratic control of arms production, intelligence, supply, operations, and procurement was heavily influenced by administrative analysts, untutored in military operations, assiduously intent on finding a single cost-effective way to national security. Burke likened the Defense Department to a sprawling and overcontrolled conglomerate. National defense would be better served, he believed, if the administration in power would establish functions for the services but not prescribe in detail how these responsibilities were to be accomplished. If those in charge did not obtain positive results, then new faces could be brought in.

Although Burke did not say so, the many-layered command channel separating the forces afloat from the commander-in-chief or his deputy, the secretary of defense, had become so ponderous and diffused that reaction to international flare-ups was dangerously slow. This diffusion in operational command also meant that fleet commanders might be left in ignorance of sensitive U.S. ship movements in their areas. With the assumption of power by Kennedy's New Frontiersmen, the Defense Department more than ever suffered from excessive centralization. Some years later, the sorry episodes of two U.S. naval "spy ships" stemmed directly from a tightly centralized (and defective) command and control system.

The Polaris Breakthrough

The development of the nuclear-propelled submarine armed with intercontinental ballistic missiles during the Eisenhower administration was spurred in large part by Soviet advances in long-range nuclear missiles and space technology. So concerned was President Eisenhower that on December 2, 1955, he announced at a National Security Council meeting that the United States would develop a reliable missile system quickly even if he had to run the project himself.[33]

Admiral Arleigh Burke, who was present, lost no time in taking up the challenge. Two days later Burke peremptorily summoned Rear Admiral William F. Raborn to his office and handed him an unique directive. Starting immediately, Raborn was to head a newly created special projects office for the development of a ballistic missile for the fleet. Fired with the urgency of the task and anticipating administrative delay within the Navy Department, Burke gave Raborn a letter addressed virtually to all hands. In it, Burke emphasized that Raborn in effect had carte blanche to cut through red tape in obtaining personnel, materiel, and whatever else he might require to achieve his goal.

Raborn, an outgoing, action-oriented officer, had attained distinction in World

War II by training thousands of pilots in aerial gunnery. In directing this program, he had displayed a talent for organizing and inspiring his people to overcome most, if not all, problems blocking the way to success. After the war he was posted to the Navy's Guided Missile Division.

Navy Secretary Thomas S. Gates reinforced Burke's instructions, adding that the need for the missile was so great as to justify violations of the chain of command. At the time, the United States lacked a strong defense against both Soviet missiles and long-range bombers. Unless America could produce its own long-range missiles, the nation's vulnerability would decline to a dangerous level.

Raborn's team received unexpected aid from the noted nuclear scientist, Dr. Edward Teller. According to a quasi-official history of the nuclear navy, in mid-1956, Teller suggested that a lighter warhead (600 pounds as opposed to the 1,600-pound warhead used for the land-based Jupiter missile) might be designed by 1963.[34] Teller's suggestion, coupled with other favorable advances in propellants, impelled Raborn to concentrate his efforts on a proposed submarine-launched missile named Polaris. It was to be 25 feet long, 5 feet in diameter, 15 tons in weight, with an estimated range of 1,500 miles. In March 1957 the Bureau of Ships completed plans for a nuclear submarine designed to carry sixteen missiles and to be operational by 1963. Simultaneously, Admiral Burke alerted all commands that the Polaris project was to be given top priority throughout the Navy.

Eisenhower's apprehension that the United States was behind in missile rocketry was confirmed on August 27, 1957, when news broke that the Soviets had launched a long-range intercontinental missile capable of reaching the United States. A month later Soviet scientists shocked Americans by putting into orbit a tiny satellite named Sputnik I. Then, rubbing salt on America's wounded pride, they launched Sputnik II a month later.

An alarmed Congress quickly appropriated additional millions for an intensified missile program. Pressed to produce plans for a new missile submarine, the Navy's ship designers took a nuclear attack submarine then under construction, cut it in two, and inserted a 130-foot hull section amidships where sixteen Polaris missiles could be emplaced. With the willing cooperation of prime contractors, such as the Electric Boat Company of General Dynamics, Lockheed, and General Electric, and with the enthusiastic assistance of civilian scientists, this modified submarine was commissioned in December 1959 as the USS *George Washington*, thus advancing the Polaris program by three years.

Rickover, Nuclear Czar

If Admiral Raborn sparked the production of the Polaris missile, Admiral Hyman George Rickover was the driving force behind the nuclear submarine's propulsion plant. A loner who had attended submarine school and served in submarines for three years, Rickover opted for a career in naval engineering, thus giving up any future command afloat. During World War II he had impressed his superiors in the Bureau of Ships by his unswerving pursuit of reliability in the manufacture and maintenance of electrical equipment for the fleet. Yet others were on solid ground when they observed that he was an abrasive curmudgeon, who sometimes was needlessly overbearing in dealing with his subordinates.

In 1947 Rickover's single-minded insistence that a nuclear-propelled submarine was feasible helped to convince Admiral Nimitz, then CNO, to lend his support to the proposal. In short order Rickover was named to head two separate offices, the Bureau of Ships' Nuclear Power Branch and the Atomic Energy Commission's Naval Reactor Branch. Like Raborn, Rickover assembled a high-powered team of scientists and naval officers. Unlike Raborn, his management methods, to put it charitably, were unorthodox. No one, however, could quarrel with the magnitude of his results. In the space of seven years, the first nuclear submarine, the USS *Nautilus*, was christened by First Lady Mamie Eisenhower at the Electric Boat Company, Groton, Connecticut. The ship represented an incredible achievement, reflecting Rickover's fanatical search for operational reliability in this revolutionary ship. The Navy's splendid record in nuclear engineering for the next 25 years was a tribute to his dedication.

In the summer of 1958 the *Nautilus* astounded the world by cruising 1,800 miles under the arctic ice cap. Shortly thereafter, the nuclear submarine *Skate*, while on a similar patrol, demonstrated its ability to surface through thin ice in locations threateningly close to Soviet territory. These "blind" undersea voyages were made possible by a navigational system that employed the inertial properties of gyroscopes to compute the ship's exact latitude and longitude. This same principle was employed in guided missiles.

Mention, too, should be made of the record-breaking, submerged circumnavigation of the globe by the submarine *Triton* under the command of Captain Edward L. Beach, Jr. The *Triton*'s performance foreshadowed the operations of nuclear missile submarines patroling for weeks on distant stations, invisible and relatively invulnerable. By December 1979 a total of 1,837 deterrent patrols had been carried out.[35]

The joint efforts of the Raborn and Rickover teams culminated on November 15, 1960, when the *George Washington*, America's first nuclear submarine capable of launching intercontinental missiles, began its first operational patrol. Over the next decade, the Polaris force grew to 41 submarines. Together with the Strategic Air Command's bombers and land-based missiles, they became part of a unified deterrent force with its own Joint Strategic Targeting Group, based at Omaha, Nebraska.

In sum, the Polaris breakthrough initially gave the United States a strategic superiority, which eventually declined to "essential equivalence." In March 1980 the number of U.S. ballistic missile submarines still stood at 41. In twenty years the Navy had developed and deployed five generations of missiles of increasing range and lethality. The obsolescent Polaris-equipped boats, of which ten remained in commission, had been or were being replaced by newer types. Over the next decade Trident submarines, of which eight were under construction and a ninth funded, were to become part of the Navy's inherently survivable-at-sea ballistic missile force until such time as technological changes took place in America's strategic force, or until political considerations, such as arms control treaties, changed the need for strategic submarines.

Three

THE NAVY
AND THE NEW FRONTIER

A New Class of Managerial Elite

IN THE 1960 presidential elections, John Fitzgerald Kennedy, a young (43) senator from Massachusetts, won out narrowly over Ike's vice-president, Richard M. Nixon. Born to wealth, the Harvard-educated Kennedy had achieved fame as a naval commander of a torpedo boat (PT-109). After the boat had been rammed and sunk by a Japanese destroyer in the Pacific, the young skipper had distinguished himself by rescuing wounded crew members, winning a medal for his feat.

In his stirring inaugural address Kennedy proclaimed to the world: "Let every nation know, whether it wishes us well or ill, that we shall pay any price, bear any burden, meet any hardship, support any friend, oppose any foe to assure the survival and the success of liberty." For the Defense Department, the president's crusading pledge was a clear mandate to be prepared for any global contingency, whether a brushfire war or a direct confrontation with Soviet ships.

President Kennedy chose as his defense secretary, Robert S. McNamara, the 45-year-old president of the Ford Motor Company, McNamara, a Phi Beta Kappa from Berkeley with an MBA from Harvard, had served as an Army Air Forces officer in World War II. He had been awarded the Legion of Merit, partly for his ability to analyze operational statistics and deduce optimum use of weaponry for combat missions. Hired by the Ford Motor Company after the war, McNamara demonstrated that he was a brilliant industrial manager. As defense secretary he quickly won the confidence and respect of the president.

Theodore Sorensen, special counsel to President Kennedy, described McNamara's ties with his chief in these words:

> The two men forged a close as well as official relationship. They reinforcd each other
> in asserting civilian control of the military . . . And aware that McNamara's ener-

getic involvement in foreign affairs was often resented by the Department of State, Kennedy had the shrewd sense of when to rely on him, and when to restrain him and when to hear from the Secretary of State.[1]

To his critics McNamara appeared the very model of the self-starting, highly intelligent, assertive executive. The new secretary construed his duties as those of a shirt-sleeves type of manager, remaining in complete control of events by constantly quizzing his subordinates, proposing new ideas, suggesting new goals, and firing those who reacted slowly to his instructions. He also appeared reluctant to delegate responsibilities to subordinates, preferring instead to pore over long, detailed reports, better left to the attention of his staff. Historian Arthur M. Schlesinger, Jr., himself a New Frontiersman, took a more kindly view, describing him as one who "lacked pretense and detested it in others," who was "tough, courteous and humane," who interpreted scientific management as a means to the rational direction of democratic government. The Pentagon, in Schlesinger's dramatic description, was an "empire without an emperor" that was rife with "internal intrigues," that had "broken able men imprudent enough to accept appointment as Secretary." Clearly, the president counted on his new secretary to curb the military.

McNamara, as a member of the scientific-technological elite that had emerged in the 1950s, drew on this new class of intellectuals "to begin the re-conquest of the Pentagon." Chief among their management tools were systems analysis, linear and dynamic programming, and game theory. Leading them was McNamara, "aggressively, questioning, goading, demanding."[2]

In developing joint defense programs, McNamara, for cost-effectiveness reasons, lumped together functions that he perceived as common to all three services. These included such activities as supply and procurement, intelligence, and research and development. No logical person could object to cost-effectiveness unless, as critics warned, those requirements unique to a single service were damaged by submerging them into a generalized class. Thus, when formulating strategic policy, McNamara's analysts began to segregate the combat arms into such discrete categories as strategic nuclear forces, conventional forces, and logistic support. Unhappy naval officers complained that the Navy's special problems as well as its singular advantages in war (or in situations short of war) either were not recognized by the analysts or were judged irrelevant.[3] In short, naval officers groused that civilian war planners, in conceptualizing war making in general terms, slighted the specific, combat characteristics of the Navy in terms of probable future missions.

An example of the shortcomings of this policy, still fresh in the minds of many critics of McNamara's innovations, was the bitter battle of the late 1960s over the F-111 fighter aircraft. The Senate Armed Services Committee finally killed once and for all this attempt to force the Navy to accept the F-111 B, essentially an Air Force 'plane that, because of its excessive weight, was unsuitable for carrier operations. Instead the Navy developed the F-14, one of the world's most effective fighter planes.

McNamara Takes Command

Kennedy aides had warned McNamara that the Pentagon was an organizational and fiscal monster where each service was inordinately concerned with defending its mission and budget requirements. The self-confident secretary had no doubt that he could introduce a firm, overall authority by emphasizing analytic techniques that he had helped to introduce at Ford. And no one would deny that, in this sense, the Pentagon profited from his introduction of new management procedures.[4] However, his critics charged that his high-handed treatment of the military probably negated these benefits.

McNamara began his seven-year tour at the Defense Department with little understanding of the Navy or the problems peculiar to the forces afloat. A technocrat first and foremost, he ran the department on the principle that all problems would yield to proper solutions if the facts could be collected and analyzed. So began the era of systems analysis in which cost-effectiveness became paramount. Typically, a McNamara staff official, in examining a program for weaponry and the like, usually asked for an analysis that would demonstrate (on paper at least) that the cost of the program was "effective" in terms of the results desired. If not, was there a better way to do it?

The hitch in this laudable goal was that some problems, such as evaluating the cost of operating a carrier, might not yield easily to systems analysis. Civilian experts, seeking quantified factors pertaining to cost-effectiveness, failed to see that elements such as the weather, the state of crew training, and the need for logistic support required intuitive reasoning based on seagoing experience. In short, the opinions of competent military professionals sometimes could not be packaged in neat mathematical units.

Nevertheless, McNamara's bright young assistants were adept at setting up assumptions on which to base their rationales for naval programs. Occasionally, senior naval officers did not agree with the solutions but could not offer effective rebuttal because of their unfamiliarity with the technical aspects of systems analysis. McNamara, in the absence of reasoned refutation, tended to accept the "proved" solutions of his staff, even though the issues involved matters that demanded professional naval judgment.

Interestingly enough, the Navy for years had been successfully using a type of systems analysis. Originated at the Naval War College after World War I, this logic form, known as the Estimate of the Situation, was one of a series of steps in the military planning process. By this sequence of reasoning, officers could order data and analyze the various combinations of time and other factors (men, weather, ships, distances) to produce several courses of action open to a commander. Moreover, many naval officers had received training in operational research at the Naval Postgraduate School. Systems analysis paralleled the Navy's methods but employed such economic concepts as marginal utility and opportunity cost in quantitative analyses for strategic decisions. In each method, however, the degree of correctness of the possible solutions (or options) depended on the soundness of the assumptions used by the problem solvers.[5]

Diffidence was not a visible McNamara trait, and it was not surprising that the defense secretary left himself open to charges of excessive pride in his own judgment. Frequently he overrode the advice of naval officers on issues that collectively affected the fighting ability of the forces afloat, and many saw signs that the secretary's so-called intellectual arrogance had seeped down to his aides.

In stressing the merits of systems analysis, proponents argued with some truth that military academies and war colleges could not state with any precision what strategy and force posture might be needed to support certain foreign policy objectives because there were no great immutable military laws to determine these requirements.[6] Conversely, it was arguable that systems analysts and quantification experts might be better qualified to decide what strategy and force posture were required for the nation.

On the other hand, those observers who remained detached from the emotional Pentagon environment credited McNamara and his analysts with making positive contributions to the strategic planning process. For one thing, perhaps unwittingly, they forced the services to gain an analytic skill in evaluating competitive weapons systems and assessing comparative risks in the procurement of armament.

The introduction of new management techniques also stimulated the services and the Congress to focus on a five-year defense plan that allowed the structure of the armed forces and their predicted costs and effectiveness to be systematized. Previously the Congress was more likely to view the defense budget on a short-term, annual basis that tended to induce unexpected gaps in the ability of each service to perform its mission. Finally, senior naval officers acquired a marked competence to hold their own in refuting the conclusions of Defense Department analysts.[7]

Creeping Civilian Control

In this tug-of-war in program decision making, officials on the defense secretary's staff enjoyed a telling advantage by virtue of their prerogative to demand administrative studies, data, reports, and the like on any issue under discussion. This power, in turn, could be used to shape the Navy and Marine Corps in ways that often clashed with the ideas of the military. Such creeping civilian intrusion in

operational matters raised the hackles of many senior officers, but as loyal
government servants, they were required while on active duty to quell any desire to
criticize this trend. But when they retired, some did not hesitate to label it
dangerous.

Admiral John J. Hyland, a naval aviator, had served successively as commander, Seventh Fleet, and commander-in-chief, Pacific Fleet, during the last years of
the Vietnam war. A 1934 graduate of Annapolis, Hyland's service reputation was
that of an outstanding combat leader. He did not pull any punches in damning the
crippling civilian influence, which, he said, had gone "much too far" in many
areas. In his view

> the professional Navy is kibitzed and closely controlled in the details of procurement,
> of operations, and the advancement [assignment and promotion] of relatively senior
> officers. This [control] comes not only from the Defense Department but from the
> Congress and its professional committee staffs, many of which have developed a
> certain superficial competence. They all have the ability to say "no" or to block or
> delay action, but none of them have to take any responsibility for the things they do.[8]

Admiral Hyland had in mind such time-wasting acts as sending down lengthy
questionnaires to the CNO calling for more data or demanding a "study" be
completed on an alternate proposal before taking action on the one under discussion. The readiness of untried civilians to manage naval operational matters was
strikingly illustrated in the Bay of Pigs episode.

Admiral Dennison and the Bay of Pigs

As noted previously, it is a maxim of the military profession that a competent
field commander knows the tactical situation best. Hence, it is folly for a superior
sitting many miles away to try to control combat developments by issuing frequent
orders. This basic precept was set aside by the White House during the Bay of Pigs
operation in a series of misjudgments initially conceived by the Central Intelligence Agency (CIA) and then compounded by administration officials.

The Bay of Pigs fiasco represents one of the great blunders in U.S. Military and
diplomatic annals. The episode merits attention as a striking violation of the rule
that a government should never mount a *military* operation unless it is prepared to
follow through with all the force needed to accomplish the objective. The incident
also exemplifies how civilian control of an essentially military operation can
magnify the chances for disaster.

The operation stemmed originally from a modest plan, approved by President
Eisenhower, to support guerrilla operations in order to assist anti-Castro Cubans in
freeing their nation from Castro's iron grip.[9] By early 1960 Operation Pluto, as

developed by the CIA, depended essentially on Free Cuban air strikes to destroy Castro's force of 30 aircraft in preinvasion bombing raids. The landing force of Free Cubans then could be expected to gain a foothold at Playa Giron, a small town on the bay known as Bahia Cochinos (Bay of Pigs) on the southern coast of Cuba. Once the beachhead was secured, the assualt troops would capture the Giron airport, knock out Cuba's power system, and move on to Havana, some 110 miles away. Apparently little thought had been given to the possibility that with Castro's huge military force plainly in charge, the Cuban populace might not rise up to support a mere 1,500 invaders.

Admiral Robert L. Dennison, who was commander of the Atlantic Fleet at the time, reveals in startling terms in his unpublished memoirs, how civilian officials of the CIA assumed control of an out-and-out combat operation involving an amphibious landing of 1,500 men, tanks, weapons, and other heavy equipment.[10] As Dennison relates, he first learned of Operation Pluto in a manner "really fantastic." One day in early 1961 he received a visit from his amphibious force commander, Vice Admiral George C. Towner, who informed him that one of his ships operating in Puerto Rican waters had been visited by two CIA men. They asked the captain if they could requisition his ship to carry landing craft and crews from Puerto Rico to a point off southern Cuba. They refused to divulge any details of this secret operation.

To this astonishing request, the skipper properly replied that any such order must be sent through the Navy's chain of command. He thereupon informed Vice Admiral Towner, who told his superior, Dennison. Dennison listened unbelievingly and promptly phoned the chairman of the JCS, General Lyman Lemnitzer, asking him, "What is all this about? I'm not going to turn my ship over to a couple of characters who say they're from CIA or any place else." On hearing the story, Lemnitzer exclaimed, according to Dennison, "My God, I'll get hold of [CIA Director Allen] Dulles or his deputy, Lieutenant General [Charles P.] Cabell."

The upshot was, as Dennison relates, that the CIA sent Richard Bissell, Jr., who was in charge of covert operations and one of the chief planners of Operation Pluto, to Norfolk to brief the admiral. Dennison heard Bissell's plan with mounting disbelief. He was incredulous that the fleet commander had been ignored in the primary planning, and he minced no words in denouncing the plan as "stupid." As Dennison recalled, "We weren't asked to approve anything. We were just being told that this was by direction of the President and this was what was to be done." Appalled at the amateurishness of it all, the admiral asked, "Didn't it occur to any of you that I'm responsible, among other things, for the defense of Guantanamo?" Dennison feared with reason that if the invasion went forward the U.S. naval base on Cuba's southeast coast might be attacked by Castro's forces. Dennison's objections were of no avail, and the planners of Operation Pluto continued on their course, serenely oblivious to the chances of spectacular failure.

The CIA's Operation Order

By mid-April 1961, according to Dennison's account, the president's men had drafted a combat operation order that, on White House instructions, was sent by the JCS to the commander-in-chief, Atlantic Fleet. The operation order went into such unnecessary tactical detail that it immediately aroused Dennison's foreboding. Once again he telephoned General Lemnitzer on the scrambler-phone:

DENNISON: I've gotten a good many orders in my life, but this is a strange one.

LEMNITZER: What do you mean?

DENNISON: Well, the last paragraph in it says the Joint Chiefs of Staff interpret this to mean, set up a safe haven [for the Free Cubans]. This is the first order I ever got from somebody who found it necessary to interpret his own orders.

LEMNITZER: Where did you get this directive?

DENNISON: I got it from you.

LEMNITZER: Who do you think wrote it?

DENNISON: You did.

LEMNITZER: No, I didn't. That order was written at 1600 Pennsylvania Avenue.

DENNISON: Well, you can just tell 1600 Pennsylvania Avenue that I am not going to do it that way. I'll do what they want done, but I'll use all the forces that I think are necessary. They don't know what's going on as much as I do.

In Dennison's eyes, this very marginal combat operation was run by untutored civilians playing at war. The admiral noted that the invasion plan had been conceived, prepared, and executed exclusively by the CIA. The JCS, which was ordered to support the operation, had correctly delegated the execution of such support to Dennison. Although the Atlantic Fleet, as directed, carried out its support mission up to a certain point, Dennison observes, "from then, the direction and control of the operation [from Washington] left a hell of a lot to be desired, and this resulted from my lack of intelligence and detailed information on the overall plan, by [Washington's] violation of basic military principles.[11]

A major reason for the collapse of Operation Pluto, critics sympathetic to the Free Cubans said, could be traced to Kennedy's cancellation (for political reasons) of the preliminary air strikes to wipe out Castro's fighter planes. Although naval aircraft were standing by on the flight deck of the carrier *Essex* to go to the rescue of the beleaguered invaders, President Kennedy refused to authorize their launching because of his publicly announced determination that the United States not be "involved." With no friendly fighter cover, the support ship of the Free Cubans was blown up by a Castro plane, one of only ten enemy aircraft reported over the beachhead. It was a stunning example of how relatively few planes in control of the air could turn the tide of battle. The Free Cubans, cut off from rescue, were rounded up and imprisoned.[12]

Off the Cuban coast, U.S. naval ship captains, in accordance with instructions, burned their copies of the operation order and revised their ships' logs to reflect only routine maneuvers, a move that was supposed to conceal from the world any U.S. participation in the aborted affair.

In Awe of the Presidency

Some years after the episode Admiral Burke, the CNO during the Bay of Pigs operation, declared that although neither he nor anyone else could prove it, "there was a complete breakdown in the ability of the Administration to take action" when the operation began to fall apart. To begin with, Burke recounted in his unpublished recollections, the JCS was not brought in on planning for the total operation. So determined were the White House and CIA that security be airtight (an impossibility as matters turned out), the JCS was given only a synopsis of an operational plan to review. [13] The chiefs informed the president, revealed Burke, that they could not intelligently comment because the synopsis lacked both a logistics plan and a communications annex. In other words, the JCS was kept in the dark as to the radio command channels between the Free Cubans and their CIA tactical commanders, as well as on the nature of U.S. follow-up support once the attack force had landed.

Secrecy was absolute, Burke recalled. "We were told that it was a CIA operation and you [the military] stay the hell out of it" President Kennedy himself made clear, whenever the JCS asked for more details, that no U.S. armed forces would be involved "so you Chiefs cannot become involved." This refrain was repeated "over and over again," Burke declared.

Based on what they could learn of the operation and assuming that all assault elements (including the planned Free Cuban air strikes) were successful, the JCS gave the opinion that the initial plan for landing at Trinidad (a small town east of the Bay of Pigs on Cuba's south coast), appeared to have "about a 50 percent chance of success."

The JCS favored Trinidad because the hills adjacent to the beaches of the town would allow the Free Cuban invaders to melt into the mountains and "go guerrilla" more easily than the swampy terrain surrounding the Bay of Pigs site. As matters turned out, many of the landing force of some 1,500 men fled to the swamps when the absence of air cover doomed the operation. They were easily captured after a few days of hiding.

In retrospect Admiral Burke candidly acknowledged that the chiefs' "big fault was standing in awe of the Presidency instead of pounding the table and demanding [more information from the CIA] and being real rough." Instead, "we set down our case and then we shut up and that was a mistake," said Burke. There was a reason for the chiefs' reticence. [14] Accustomed to a military-like relationship with the Eisenhower White House, their unwillingness to pound the table in Kennedy's Oval Office was understandable. As military advisors, the chiefs felt free to offer advice on matters within their jurisdiction. But once the president had chosen his course, his decision was not to be questioned. Thus, during the early months of 1961, the JCS gave its opinions on Pluto only when asked.

Initially they had protested Kennedy's order that the services would not be permitted to "staff the operation." Burke remembered that "it took some time to convince the President that we needed a very small staff, at least, to handle the papers [correspondence, plans], etc. . . . [but] the emphasis on secrecy, the insistence that this was a CIA-run affair, impressed me and, I think, the other Chiefs that this was not our baby. It was the CIA's . . . We had not even been informed when the plans were drastically changed, such as the time when the President cancelled the air strike. Our advice was asked for when the [the CIA or White House] wanted it, and it was not asked for during the operations themselves.[15]

The Bay of Pigs, Burke concluded, "was a military operation which was conducted by amateurs all, from top to bottom, and it was a horrible fiasco." The Kennedy staffers, all "ardent, enthusiastic people without experience in administering anything," had no conception of the need for channels of command, without which any organization, especially the military, cannot function.[16] Military officers were disposed to believe that when nonelected and nonaccountable officials in the executive branch arrogated to themselves control over an amphibious landing, they failed to sense that they might jeopardize not only the assault itself but also the reputation of the United States as a major power. Specifically this disposition to take charge of naval combat operations must be kept in mind when we examine the Cuban missile crisis and the Indochina war.

Admiral Burke remained as CNO for about a year with the Kennedy administration. Asked if the CNO's relationships with the White House and defense secretary changed under the new regime, Burke left no doubt that the arrangements with Eisenhower and Gates, which were characterized by mutual trust and confidence, had ended abruptly: "Mr. Kennedy was all right but many of his subordinates were young, inexperienced, arrogant and bullheaded with the preconceived [notion] that the military had to be curbed."[17]

Scapegoats and the Presidential Image

Oddly enough, the bungling of the Bay of Pigs operation apparently taught the Kennedy administration little about the proper direction of military operations. Scapegoats were found in the CIA, and the JCS came under what many believed to be undeserved criticism for not injecting itself into the operation sooner and possibly saving it.

Subsequently, Kennedy publicly assumed full responsibility for the disaster, but Arthur Schlesinger wrote: "The President said he could not understand how men like Dulles and Bissell, so intelligent and so experienced, could have been so wrong.[18] Taking an opposite view, Arthur Krock, the *New York Times* journalist and longtime friend of the Kennedy family, declared that the president's half-in, half-out support had foreordained the debacle. Krock noted disapprovingly that "Kennedy's transfer of blame from himself to the Chiefs of Staff for the Bay of Pigs disaster was leaked to the press to preserve for him the reputation for resolute leadership that he had definitely failed to demonstrate in this instance."[19]

The study of error often discloses the truth. Military men believed that it was absurd for President Kennedy to assume that the United States could secretly mount a military invasion involving thousands without its security cover being blown. But once he had decided to proceed with the plan, he should have viewed it as an outright war operation and not a large-scale James Bond–type adventure. That is, he should have either canceled the operation or, having decided to go on with it, let the military run the show. Instead, he resorted to feeble compromises that made catastrophe inevitable.

Probably one of the grim consequences of the Bay of Pigs blunder was Khrushchev's decision some months later to emplace long-range missiles in Cuba on the assumption that the young U.S. president would shrink from taking any counteraction. The mercurial Russian thus set in motion the missile crisis of October 1962, an episode in which White House strategists again chose to become involved in the supervision of fleet operations.[20]

The Blockade of Cuba

Ill-feeling between Cuba and the United States continued to fester after the Bay of Pigs blunder. It is not surprising that the crafty but impetuous Nikita Khrushchev, chairman of the Supreme Soviet, persuaded a willing Castro to become an active ally in the cold war. The Kremlin saw Cuba as a made-to-order base from which to launch Soviet-backed operations into all of Latin America, particularly the Caribbean and Central America. Not surprisingly, Moscow secretly decided to install ballistic missile launchers on the island, presumably to intimidate the United States, specifically its young, untried president, into acceding to future Soviet demands in Berlin, Turkey, or elsewhere.

The story of the missile crisis that followed U.S. discovery of the weapons sites has been told and retold.[21] But not apparent to most Americans at the time was the pattern of control exercised by civilian officials from the White House and the Pentagon over the naval blockade. The confirmation of the missile sites in October 1962 by a CIA U-2 spy plane prompted President Kennedy to convene an ad hoc executive committee to deal with this test of U.S. resolve. Chief among its members was Defense Secretary McNamara, who reportedly argued that a naval blockade, not an air strike against the sites, was preferable because it "would maintain our options" (interpretation: it would not commit the president to a shooting war that might impel Khrushchev into an irrational use of nuclear missiles).[22]

On October 22, 1962, two days before the naval blockading force got under way, Kennedy announced over a nationwide television broadcast that the "quarantine" (blockade) would remain in effect until the missiles were removed. That same day Vice Admiral Alfred G. Ward, commander of the Second Fleet, based in Norfolk, Virginia, received orders for his ships to seal off Cuba.

To carry out the mission Ward positioned a task force of two cruisers, 22 destroyers, a carrier (the *Essex* of Bay of Pigs fame), two oilers, and an ammunition ship to cover the sea approaches. Two more carriers furnished air cover and prepared to support an amphibious landing by 11,000 Marines on board 85 ships standing by. In far-off San Diego, California, 21 vessels stood ready to receive another 11,000 Marines for transport through the Panama Canal to Cuban Waters. In all, 183 U.S. naval ships, plus over 30,000 embarked Marines, took part in the quarantine. To give the operation an inter-American character, warships from Argentina, the Dominican Republic, and Venezuela joined the U.S. task force. Meanwhile, 25 Soviet or Soviet-chartered ships were on the high seas steaming toward Castro's island.

Back in Washington, Defense Secretary McNamara, fully conscious of his status as President Kennedy's deputy commander-in-chief, let no one doubt that he was in charge even down to tactical details. One likely explanation of McNamara's assumption of operational matters stems from the possibility that the president did not fully trust his ship captains. He may have been apprehensive that a trigger-happy U.S. naval skipper might overreact if a Soviet captain refused an order to heave to for visit and search, thus precipitating a full-scale war.

Apparently Kennedy communicated his fear to McNamara, who took it upon himself at ten o'clock at night to enter Flag Plot, the Navy's command center in the Pentagon. Here he encountered the CNO, Admiral George W. Anderson. Flag Plot's charts and display panels pinpointed the positions of the Navy's ships and the approaching Soviet vessels. Anderson, a tall, imposing figure, was regarded as one of the Navy's ablest flag officers. McNamara, the sharp-eyed, take-charge, industrial executive, allegedly was relentless in his questioning on the minute details of the operation, a procedure that Admiral Anderson must have resented. Both men were exhausted, and a clash of personalities probably was inevitable. Detzer, without citing his evidence, has McNamara "barking questions" at Anderson. Abel states that no secretary of defense had ever spoken in such a manner to a member of the JCS.[23]

No one could fault the president or McNamara for making certain that no ship's commanding officer took hasty, aggressive action, but one could question

McNamara's methods of imparting the president's instructions to Admiral Anderson before a host of naval subordinates. Had he called the CNO into his office for a quiet talk to nail down any doubtful issues and to hear Anderson's account of actions already under way, the contentious jaw-to-jaw scene might never have happened. The two men could have visited Flag Plot later, thus avoiding an awkward, if not painful, episode.

The missile crisis ended on October 28, 1962, when a chastened Khrushchev agreed not only to ship his missiles out of Cuba but to refrain from placing any offensive weapons there in the future. In return Kennedy agreed not to invade Cuba. Moreover, a few months later the United States dismantled its missile sites in Turkey and Italy, thus for the time being removing a prickly point of contention with Moscow. The Kremlin's pullout of weaponry did not apply to the thousands of Soviet military "advisors" who continued to serve in the Pearl of the Antilles. And in succeeding years right down to 1979, the Soviets continued to test the level of U.S. acquiescence to Russian military activities on the island.

The Bitter Fruit of the Missile Crisis

The jubilant New Frontiersmen had reason to celebrate their victory. After all, they had used controlled naval power to coerce the Kremlin into removing its lethal missiles from the Western Hemisphere. If their successful handling of the confrontation had avoided violence, it also reinforced their readiness to manage future crises by the measured use of force or, as it became known, flexible response. Although they had no way of knowing it, their opportunity would come in a few short years in the Far East.

Even as the champagne glasses were clinking in Washington, Kremlin strategists realized with piercing clarity that until now they had not fully appreciated the need for naval power in plotting Soviet global strategy. Not only had their cargo ships been turned back, but six of their submarines had been detected and kept submerged by the Navy's ASW planes and destroyers until ignominiously forced to the surface. Admiral Anderson declared that it was the most productive antisubmarine operation since World War II.[24] Conscious of profound national humiliation in the eyes of the world, the Soviet deputy foreign minister prophetically warned a U.S. official that never would the Soviet Union allow itself to be "caught like this again."[25] This bitter remark carried ominous implications for the U.S. Navy, for in short order the Kremlin directed that the Soviet Navy's surface ship—building program, already proceeding at a moderate pace, be accelerated.[26] Although Khrushchev had leaned toward long-range missiles and submarines, Kremlin strategists now sensed that if they were to engage in worldwide operations as a military power, a balanced fleet of submarines, surface ships, and naval aircraft was absolutely essential.

Meanwhile, the newly centralized control of U.S. naval operations was setting in motion a chain of circumstances that produced two embarrassing blunders in quick succession.

The Muddled Liberty Affair

On June 8, 1967, as the Arabs and Israelis were locked in their third bloody war in two decades, the USS *Liberty* (AGTR-5),[27] a converted World War II cargo ship, was cruising some fifteen miles off the Egyptian coast, engaged in the collection of electronic intelligence. Shortly after two o'clock, in broad daylight, Israeli planes hit the ship with rockets, napalm bombs, and strafing attacks.[28] Within thirty minutes, three torpedo boats raked the stricken ship with 20 mm and 40 mm shells. A torpedo struck amidships, exploding in the hold. Amid a jungle of twisted metal and escaping steam, 34 men were killed and 170 wounded.

The ship was plainly marked with a large GTR5 on both sides of its bow, the "5" measuring over 9 feet. The U.S. colors (5 by 8 feet) were flying from the 100-foot tripod mast. Nevertheless a subsequent Israeli investigation revealed that it was a case of mistaken identification. The circling planes had assumed the *Liberty* to be an Egyptian ship that allegedly had shelled Israeli army troops on the shore.[29]

A nagging question was Why had not the Israeli planes seen the U.S. colors at the masthead? A U.S. naval court of inquiry found that "flat, calm [sea] conditions and the slow five-knot patrol speed" of the ship may well have produced insufficient wind for the colors to stream out enough to be seen by the Israeli pilots.

These reasons, valid though they may be, failed to explain, at least to U.S. naval officers, why the Israeli pilots did not correctly identify the ship. The best that can be said is that in the heat of battle, recognition of friend and foe became hurried, leading aggressive warriors to shoot first and identify later.

Why had the ship sailed into a war zone close to the African coast? The *Liberty* was under the control of the Joint Reconnaissance Center (JRC) in far-off Washington. It is likely that the skipper assumed that because he had informed the JRC of his location and received no countermand, his proximity to the coast was approved. Obviously, he did not consider that his ship would be taken for a small Egyptian cargo vessel. It is difficult to avoid the conclusion that the ship never would have been placed in jeopardy if an effective command and communications system had been in effect. We know now that at least five important messages addressed to the ship before the attack never were received because of misrouting, delays, and other personnel errors.

Some fourteen hours before the Israelis struck the ship, a staff officer in the JRC became concerned over the *Liberty's* nearness to the combat zone. He immediately telephoned the London office of the commander-in-chief, U.S. Naval Forces

Europe, directing him to order the *Liberty* 100 miles out from the coast. The officer confirmed this oral order by a message to the *Liberty* from the JCS. Sadly, the ship never received it.

Ironically, on June 7, 1967, the commander of the Sixth Fleet, in the Mediterranean, complying with JCS instructions, had ordered *his* ships to remain at least 100 miles distant from Egyptian shores. Unfortunately, the *Liberty* was not under his command at the time.

This tragic episode highlighted the dangers inherent in the new command system. Naval officers were quick to note that under the old system of functional command, once the *Liberty* had sailed into the Mediterranean it would have come under the operational control of the commander of the Sixth Fleet.[30] There is no doubt that Sixth Fleet command communications in the Mediterranean would have been sent directly (not relayed) to the ship and that the *Liberty* would have escaped its fate. Admiral Anderson, in noting the lack of direct naval operational control, observed that "*Liberty* paid part of the price of excessive centralization" in Washington.[31]

Regrettably, the lesson of divided command was lost on Secretary McNamara, whose reaction seemingly reflected his constant concern with the judgment and stability of senior flag officers. On learning the facts, he reportedly observed: "I thought the *Liberty* had been attacked by Soviet forces. Thank goodness, our carrier commanders did not launch immediately against the Soviet forces who were operating in the Mediterranean at the time."[32]

The Pentagon collectively was put in a bad light by its failure to recognize that ships or planes bound on intelligence-gathering missions are not likely to be protected by international law. Some seven months later, Secretary McNamara and the JCS were to learn all over again the lessons of the *Liberty*, this time in the Far East.

The Capture of the Pueblo

A major defect in the U.S. operational command system came to light off the shores of Korea while the United States was mired in the Indochina war. On January 23, 1968, the USS *Pueblo,* a so-called spy ship, was steaming in international waters off North Korea, engaged in its mission of electronic intelligence collection. A North Korean naval force surrounded and captured the tiny ship, its 83-man crew, and all its secret equipment. A Pentagon investigation later revealed that so many federal agencies and commands had a hand in the *Pueblo's* mission that responsibility and accountability for the safety of the ship were fatally flawed. Clearly, the vessel had been placed in an untenable situation from which rescue was not feasible.

When McNamara called for the facts on the capture, he learned that the *Pueblo* gathered intelligence for the National Security Agency. It had sailed from the west coast to Pearl Harbor where it was inspected for operational readiness by the commander, Service Force, Pacific Fleet. Its operational superior in the Far East was the commander, Naval Forces, Japan, based at Yokosuka. In retrospect, it appeared that no one in the command system was particularly worried over the *Pueblo's* dangerous mission in spite of recent warnings broadcast by the North Koreans against alleged intrusion into their so-called coastal waters. When the North Koreans carried out their threat to take action, the little ship was already in extremis, too distant for U.S. forces to come to its rescue.

Veterans of World War II, accustomed to the effectiveness of the close-knit fleet command structure of the task force, task group, task unit, and task element, were mystified that an operation involving super-sensitive electronic intelligence equipment and a U.S. Navy ship could be so loosely handled. Very plainly, fragmented operational control of ship movements, stemming from the 1947 Unification Act and its subsequent amendments, had laid the foundation for the foul-up.

The *Pueblo* affair was a vivid example of the growing bellicosity of smaller nations that refused to be impressed by American sea power or nuclear might. Although U.S. public feeling ran high and many outraged citizens called for a military rescue operation, President Johnson, already bogged down in Vietnam, decided to negotiate rather than risk fighting a second war. After spending a year in a North Korean prison, the officers and crew were released following an official charade in which the U.S. government signed an apology for intruding in North Korean waters and instantaneously repudiated it. Some months later, the Navy decommissioned the *Pueblo* and its two sister ships. Evidently, electronic intelligence collection henceforth would be accomplished by satellites and shore-based equipment.

A Cumbersome Chain of Command

Inevitably, the *Pueblo* capture evoked memories of the Israeli attack on the *Liberty*. In each case the operational commander was located at a distant shore base, making communications difficult. In the *Liberty* affair, the commander of the Sixth Fleet was not given operational control until the attack was imminent. In the *Pueblo's* case, the commander of the Seventh Fleet was not called in until the capture had taken place.

What lessons were to be learned from both dismal misadventures? A congressional investigation disclosed "serious deficiencies in the . . . military command structures of both the Department of the Navy and the Department of Defense."[33] A special congressional panel concluded that the civilian-military command channels in the Navy and Defense Departments were so cumbersome as to be incapable of responding to critical contingencies. Taking corrective action, the new defense secretary, Melvin Laird, directed an over-haul of the command system. Understandably, no details were released.

Admiral Edwin B. Hooper, who had served in the Pacific Fleet at the time of the *Pueblo* incident, revealed that the *Pueblo's* chain of command was "structured to accommodate the requirements and authority of intelligence organizations" such as the National Security Agency in Washington, and not that of the fleet that presumably would be called on to protect the ship from attack.[34] Clearly, the Defense Department's command-and-control communication channels were so divided as to be unworkable.

The American people soon forgot the *Pueblo* affair amid the national turmoil of racial unrest, student riots against authority, and protests against the Indochina war. But for many in the Navy the incident remained an unforgetable example of what could happen to operational missions when a defense organization ignores the fundamental military principle of unity of command.

Some years after the event Admiral Hyland, who had been Seventh Fleet commander at the time of the *Pueblo* capture, commented that Commander Lloyd Bucher, the skipper, was gravely at fault in not sensing the potential danger and doing nothing to meet it.[35] Hyland recalled that the U.S. Navy routinely sent aircraft, ships, and submarines on peripheral reconnaissance missions against the Soviets. (The Soviets did likewise, but their forays were facilitated because an open U.S. society made it relatively easy for the Soviets to collect information, either by electronic intelligence ships twelve miles off U.S. shores or by scores of newsmen and diplomatic and consular officials traveling around the United States.)

At any rate, Hyland said, all of these reconnaisance missions entailed a certain danger. Some of them were and continue to be extremely risky. Nevertheless, the naval command depended on the individual pilot or skipper to use sound, prudent judgment. "He knows before he leaves that there are things which could happen . . . [where] he will end up out on a limb and nothing can be done to save him except his own action."

Perhaps the Navy Bureau of Personnel erred in not assigning a more qualified officer to lead a mission beset with peril. Perhaps the Navy's personnel staff in Washington had only the vaguest appreciation of the hazardous nature of the *Pueblo's* mission and failed to place a top-notch commander in charge. And perhaps from the start—before the ship ever sailed for Korean waters—the *Pueblo's* mission should have been under the direct control of the Seventh Fleet. But the central truth remains: divided responsibility in any project promotes confusion and may lead to disaster.

Four

THE VIETNAM WAR: CIVILIAN CONTROL AND COMMAND ACCOUNTABILITY

The Drift into Asian Shoals

THIS IS NOT THE PLACE to discuss whether the U.S. decision to enter the Indochina cockpit was a political mistake. It is enough to recognize that it was, beyond doubt, a war marred by U.S. strategic ineptitude and a failure to grasp that North Vietnamese territory was the source of the threat to South Vietnam. When President John Kennedy made his foredoomed decision in 1961 to send thousands of U.S. "military advisors" to Indochina, he unknowingly committed the Navy to a frustrating, unproductive, twelve-year war. He then compounded his initial error by condoning the plot to unseat President Ngo Dinh Diem in Saigon; by his acquiescence in the proposed coup, he assumed for the United States a grave moral responsibility for the security of South Vietnam. Because the United States took on this task with no clear understanding of the combat objective and a less than all-out resolve for victory, the calamitous consequences were predictable.

Kennedy's reasons have been ascribed partly to his idealistic belief that the American people were prepared to patrol the globe indefinitely as the cop on the beat to enforce international law and order. Others believed that his desire to recoup the prestige lost in the Bay of Pigs fiasco and to impress Soviet Premier Khrushchev as a resolute, two-fisted protector of democracy led him to take a stand in Southeast Asia. Significantly, on April 20, 1961, as the Bay of Pigs disaster lay heavy on the young president's shoulders, McNamara, unquestionably on Kennedy's orders, instructed Deputy Defense Secretary Roswell Gilpatric to develop a program to save South Vietnam from a communist takeover by Ho Chi Minh's forces from the north.[1]

By late 1963 over 15,000 Americans were serving in Indochina. Within a few years this number had multiplied to 550,000 fighting men, of whom some 55,000 were killed and 300,000 were injured. Besides the appalling casualties, the war generated a horrendous dollar drain of some $150 billion which, among other things, crippled the Navy's shipbuilding program. Ultimately, Lyndon Johnson's blindness to the war's winner-take-all nature led directly to a catastrophe for South Vietnam and Cambodia. Indirectly, it caused a serious erosion of the once invincible U.S. fleet. Basic to an understanding of the war and its consequences is the concept of flexible response.

A New Theory of Making War

One of Kennedy's campaign pledges was the promise to modify the doctrine of massive retaliation by developing a strategy of flexible response. Kennedy's aides argued that rather than reacting to a crisis with nuclear bombing, the United States also have at hand conventional forces trained to extinguish brushfire wars.

Interestingly enough, President Eisenhower, despite his acceptance of massive retaliation, well understood the need for conventional forces in the cold war of the 1950s. In January 1959, he warned the Congress that such forces were required to "prevent war at any place and in any dimension."[2] Chief among them were carrier task forces and the Marines. Moreover, he himself employed flexible response (although he had not so labeled it) successfully in several situations, notably in the Lebanon landings of July 1958 and the defense of Quemoy and Matsu.

It could be argued that the Eisenhower concept of flexible response failed to recognize the threat of subversion of friendly governments and to devise necessary countermeasures. To plug this gap in U.S. strategic thinking, Kennedy pressed for more funding for conventional forces, especially countersubversion troops, later to become famous as the Green Berets.

The global role thrust on Washington policymakers after World War II, coupled with nightmarish thoughts of a possible nuclear war, attracted the attention of scholars seeking theoretical insights into the use of power. In probing the ethical aspects of war and the use of force in international relations, certain academicians grappled with the question of the amount of force required to win a victory in a given situation.[3]

The theory of flexible response that emerged in the 1950s held that wars could be "limited" if U.S. armed services were capable of shaping their military response to a threat with a military force tailored to the particular challenge. As proponents of flexible response pointed out, the aim was to avoid an all-out nuclear war. Understood in these terms flexible response was a commendable concept.

Yet the notion contained the seeds of potential danger because it was based on the assumption that the relative magnitude of the U.S. flexible response would signify to the enemy the value placed on the military objective. In other words, the doctrine of flexible response encouraged piecemeal operations that would fail to bring the enemy to terms. At that stage flexible response would cease to provide an acceptable solution and would instead lead to a gradual escalation of a limited war.

Gradualism implied the incremental application of military force, with pauses between each step to give an enemy a chance to respond. Sooner or later, he would realize that further resistance was futile and come to the negotiating table. In other words, everyone had his limit of pain. Thus, by gradually increasing the level of agony, then stopping temporarily to allow the enemy to reflect, one could bring an adversary to terms.

The idea of gradualism, which seemed to deny the principle of a vigorous offensive against the objective, found little favor with military professionals who pointed out that if you attack your enemy in a series of nibbles, you then allow him to reinforce his defense and foresee your next attack. The result (as proved in Indochina) is stalemate instead of victory.[4] Other critics correctly argued that the doctrine, as developed in Vietnam, seemed sane enough but contained a lethal logic—namely, that if it potentially lowered the level at which diplomacy would give way to shooting, it also opened the door to a progressive stepping up of the use of force.

Nevertheless, to the administration in Washington the doctrine of strategic gradualism seemingly offered a rational approach to the management of violence in combat situations. Naval officers such as Admiral U.S. Grant Sharp, trained in the belief that wars were won by destroying the enemy's will to resist through the decisive use of arms, were skeptical of the new theory. To them it meant self-imposed limitations on targets, combat areas, and the use of certain weaponry, for example, sea mines. Their worst doubts were realized when the Johnson administration, fearful of enlarging the war, refused to accept the idea that American air and naval power, properly applied against specific targets in North Vietnam, very possibly could bring the enemy quickly to his knees. For the Navy, this fateful decision meant a continuation of the limited-air-war strategy inherited from Korea. It also signaled to the Seventh Fleet that the brunt of the naval war (and the casualties) would be borne by carrier pilots and their air crewmen.

Gradualism or Equivocation

The doctrine of strategic gradualism had a particular appeal for Lyndon Johnson, who assumed the presidency after the tragic events in Dallas in November 1963. He desired, above all, to fight a small war, while pushing through costly welfare legislation in support of his Great Society programs.

The doctrine also appealed to McNamara, who—as a systems analyst—saw opportunities for controlling the war by measured quantification of combat actions and the assessment of results in terms such as body counts and aircraft sorties.[5]

In all likelihood, the unflappable defense secretary, encouraged by the success of the ad hoc White House group in handling the Cuban missile crisis, experienced no qualms in moving confidently into combat operations to a degree unknown in American history. His role was made easier by the irresolute Johnson, who hoped to wage war cheaply and therefore opted for what his opponents dubbed a strategy of equivocation.

So closely did Johnson, with McNamara at his side, control the fighting that the uninhibited president, reverting to the homely language of rural Texas, reportedly declared: "My boys [the fighting forces] cannot even bomb an outhouse without my approval."[6] Unintentionally, Johnson had summed up the crippling restrictions placed on U.S. combat arms, restrictions that completely ignored two principles of war: the offensive and surprise.[7] As a result, the fighting men, as his political critics repeatedly reminded the president, were forced to fight with one hand tied behind their backs.

Basic flaws existed in American strategy and tactics in Indochina. Clark Reynolds aptly describes the confusion of U.S. roles and missions in his book *Command of the Sea*. According to Reynolds, the Army viewed the conflict as a guerrilla war and forgot the Clausewitzian principle of "breaking the enemy's will in favor of ridiculous body-count statistics during halfhearted search and destroy patrols." The Marine Corps was surprised to see the Army take over its vertical envelopment tactics with "airmobile" troops transported by helicopters, which consequently meant the Army once more possessed its own air corps. The Air Force used its B-52 strategic bombers, startlingly, for tactical air support. The Marines found themselves used in positional army-type operations rather than as an amphibious assault command. The Navy's carrier planes conducted strategic bombing of enemy targets using piston-driven A-1 Skyraider aircraft, which were designed (and would have been more effective) for close air support.[8]

The basic flaw in Washington's strategy was rooted in Johnson's stubborn belief that the war could be won by fighting the Viet Cong inside South Vietnam. By 1972 when President Nixon ordered Hanoi bombed and Haiphong harbor mined, it was too late to save South Vietnam even though these strikes brought the enemy quickly to the Paris peace talks. In effect, U.S. policymakers, who tried to "keep the war small" by resorting to half-measures, succeeded only in stringing out the destruction and killing.

The Guns-and-Butter War

As U.S. involvement in Vietnam edged upward to $30 billion a year, McNamara's managers sought to reduce the skyrocketing costs by management and control techniques. To the extent that the defense secretary could assure the Congress and the U.S. public that the Navy's ship and aircraft procurement could be safely cut back, President Johnson could push forward his social programs.

Perhaps the beleaguered president, single-mindedly dedicated to helping the underprivileged, was not aware that by curtailing future shipbuilding programs, he was sacrificing a whole generation of naval ships. This serious setback to the fleet became glaringly evident in the late 1970s when many World War II–vintage vessels, finally at the end of useful service, were decommissioned without being replaced.

What was McNamara's explanation? According to one of his trusted subordinates, former Secretary of the Navy Paul Ignatius, the defense secretary, sitting in judgment on budget estimates, counted on the services to prepare their annual military requirements without being restrained by any prior budget ceiling. Thus, the reasoning went, the "force structure" of the respective armed forces could be determined without fiscal shackles. "Ultimately, of course," Ignatius admitted, "budgeting considerations were undoubtedly a factor."[9] After he had received the service's requirements or "wish list," McNamara demanded of his own staff a detailed analysis before he decided on the respective weapons systems that each service would receive. The Navy's budget cuts could be traced to McNamara's determination to fight the war with current defense "assets" (ships, planes, ammunition, spare parts, etc.). So he shunted aside any proposals for future replacements that would increase the already soaring defense costs.

In order to reserve all final verdicts on individual service proposals for his own decision, McNamara never disclosed budget limits for the Navy and the other services while they were preparing their force recommendations. Ostensibly he desired to know in advance the relative priority each service placed on its programs. Thus the defense secretary could conduct a review of all proposals and make his choices in accordance with their relative value to the nation's needs and strategic policy.

To naval planners it appeared that such highly centralized control in the hands of a cost-conscious secretary dedicated to holding down the expenses of a highly unpopular war destroyed the relevance of a naval budget based on the Navy's need for a realistic ship and aircraft replacement program. In fiscal year 1969, the Navy's budget was $26.7 billion, of which only $800 million was allotted for shipbuilding. Navy Secretary Ignatius, who had served as a naval combat officer in World War II, rightly considered the latter sum to be inordinately low and went on record as supporting more for the ship program.

It was a poor time for the Navy to ask for a substantial increase in funds, despite the obsolescence of a major part of its fleet. Washington's attention was increasingly focused on domestic problems. The nation was torn apart by racial conflict, antiwar demonstrations, inflation, the decline of the dollar, and troubles in the Middle East. Because of the stepped-up tempo of naval operations and a lack of sufficient maintenance time, the fleet suffered from troublesome materiel deficiencies.

The spare parts problem was acute, especially for complex electronic and mechanical equipment, as Congressman Porter Hardy of Virginia proclaimed in August 1968.[10] Basing his conclusion on an inspection conducted on board various ships, Hardy found the operational readiness of the Sixth Fleet in the Mediterranean to be "marginal." The report emphasized conditions of poor materiel maintenance and deterioration of equipment, both attributable to a lack of technicians, spare parts, and time for repair and upkeep. In a policy best described as borrowing from Peter to pay Paul, Hardy disclosed that in order to supply and maintain the ships of the Seventh Fleet off Indochina, the Navy had been forced to send repair ships, tankers, and skilled naval technician—petty officers from the Atlantic Fleet to the Far East, thus magnifying upkeep problems for the Sixth Fleet. In addition to the vexing problem of maintenance, the Atlantic Fleet's ammunition stocks had been drawn down to a dangerously low level in order to keep the Pacific Fleet supplied.

As if all this were not enough of a problem, the Navy's slender budgets practically compelled the CNO to mothball more ships from the fleet, with very little expectation that new vessels would be coming off the shipways. Clearly in terms of operational capability, the Navy of 1969 was not qualified to fulfill its worldwide mission on the scale of the previous decade. Particularly, the Navy was deprived of sufficient ASW forces, and the Marine Corps needed amphibious ships.

In 1967 McNamara had cut funds for antisubmarine programs, forcing the decommissioning of the carrier *Randolph* and other ASW units. Navy Secretary Ignatius reluctantly concurred on the dubious grounds that this dollar-saving expediency would not affect the safety of the fleet off Vietnam, where no submarine threat existed. Nevertheless, a worrisome fact remained: as the Soviet submarine force was expanding, the U.S. Navy's ASW strength was shrinking.

Running the War from the White House

The degree of tactical control exercised by the president, with the defense secretary at his side, was unprecedented. Johnson put his stamp of approval on all air targets. These lists, known as packages, were at first doled out weekly and later monthly, provoking bitter reactions from Seventh Fleet combat officers "on the line" off Vietnam.

As the system worked, the commander-in-chief Pacific Unified Command, initially transmitted a list of recommended targets to the JCS, which reviewed it. The list then was sent to many civilian levels in the Defense Department (notably, International Security Affairs) and the State Department for recommended changes. The amended version ended up on the president's desk.[11] It is safe to assume that in many cases the original list bore little relation to the final choice. Clearly, in May 1967 when the president approved attacks on Hanoi the political aspects exercised a dominant influence on the target list. The strikes were successfully carried out, but Johnson, now worried about the outcry cleverly exploited by the North Vietnamese in the world press over the death of innocent civilians, terminated all further attacks within ten miles of the North Vietnamese capital.

Lieutenant General Victor H. Krulak, USMC (Ret.), an expert in guerrilla warfare who was a member of the Joint Staff in the mid-1960s, some years later recalled an occasion at the White House when he watched in wonderment as President Johnson selected his targets. Standing firmly before an operations map of Vietnam, the grim-faced Texan, intent on "nailing the coonskin to the wall,"[12] placed his finger on specific sites to be bombed. Around him stood a circle of assenting advisors, all civilians.

According to Krulak, the chairman of the JCS, General Earle G. "Bus" Wheeler, tended to be too pliant in his relations with McNamara and Johnson. This criticism found a supporter in Hanson W. Baldwin, for years the military editor of the *New York Times*. Baldwin, who had excellent sources, related in his unpublished oral memoirs that McNamara, in his talks with Johnson, filtered and reinterpreted the opinions of the JCS. Baldwin recorded that he was told by General Wheeler and others of McNamara's habit of twisting words. "You know, when he'd go to the White House with McNamara, Wheeler would answer the President's question but McNamara would then interject and say, 'But look, Buzz [Bus], it's this way, isn's it?' and then he would put his own interpretation on it and get it shifted around."

Baldwin was a graduate of Annapolis, class of 1924, and had served several years in the fleet before his long and distinguished career with the *Times*. In reflecting on the strong-willed McNamara's apparent domination of General Wheeler, Baldwin said:

> I am sure that the fundamental factor in representation of the Pentagon [at the White House] was McNamara and not Wheeler. Wheeler was not a strong man and, although I think he did his best, he interpreted his job as Chairman as bridging a gap between the Secretary of Defense and the Joint Chiefs and the White House, and he did not pound the table and say, "Mr. President, these are the military considerations and it's no use doing it that way unless you take account of those."

By way of contrast, observed Baldwin, McNamara "was absolutely ruthless with anyone who said, 'We can't do it this way, Mr. Secretary.' "[13]

The Temptation To Take Charge

In a series of devastating reports on McNamara's meddling in combat-related issues better left to the professionals, Baldwin wrote a number of articles critical of the Pentagon's systems analysts ("people who had never done anything except go to school or teach school"). These officials, part of McNamara's staff, visited the fleet and the armed forces abroad while conducting surveys on matters of which they knew nothing, declared Baldwin. Understandably, relations between the two men were frigid. What irritated the defense secretary most of all were Baldwin's criticisms of McNamara's "extreme emphasis on theoretical analysis and on his subordination of military professionalism and judgment."[14]

As the Vietnam war expanded, Baldwin uncovered dangerously low stockpiles of military equipment from sources on the Senate Armed Services Committee.[15] Matters reached the point where McNamara finally snapped, "You're the most inaccurate reporter I've ever known." To which Baldwin retorted in effect that McNamara was the most dishonest secretary he had ever known. According to the journalist, McNamara never learned to put a good man in charge of a program "like [Admiral Raborn, who headed] the development of the Polaris missile system." Instead he acted as his own project officer and interfered at every level.[16]

Baldwin summed up his impressions in these words:

> He was the most egocentric man I think I've ever met, a man who did more damage, in my opinion, to national defense than any other one man in my experience. It was primarily due to a defect in personality and to the fact that when he was criticized, instead of becoming self-analytical a little bit, he built up a hedgehog [*sic*] around him [self] and became so protective and defensive. The other defect in character, which I think was of supreme importance to the military, was that he owed impeccable loyalty up but very little down, very little down.[17]

Concerned over the possibility that the Defense Department might have a great surplus of armaments after the war, and to avoid "waste," Defense officials cut back on war production so as to "come out to the last bullet" at war's end. Upset by such insensitivity to the life-and-death problems of the fighting men, Baldwin asked an assistant defense secretary, "Isn't it better to have a surplus than to have a loss of life?" The question, he acknowledged later, did not endear him to McNamara's staff.

One officer who paid dearly for the Pentagon's penny-pinching was Lieutenant Commander Richard A. Stratton of the carrier *Ticonderoga*.[18] As a carrier attack plane pilot, he was required to use air-to-air rockets (because of a shortage of munitions) as weaponry for air-to-ground attacks. These weapons were left over from the Korean War, and some were defective. On a combat mission over enemy territory, one of these malfunctioning rockets damaged Commander Stratton's plane. He bailed out, was captured, and spent six years as a prisoner at the so-called Hanoi Hilton prison. It seems beyond question that similar instances, which will never be known, occurred with fatal results.

Admiral Hyland, from his vantage point in the Seventh Fleet and later at Pacific Fleet headquarters, saw a danger in the growing tendency of senior civilians in

Washington to transmit verbose instructions to the forces afloat through the Navy's rapid communication system:

> Since it is possible, many times, because of the miracle of modern communications, to send out detailed orders, the civilian masters enjoy doing it. Almost any decision of importance is now made in Washington and the people on the scene have really little to say.
>
> I worry that this highly centralized system won't work in wartime. We are raising whole generations who expect to be told what to do, in detail. What will happen when the system is damaged in battle, and nobody tells the warrior what to do?[19]

As a combat commander off Indochina, Hyland was the recipient of many messages from the secretary of defense, detailing what targets were authorized, the number of sorties allowed, and the tactics to be used by naval pilots.

Admiral Hyland observed that civilian control had expanded since World War II, possibly because political and military affairs had become so entwined that appointed officials found it difficult to withdraw from political crises when the fleet became involved. Another reason could be ascribed to modern technology. In the years before the cold war, civilian officials were less apt to intervene in ongoing ("real-time") military field operations. But in the 1960s, when reliable voice and radio communications extended worldwide, the temptation was too great for many of them to resist.

Limited War and All-out Commitment

The administration's seeming indifference to the dangers encountered by naval men fighting a limited war had a special relevance for carrier pilots under orders to hit secondary targets protected by deadly Soviet surface-to-air (SAM) missiles.

Consider the outlook and attitude of a senior U.S. naval aviator who was finally shot down and spent over seven years as a prisoner of war in Hanoi. Commander James B. Stockdale, a down-to-earth midwesterner, was graduated from the Naval Academy in 1947. He had spent most of his career in the naval air arm, save for two years at Stanford University where he earned a master's degree in political science. In September 1965, on a mission over enemy territory, his plane was hit. He parachuted to earth, badly injuring his leg in the landing, and was captured. His valorous leadership as the senior officer of all POWs in Vietnam marked him as one of the many brave men largely unnoticed in a business-as-usual war. Having written down his thoughts beforehand, Commander Stockdale spoke to the 120 pilots of his air wing on board the carrier *Oriskany* April 29, 1965, while the ship was steaming toward Tonkin Gulf (see Appendix A for text of talk). One week later, these pilots were in combat. The commitment of the fighting men, as embodied in his stirring words, was in stark contrast to the limited war mindset of Pentagon analysts.[20]

Anticipating that his men were asking themselves how they could fight a war under "this limited war, measured response" concept, Stockdale told them that there could be nothing limited about their personal commitment to bore in on the target, no matter what the opposition. National commitment and personal commitment were two different things:

"Limited war" means to us that our target list has limits, our ordnance loadout has limits, our rules of engagement have limits, but that does *not* mean that there is anything "limited" about our personal obligations as fighting men to carry out assigned missions with all we've got. If you think it is possible for a man, in the heat of battle, to apply something less than total *personal* commitment—equated perhaps to your idea of the proportion of *national* potential being applied—you are wrong . . .

Let us all face our prospects squarely. We've got to be prepared to obey the rules and contribute without reservation. If political or religious conviction helps you do this, so much the better, but you're still going to be expected to press on with or without these comforting thoughts, simply because this uniform commits us to a military ethic—the ethic of personal pride and excellence that alone has supported some of the greatest fighting men in history. Don't require Hollywood answers to "what are we fighting for?" We're here to fight because it's in the interest of the United States that we do. This may not be the most dramatic way to explain it, but it has the advantage of being absolutely correct.

Stockdale ended his attention-riveting talk by pointing out that, like all forms of caution, "caution in war" has a fatal effect on a fighting man's future self-respect:

When that Fox Flag is two-blocked in the Gulf, you'll be an actor in a drama that you'll replay in your mind's eye for the rest of your life. Level with yourself now. Do your duty. [21]

Years later Commander (by then Vice Admiral) Stockdale recalled that none of his officers came forward with reservations. Of this group of 120 pilots, 8 were destined to be killed in action, 1 was declared missing in action, and 4, including Stockdale, spent years of their lives in barely survivable conditions in Hanoi. [22]

How can one account for such heroism under conditions of intermittent combat that allowed the enemy time to regroup before the next series of attacks? Vice Admiral Ralph W. Cousins was commander of the carrier force in late 1967 and early 1968 when American naval aircraft mounted major strikes against North Vietnam in the face of furious opposition. In praising his airmen, he noted that they had taken the war to the enemy in "downtown Hanoi and Haiphong" where the flak and SAMs presented air crews with "the most hostile environment in the history of warfare." In spite of the loss of hundreds of the finest fighting men, many of whom were captured, the morale of his air squadrons never wavered. It was only by virtue of this resolute, single-minded devotion to duty by the men flying the A-6 attack planes, declared Admiral Cousins, "that Hanoi decided that they had better go to the Paris Conference to see what relief—and concessions—

they could win by negotiations." He concluded that never in any previous U.S. war had "young men been as courageous—as competent—as they have in this one."[23]

Over-the-Shoulder Combat Control

Naval combat commanders viewed the Navy's role in the war with mixed emotions. Rear Admiral Malcolm Cagle served as commander of a carrier division in combat during 1968 and 1969. During the previous three years he had observed the Pentagon's direction of the war as a senior staff officer of the CNO. Cagle later wrote that civilian control over combat operations in Southeast Asia was "complete, unquestioned, ubiquitous, and detailed, not only at the higher levels of strategy and political decisions, but also—very importantly—at the lower levels of operations and tactics."[24]

Rear Admiral Henry L. Miller, who commanded the carrier task force off Vietnam in 1965, later recalled the flood of operational dispatches daily transmitted from Washington. Some of the messages directed what targets to hit, when to hit them, and what combat units (Navy or Air Force) would carry out particular strikes. It was a "stop-and-go war" that was new in his experience, said Miller.[25]

A minor annoyance was a steady stream of visitors, including ambassadors, generals, senators, congressmen, newsmen, and Pentagon officials, who came on board the ships off Vietnam to see the carriers in action. Such VIPs have visited fighting fronts ever since the Civil War, but the practice reached new heights for the Seventh Fleet off Indochina. What drew these visitors to the front line of the war? At best, some had an honest curiosity in the mechanics of an air launch at dawn or the debriefing pilots and the like. At worst, ego was involved. Some wanted to show their importance, perhaps to return home and tell listeners how the "real" war was being fought. In this latter sense their visits were unproductive and slowed carrier operations.

For all the over-the-shoulder direction of the naval war, the military—from the JCS down to the junior officers piloting the attacking aircraft—were in the words of Admiral Cagle, "conscientiously obedient, subservient, and responsive to their civilian control. Not once did a responsible [naval] commander exceed his authority or disobey his orders. Not once did any naval airman succumb to the temptation of dropping a string of bombs on a loaded merchant ship, or fire into a huge stockpile of oil drums and war materials on the Haiphong piers."[26]

Senior naval officers in key posts during the Indochina conflict generally have chosen not to write of their reactions to the Johnson-McNamara takeover of tactical direction of the war and of the President's rejection of military advice. An exception was Admiral U.S. Grant Sharp, the commander-in-chief of the Pacific command during much of the Vietnam war. A brainy officer devoid of pretension,

Sharp was a 1927 graduate of Annapolis and a combat veteran of World War II and Korea. Later, as director of strategic plans and as deputy chief of naval operations (plans and policy), he had become intimately acquainted with Washington's web of power. [27]

Ordered to the command of the Pacific Fleet in 1963, he was promoted a year later to overall command of the entire theater, including forces in Indochina. For four years from his headquarters at Pearl Harbor, Sharp—supported by the JCS—kept up a drumfire of opposition to the Johnson-McNamara concept that stopping enemy infiltration to the south was the objective of the war. The U.S. purpose in fighting, declared Sharp, was to destroy North Vietnam's source-targets (ports, factories, airfields, power plants) in order to destroy its will to fight. Incomprehensible to him, and to many senior officers, was the administration's refusal to carry the war to the enemy.

In Sharp's view, President Johnson, in disregard of military advice, grievously erred by refusing to employ the immensely superior air power of the Navy and Air Force in a sustained hammering of critical targets in North Vietnam. Instead, a fear of Soviet and Chinese communist intervention, coupled with an obsession to contain the war in the south, prompted Johnson to compromise on so-called tit-for-tat air attacks against North Vietnam and then only if any U.S. unit in the south was attacked. The president also authorized a display of force by the dispatch of U.S. naval ship patrols off North Vietnam. A mystified Sharp labeled these reactive moves mere demonstrations rather than aggressive actions. [28]

Hanson Baldwin has speculated that "some of the younger and [more] enthusiastic" Air Force officers might have sold, indirectly, the idea that "a few [bombs] dropped selectively here and there" on the north would force Hanoi to capitulate. When the initial attacks failed to budge the enemy, the attacks were reduced. "In other words," said Baldwin, it was "the same over-estimation of air power . . . [that occurred] in many cases in World War II." Baldwin believed that Johnson never grasped "the sound use of air power—continuous interdiction." [29]

Holding the Carriers in Check

In December 1964, seemingly persuaded that the war should be stepped up, Johnson agreed to an air-bombing campaign, known as Rolling Thunder, against North Vietnam. But, as Admiral Sharp observed, the president approved this bellicose move only in theory. The JCS and Sharp had argued that only a "dramatic and forceful application" of power would erode the enemy's will to continue the fight. To the military's regret their counsel did not prevail. As Admiral Sharp recalled, most civilian officials in the State Department, the White House, and on McNamara's staff argued for a restrained, gradual schedule of attacks on the principle, ultimately proved wrong, that future U.S. attacks of greater violence would run the risk of impelling Russia and China to declare war. Ever sensitive to world opinion, Johnson's advisors convinced him that he must forgo large-scale attacks in the north. Presumably he was prompted to do so after McNamara informed him in July 1965 that a wider war would "appall our allies and friends."[30]

The lack of progress of the limited air war ultimately led the reluctant president to change the course of the conflict by dispatching vast numbers of ground troops, both Army and Marines, to South Vietnam. Curiously enough, by this action he tacitly accepted the military's view that limited, gradual attacks would not bring the enemy to the peace table. Abandoned was his original plan for the incremental use of force. Instead, he hoped to signal Hanoi that its forces could never achieve victory in the south because it was defended by a huge U.S. ground force. Thus began an ugly ground war in the jungles and rice paddies, a self-imposed Sisyphean task in which most of the advantage lay with the North Vietnamese.

In a larger sense, by refusing to mobilize the reserve forces and declare a national emergency, and by wrongfully deferring college students from the draft, Johnson set in motion a program that sent thousands of poor, less educated youths to the combat front, while many of their more fortunate contemporaries remained at the universities. The damage to the morale of fighting forces in Indochina and to the social fabric of American life wrought by this latter decision was incalculable. Its harsh consequences surfaced in the Navy and, to a lesser extent, in the Marine Corps in the late 1960s, as racial tensions, drug problems, and sabotage hampered operations both afloat and ashore.

The Senators and the Strategists

For the Navy the most frustrating feature of the war was Johnson's reluctance to mine the ports of North Vietnam. Repeatedly Admiral Sharp, backed up by the JCS, sought permission to lay mines by aircraft and to bomb the harbors. Meanwhile, the enemy continued to unload arms cargoes 24 hours a day from Soviet bloc vessels at Haiphong while, offshore, the Seventh Fleet carriers were held in check. Loathe to make the critical decision that might mean the destruction of Soviet ships, the vacillating Johnson continued to waffle.

Sharp's reasoning seemed sound enough.[31] Accurate nighttime planting of mines could have been accomplished by carrier A-6 Intruder attack planes under cover of diversionary air strikes. Mining posed the least threat to civilians and would not have directly involved third nations. Closure of the ports by mines would have imposed severe hardship on the North Vietnamese at a cheap price to the U.S. Navy. Only a few aircraft were needed for the task, and even fewer planes would have been required to replant the mine field. Last, 95 percent of the huge flow of foreign imports from the Soviet Union and other European nations entered through Haiphong. Sealing off this port would have been a major step toward victory.

By now, Admiral Sharp was resigned to the probability that Washington would continue to reject any forthright action against Hanoi and Haiphong. And he was not surprised when his recommendation was buried in the Pentagon files. As the seemingly endless fighting ground on, certain senators and congressmen demanded explanations on the conduct of the war.

Matters came to a boil in August 1967, when a panel of the Senate Armed Services Committee heard testimony on the inconclusive air war against North Vietnam.[32] Conducted by shrewd and knowledgeable John Stennis, the panel included Henry M. Jackson, Stuart Symington, Howard Cannon, Robert C. Byrd, and Strom Thurman. The closed hearings revealed in some detail the futility of fighting a war by half-measures. Interestingly enough, as Sharp later recalled, just hours before he was scheduled to testify before the panel, the administration apparently had a change of heart on target lists:

> The night before my testimony we [Pacific Unified Command] received authority for sixteen targets that I had been trying to hit for some time. They included the Hanoi thermal power plant, three railyards, two bridges, and some lines of communication targets in the ChiCom [Chinese communist] buffer zone. It didn't take the Committee long to figure out that giving permission to hit these sixteen targets might have been an attempt [by the administration] to spike my guns.[33]

The panel met for three weeks, taking testimony from Admiral Sharp, General Wheeler (then chairman of the JCS), Secretary McNamara, and various senior military officers. Understandably, the panel's hawks, among whom were Symington, Jackson, and Thurman, appeared more sympathetic to the military than to McNamara. After six years of testifying before congressional groups, the self-assured defense secretary, who could rattle off detailed responses loaded with statistics, had lost favor with many of Capitol Hill.

McNamara Sticks to His Guns

The official transcript of the hearings reveals McNamara's firm refusal to agree with Admiral Sharp and the military witnesses that an accelerated air campaign in the north would reduce casualties in the south. The secretary testified that he had "seen no evidence" to change his mind despite what the panel termed "the overwhelming weight of the testimony of military experts" to the contrary. Instead, he clung steadfastly to his belief that the North Vietnamese leaders ultimately would recognize that continued heavy defeats on the ground would lead them ''to see that they face self-destruction'' if they continued ''their efforts to subvert the institutions of the South.''

A facile debater, the secretary parried hostile questions by advancing his thoughts on how General Westmoreland, Admiral Sharp, and the JCS would answer the same questions. McNamara argued that it was ''incumbent upon us to take such military action as to achieve our objective at the lowest cost in American lives and the lowest risk to this Nation.'' Not surprisingly, militant Senator Thurmond, a Republican from South Carolina, a major general in the Army Reserve, and a decorated combat officer in World War II, expressed deep disappointment over what he described as a ''statement of no-win.''

Quizzed by Senator Jackson on how the United States could end the war without stopping the constant flow of Soviet supplies that formed the bulk of the enemy's arsenal, McNamara persisted in his answer that aerial mining of the ports could not ''cut them off'' and would carry ''very serious military risks.'' The rest of his response was deleted, suggesting that he raised the possibility of Soviet and Chinese intervention.[34]

General Wallace M. Greene, commandant of the Marine Corps, was asked by Senator Margaret Chase Smith, a Republican from Maine, if he opposed ''the concept of gradualism which we have adopted as national policy with respect to the air campaign against North Vietnam.'' Greene, conscious that he was voicing a controversial view, replied that in his ''own personal view'' he was strongly against it.[35]

"Unskilled Amateurs" and Partisan Politics

In a report published on August 31, 1967, the senators came down resoundingly against civilian meddling in tactical operations.[36] The panel found a ''sharp difference of opinion'' between the administration's civil officials and the top-level military witnesses who testified on ''how and when our air power should be employed against North Vietnam.'' The report went on to say that the plain facts revealed in the testimony

> demonstrated clearly that civilian authority consistently overruled the unanimous recommendations of the military commander and the Joint Chiefs of Staff for a systematic, timely, and hard-hitting integrated air campaign against the vital North Vietnam targets. Instead, for policy reasons, we have employed military aviation in a carefully controlled, restricted and graduated build-up of bombing pressure which discounted the professional judgment of our best military experts and substituted civilian judgment in the details of target selection and the timing of strikes. We shackled the true potential of air power and permitted the build-up of what has become the world's most formidable anti-aircraft defenses.

The senators expressed their low opinion of civilian control of the war by noting the "diametrically opposed views" of the defense secretary and the military leaders.

> In such circumstances and in view of the unsatisfactory progress of the war, logic and prudence require that the decision be with the unanimous weight of professional military judgment . . .
>
> It is high time, we believe, to allow the military voice to be heard in connection with the tactical details of military operations.

The panel concluded that the administration's policy of throttling the aviation forces had not "done the job" and was contrary to the best military judgment.

Predictably, the Stennis report caused alarm bells to ring in the White House. Johnson immediately convened a press conference to assure the public that there were no differences on war policy in his administration.[37] He even went so far as to order an escalation in the attacks on North Vietnam's ports. But the time had long passed for Johnson to turn the tide.

With only months remaining before McNamara's departure from the Pentagon, the panel evaluated his role in the war in words that represented a harsh condemnation for strategy conducted by what the panel called "unskilled amateurs."

> That the air campaign has not achieved its objectives to a greater extent cannot be attributed to inability or impotence of air power. It attests, rather, to the fragmentation of our air might by overly restrictive controls, limitations, and the doctrine of "gradualism" placed on our aviation forces which prevented them from waging the air campaign in the manner and according to the timetable which was best calculated to achieve maximum results.[38]

The panel took pains to make clear that it did not derogate the principle of civilian control of the military, "one of the truly great bulwarks of our system of government. The best traditions of the military uphold this principle and it has been scrupulously adhered to in both the conduct of this war and during the hearings." Nevertheless, an editorial in the *New York Times* entitled "Generals out of Control" expressed alarm over the erosion taking place in the constitutional balance that supposedly puts the military under civilian direction.[39] The *Times* editorial writer apparently was unaware that military officers traditionally have responded to direct questions in congressional hearings that seek their personal views. In fact, the real issue revealed by the hearings, that of allegedly excessive and damaging civilian direction of combat operations, was completely overlooked by the *Times* writer.

In retrospect, the panel's strong criticism could be traced partly to opposition to the administration's strategic blunders and partly to the Senate's realization that it had relinquished too much of its power when it had passed the Tonkin Gulf Resolution in August 1964, giving Lyndon Johnson a license to escalate the war to its by then unmanageable state. Partisan politics were very much a factor in the hearings, which gave the hawks a forum to counterblast those who ridiculed their views on hitting the enemy on his own ground. Last, the hearings helped to persuade Johnson to step up the Seventh Fleet's strikes against Hanoi and Haiphong, a move that eventually forced the North Vietnamese to the conference table in Paris. Korean War veterans recalled that similar tactics had compelled the North Koreans to meet with U.N. negotiators at Panmunjom.

The Joint Chiefs: The Silent Military

A best-seller first published in 1969, *The Best and Brightest* by David Halberstam, is a revealing but undocumented account of the civilian officials who directed the disaster of Vietnam. Halberstam pictures the Joint Chiefs as mystified that as the war escalated, they as professionals were allowed so little control and instead were eased aside by civilians around the president. He ascribes (correctly) to the Joint Chiefs the feeling that McNamara did not really represent their position to the president and that they were on the outside looking in. But he falls into error when he describes the chiefs as "simple men" convinced that "if you had to go to war you used force . . . maximum warfare. If we were going to bomb then it had to be saturation bombing . . . Obliteration of the enemy." In particular, Halberstam wrongly depicts the CNO, Admiral David McDonald, as "anxious to show that the carrier still worked and to get its share of roles and missions in what had been largely an Army show."[40]

This unflattering description of the chiefs fails to take into account the testimony of Admiral Sharp and other military officers at the Stennis hearings. In fact, Halberstam devotes just two paragraphs in his 665 pages of text to the Stennis hearings, failing utterly to grasp the point that the proposed air attacks in the north were pinpointed at source-targets, such as the Haiphong wharves, and were designed to destroy the enemy's capability to fight—not to control the degree of violence by limiting the war in the south. Halberstam dismisses the hearings as "primed by frustrated and unhappy generals."[41] However, he correctly concludes that when McNamara in his testimony sought to "remove bombing as a means of attaining victory," he enraged Johnson, who no longer considered him a trusted strategic advisor. Within three months the defense secretary was happy to be transferred out of the Pentagon and into the presidency of the World Bank, a position he holds as this is being written.[42] He left behind a record that, his critics said, epitomized the folly of war management by civilians whose primary aim was not victory but limited political goals.

Halberstam discloses the shadowy status of the Joint Chiefs as the legally authorized principal defense advisors to the president in a brief passage.

It was years later, when the decision making in this war was analyzed that the names and faces of the civilians came easily to mind, but the names and faces of the Chiefs remained a mystery. Was it Earle Wheeler or Harold Johnson at Army? Curtis LeMay or John McConnell at the Air Force? David McDonald or Thomas Moorer at Navy?[43]

Neither Admiral McDonald nor Admiral Moorer, as yet, have made public their oral histories recorded in manuscript form by the U.S. Naval Institute at Annapolis. The same is true of General Greene of the Marine Corps. One need not doubt that their recollections of relations with their civilian superiors pertaining to the conduct of the war will prove blistering.

Future historians may well reveal that once the White House made the decision to fight in Southeast Asia, military operations should not have been shackled by political factors. In reviewing the record, Admiral Sharp is of the opinion that the Joint Chiefs did not exercise "to a sufficient extent" their legal right to carry their opposition to gradualism directly to President Johnson. Admiral Sharp seems to be saying guardedly that (like Admiral Burke at the time of the Bay of Pigs planning) the chiefs failed to "pound the table" in the Oval Office, insisting on a "dramatic, forceful, and *consistent* application of air power in the North."

Nor does Sharp spare himself, acknowledging that "I should perhaps have injected myself, early on and more than once into the Washington arena with *personal* briefings of the sort I gave to Secretary McNamara at Saigon in mid-1967." He admits that, in any event, there was more than enough "responsibility" to go around for each to take his share.[44]

Admiral Sharp raises an arresting moral question for serving senior officers. At what point does an individual officer who disagrees strongly with administration policy march into the office of the president and express his strong opposition? Conventional wisdom advises caution. The president can hire and fire senior officers at any time. Wave-makers can be replaced by more pliant officers willing to accept the administration's defense policies unreservedly. One can only speculate on the effect on the war's course if the Joint Chiefs collectively had pounded Lyndon Johnson's table.[45] Would the harried Johnson have sent them packing, thereby risking an inevitable, unwanted public uproar? Or would he have accepted their advice, for example, to mine Haiphong as eventually ordered by President Nixon?

Yet another aspect of the civilian-military relationship was raised by Admiral Hyland. Expressing concern over the trend toward politicization of the service, he wondered if a bright, ambitious young officer might very well decide that the impression he made on his civilian superiors would advance his career more than his service reputation with his professional seniors. Such an officer, reasoned Hyland, could decide to try to seek promotion through the tactic of pleasing civilian officials in Washington, counting on their influence, rather than seeking command at sea where his talents would not be visible to them. Presumably,

Hyland was referring to the dominant role played by not only the secretary of the navy but the secretary of defense and the deputy defense secretary in the assignment of three- and four-star flag officers—including fleet commanders. Thus in Hyland's view the professional assessment of these officers as potential combat leaders at sea lay essentially in the judgment of civilians who lacked the competence to do so. Obviously this was no way to run a navy, in the view of one former fleet commander-in-chief.[46]

Five

THE NIXON YEARS
AND NAVAL DECLINE

Nixon and a New Pentagon Team

RICHARD M. NIXON, a complex personality whose role in history will absorb the attention of scholars for decades, won the presidency in 1968, defeating Johnson's vice-president, Hubert Humphrey, by the barest of margins. A native Californian, reared in modest circumstances, Nixon had won a law school scholarship at Duke University. After Pearl Harbor, he became a naval combat intelligence officer, serving at various bases in the Pacific. Entering politics after the war, he won attention as a strong, if opportunistic, anticommunist first in the House and later in the Senate. As Eisenhower's vice-president, while on a visit to Moscow, he engaged in a spontaneous, finger-jabbing debate with the blustering Khrushchev. The press photographs of the incident seemingly demonstrated to the world that he was not easily intimidated by the Soviets.

Nixon appointed as his defense secretary, Melvin Laird, a seasoned political professional who had been an eight-term congressman from Wisconsin. In World War II he had fought in the Pacific as a destroyer officer and later authored several books on national defense policy. Senior naval officers correctly anticipated that their relationship with civilian leaders of the Defense Department would greatly improve.

Shortly after the Republican victory, Laird visited Vietnam where he met Vice Admiral Elmo R. Zumwalt, Jr.[1] Zumwalt, as commander of Naval Forces Vietnam, headed the "brown-water Navy," the many small craft patrolling the Mekong delta waters to prevent enemy infiltration. Part of Zumwalt's responsibility was the development of a program to turn his command over to the South Vietnamese, a process later known as Vietnamization. President Lyndon Johnson, reports

Zumwalt, originated the idea in the dying days of his administration.[2] Vietnamization had a special appeal for visiting Secretary Laird as a modus operandi under which the U.S. forces could pull out "with honor." Interestingly, when Zumwalt briefed the secretary on the accelerated turnover procedure, he evidently made such a lasting impression that two years later Laird was instrumental in his selection as CNO.

Highly critical of McNamara's custom of "sizing out" the respective service budgets, Laird promptly laid it to rest. McNamara, during the annual budget-planning period, had refused to disclose the approximate dollar amount to be allotted each service because he alone wished to decide on an overall priority list for the services. Recognizing that this process made any realistic planning by the Navy virtually impossible, Laird informed each service of its budget limit.[3] In another move welcomed by the Navy Department, Laird unobtrusively let it be known that henceforth the systems analysts would not review programs but instead would play only an advisory role. The JCS now sensed that it could have a more dominant voice in military policy.

In the search for a solution to postwar national security, the administration announced the Nixon Doctrine on July 25, 1969, at Guam, pledging that the United States would keep its treaty commitments with allies and provide them with a nuclear shield. But, and this was the heart of the new policy, U.S. forces no longer would rush into Asian wars. True, Washington would send arms to its allies, but henceforth, any U.S. ally involved in conflict would have to bear the main burden of fighting its own war. To support the Nixon doctrine, U.S. war planners devised a new ocean strategy based on a deterrent force of missile submarines and a general-purpose fleet. The latter presumably would allow the Navy to dominate selected sea areas, project power abroad, and maintain a naval presence where needed. The catch was that the Navy would be required to carry out these missions with a much smaller force.

The administration left no doubt about the rigors of the new austerity, emphasizing that smaller defense budgets were necessary so that the White House could support more urgent social programs for housing, medical care, and education. The fleet felt the impact on August 21, 1969, when 100 ships were decommissioned and 72,000 personnel discharged from the service. The move, obviously in response to White House instructions, was the first of a series of cutbacks with ominous long-term consequences.

Some ten years later, Henry Kissinger, who served Nixon initially as national security advisor and later as secretary of state, charged that a Democratic Congress (ignoring the need for a strong U.S. defense posture) was responsible for the cutbacks. So determined were the legislators to reduce defense programs that even when the White House, knowing in advance the mood on the Hill, submitted a bare-bones budget, the Congress made further cuts.[4]

Chafee, Zumwalt, and Progressive Reform

The new secretary of the navy on the Nixon team was John Hubbard Chafee, a Republican from Rhode Island. Reportedly, he had been offered the post to give some representation to the liberal, East Coast wing of the GOP. Chafee became secretary at a time when the national temper was marked by disillusionment with war, racial strife, and widespread rebellion against authority. The new secretary was filled with an earnest desire to introduce changes in the Navy, designed to make the service more palatable to what he interpreted as youth's desire for recognition, self-expression, and well-being. In assessing his performance at the Pentagon, certain senior officers regretted that although he did not consciously order any specific action to lower naval standards, he was in charge during the years that naval standards in discipline, appearance, and behavior deteriorated to a point where the fighting effectiveness of the fleet was affected.[5] Proponents of Chafee argue that he supported long overdue changes, which in the long run strengthened the Navy.

The new secretary, with the strong endorsement of his superior, Defense Secretary Melvin Laird, chose Vice Admiral Zumwalt as his CNO. "Bud" Zumwalt, only 49 years old, handsome, competent, and possessed of an astute, analytical mind, was picked over 33 senior admirals. He was the youngest officer ever to hold the post.[6]

Some of Zumwalt's naval superiors, notably outgoing Chief of Naval Operations Moorer, believed that Zumwalt's selection was premature. No one denied his inherent brilliance, but many were uneasy about his relative lack of experience. Zumwalt himself tells how Admiral Moorer (soon to be chairman of the JCS) advised that Zumwalt "be saved for the top slot for four more years," that is, his appointment be delayed for the present.

Moorer's reasoning proved sound in the opinion of many firsthand observers of Zumwalt's turbulent tenure. For one thing, he had commanded only destroyer-type ships before being promoted to rear admiral. His only sea command as a flag officer was a minor one, that of a cruiser/destroyer flotilla based at San Diego. He had received an early promotion to rear admiral largely because of the strong recommendation of Secretary of the Navy Paul Nitze.[7]

One of his contemporaries, Vice Admiral Gerald E. Miller, regretted that in view of his unique talents and great desire to excel, Zumwalt never had the opportunity to command a unit similar to a 90,000-ton aircraft carrier with a ship's company of 5,000.[8] Such a command, Miller declared, would have brought Zumwalt "closer to the realities of modern command at sea." In brief, Zumwalt had spent relatively much time in Washington wrestling successfully with conceptual and technical problems but relatively little in facing tough operational and morale problems encountered by major fleet commanders. Zumwalt's subsequent stormy record in eliminating so-called Mickey Mouse (outmoded customs) in the Navy confirmed to many that he had been promoted too soon. But, as Zumwalt wrote later, he "believed so deeply in the need for changes in the Navy . . . that I could not refuse to the job [of CNO]."[9]

A multifaceted individual, Zumwalt undoubtedly could have become a noted political figure had he not chosen a naval career. An accomplished speaker who was sensitive to changing social values, he would have moved easily with Theodore Roosevelt's progressive reformers and their political descendants.

In 1970, as in the early 1900s, America was going through a fundamental social, economic, and political transformation. The Chafee-Zumwalt reforms; like Theodore Roosevelt's progressivism, advocated and, in some cases, achieved the goals of social justice and equality for the underprivileged. Reformers as a group tend to show traces of self-righteousness and moralistic militancy in trying to repair deficiencies arbitrarily and too fast. No one doubted Zumwalt's dedicated sincerity, but his critics faulted him for not foreseeing obvious pitfalls.

A Cloud of Z-Grams

On taking command on July 1, 1970, Zumwalt announced that he would institute certain personnel procedures "to conform to certain social attitudes." In short order a torrent of directives streamed out of his office. Dubbed Z-grams, they were intended to promote new social attitudes and to make naval life more attractive by eliminating "demeaning and abrasive regulations."[10] The Z-grams were not designed to relax good order and discipline but to improve the quality of naval life.

Unfortunately, looser regulations tempted less motivated enlisted men and officers to disregard traditional discipline. Unkempt uniforms, nonsalutes, and a general lack of smartness became more and more obvious. Enlistment into the Navy of many underprivileged youths created problems. Some of them, reared in black ghettos, assumed that because their superiors were white they could not be trusted, a development that led to disciplinary and racial troubles.

In extenuation, we should bear in mind that the changes introduced by Zumwalt, with Chafee's support, were presumed to be supportive of White House and Pentagon affirmative action and equal opportunity programs. Both officials were motivated, as Chafee put it, by a desire to "provide a high degree of job satisfaction to all hands."[11] Unfortunately, when naval enlistment fell off, the Navy lowered its entrance requirements, thus attracting many members of various racial backgrounds who lacked a knowledge of elementary science and mathematics. Failing to qualify for the Navy's technical schools, they were assigned to jobs in the deck force, the ship's laundry, or the galley—work that they considered menial. Militants in the fleet quickly found these discontented sailors a fruitful source of troublemakers.

In sum, Zumwalt's supporters praised him for dragging a reluctant Navy into the twentieth century. But many held that his reforms ultimately led to a tolerance in the fleet of unruly and eventually mutinous conduct.

By late 1972 four mutinous riots or free-for-alls had erupted in two aircraft carriers and a fleet oiler. Such widespread violence, much of it reportedly traceable to racism in the Navy, brought on a Congressional investigation.[12] Following the uproar, Navy Secretary John Warner (who had succeeded Chafee in April 1972) and Admiral Zumwalt took steps to raise enlistment standards and to rid the service of marginal performers through the device of early discharge.

In his memoirs, Zumwalt devotes forty pages to his version of the flare-ups, arguing that the great majority of the Navy had the good sense to recognize "the personnel changes we had made had benefitted all hands and were not a fit subject for politicians to tinker with."[13]

Former CNOs invited to confer with Zumwalt at the Pentagon privately expressed their disagreement on one important aspect of his reforms. It was the opinion of the Navy's elder statesmen that by setting up committees on board ship (the human relations councils), which were designed to promote the human goals program, Zumwalt had undermined the chain of command, the keystone of all successful military organizations. At the meeting Admiral Carney, the most senior of the former CNOs, later recalled that having sent all staff personnel out of the room, he delivered this judgment to a somber Zumwalt:

> After requesting staff members to leave the room—what I was going to say should not be said in the presence of Zumwalt's subordinates—I told Zumwalt that I had two points to make:
>
> (a) That he violated accepted principles of leadership and command when he upbraided his flag-officer subordinates in the Pentagon, and then released his remarks to Congress and the press.
>
> (b) By establishing minority representatives in every command, and authorizing them to submit their complaints to higher authority without reference to the legal established military chain of command, was no different from the Russian commissar system, and undermined the authority and positions of those in the chain of command.
>
> I summarized by saying that I considered those actions to be in direct violation of the proven and accepted principles of leadership and command.
>
> Zumwalt did not respond.
>
> I was blunt—and meant to be.

Admiral Arleigh Burke recalled that Admiral Carney had the full concurrence of the former CNOs who were present and they all added to Carney's thoughts. According to Burke, Admiral Zumwalt had bypassed his senior subordinates who bore the responsibility for their respective commands, thereby undercutting their authority. Burke added, "I also believe that was the last time that the old past CNOs were invited to confer with Zumwalt. Bud was not a man to want his ideas discussed adversely."[14]

As Vincent Davis observed, in the U.S. Navy a typical advocate of innovation is likely to be a vastly self-confident person who has already carved out a promising career and is accustomed to "winning." He abhors inefficiency, obsolete practices based on tradition, and conventional thinking. He suffers, more often than not, from a certain intellectual arrogance. If he attracts followers by his charm, dedication, and intellect, he also becomes a target for critics who prefer a calmer, more cautious approach.[15] So it was with Zumwalt, who was determined to steer the Navy into the modern age. Significantly, he and Navy Secretary Chafee reportedly asked for the early retirement of senior flag officers. In their stead they appointed relatively young admirals impatient to implement Zumwalt's reforms.

In one notable appointment, Rear Admiral Stansfield Turner was named president of the Naval War College, reportedly with instructions from Zumwalt "to shake the place up." Turner, a former Rhodes Scholar, later was appointed by President Carter, his Naval Academy classmate (class of 1947), as director of the CIA, where he again, stirred controversy by his administrative changes.

Two years after the fleet disorders, Admiral Zumwalt was asked by a journalist to comment on his human goals program. He replied that he "would have been more methodical and painstaking about being sure that all hands understood what was behind each change."[16] One senses an acknowledgment that he might have been too swift in taking actions that, some said, had the effect of diluting the Navy's time-tested system of discipline and its combat effectiveness.

When more senior naval officers and public officials have written their memoirs or released their oral histories, thus providing evidence, future historians will be able to evaluate the impact of Zumwalt's reforms on the fleet. From the evidence at hand, his naval critics concluded that in 1974 his successor, Admiral James L. Holloway, III, inherited the rather formidable task of getting the Navy back on course, an accomplishment that was to win Holloway many plaudits.

Calculated Risks: Possibilities Versus Probabilities

From the standpoint of the Navy the conclusion of the Vietnam war meant a gradual loss of U.S. naval dominance at sea as the fleet drifted into obsolescence. By the late 1960s and early 1970s it was clear to Moorer and Zumwalt that budget cutbacks had reached the point where there was no alternative but to decommission large numbers of ships, in effect gambling that no crisis would occur in the decade ahead that could not be handled with a reduced fleet.

Naval officers, in evaluating the combat capability of their fleets, generally take a worst-case view of their potential enemies. They are well aware that when the chips are down they alone will be responsible for the maritime defense of the nation and any underestimation of the adversary would constitute dereliction of duty. Simply put, in drawing up strategic plans, officers tend to look at those combat scenarios that the enemy is *capable* of executing (possibilities), not those he is *likely* to carry out (probabilities). Conversely, nonmilitary planners lean to the latter because it allows them to factor into their estimate economic, political, and psychological elements that, in their view, will sway the enemy's course of action.

But one is reminded that before the attack on Pearl Harbor Washington officials including the military, intellectually acknowledged that the Japanese Navy was technically capable of striking Hawaii; yet the tacit consensus was that the Tokyo government was unlikely to carry out such a foolhardy act. Almost forty years later Washington policymakers similarly continued to accept a controversial nuclear equivalence with Moscow while allowing U.S. naval strength to erode. The conventional American belief, current in the 1970s was that Moscow was not likely to take any significant international actions threatening to the interests of the United States that could not be met successfully by the U.S. Navy. Those who held this comfortable opinion were rudely surprised by the sudden discovery in the summer of 1979 of an armored brigade of Soviet troops in Cuba, coupled with reports of a Soviet submarine and missile base at Cienfuegos.[17] The episode raised doubts about the validity of the theory that the Soviets would adhere to the Kennedy-Khrushchev understanding.[18] Also apparent was a growing Russian inclination to test U.S. resolve in situations where, in the past, a powerful U.S. fleet might have deterred such actions.

One-and-a-Half Wars and Political Pragmatism

A concept that attracted U.S. policymakers in the years before Vietnam was the notion that U.S. forces should be capable of handling two-and-a-half wars; for example, a major campaign in Europe, another in Asia, and a small brushfire conflict in the Caribbean. Because the two-and-a-half wars never materialized, the theory fortunately was never put to the test. Had it been, U.S. strategists who espoused it would have quickly discovered that the Navy lacked the sealift capability to support two major wars.

So long as the United States possessed nuclear superiority, U.S. planners relied on nuclear weapons, or the threat of "massive retaliation," to prevent big wars and on conventional forces to fight "half wars." However, after Moscow successfully negotiated for nuclear parity, "massive retaliation" became impracticable.

At the same time minor brushfire wars became commonplace.

Concerned with presenting a firm front to Moscow, the Nixon administration doggedly insisted that the services must be capable of fighting if not two-and-a-half then one-and-a-half wars. This new policy required that the armed forces should be prepared to wage a conventional (nonnuclear) war against a major adversary while simultaneously fighting a half-war, say, in Asia. The Joint Chiefs, wrote Zumwalt, to a man believed that the U.S. forces could not do so but were pressured by the administration not to admit publicly this politically damaging truth.[19]

Admiral Moorer, recalling the *Pueblo* crisis, is quoted as stating that it was the Indochina half-war that prevented the United States from even threatening a second half-war against North Korea.[20] Nevertheless, the White House continued to cling to its illusion while the Joint Chiefs pondered the question of how to alert the U.S. people or the Congress to the actual decline of America's defense without—as Zumwalt put it—going over the heads of their civilian masters. The Joint Chiefs unanimously agreed, now that U.S. military reductions had advertised a lesser capability than that of the Soviet forces, that the Middle East soon would feel the pressure of Russian military muscle.

The danger, according to Moorer, speaking in July 1970, was not a shooting war. Instead, he feared that the deterioration of U.S. military strength would sag to a point where the Soviets would win by U.S. default. Or, worse, the Russians would blackmail the United States, forcing it to back down in a given confrontation, a situation that could produce (as Moorer termed it) "a Cuba [missile crisis] in reverse."[21] To avoid an obvious loss of face, diplomatic window dressing might permit the United States to withdraw "gracefully." Nine years later another former CNO and onetime chairman of the president's Foreign Intelligence Advisory Board, retired Admiral George W. Anderson, voiced the same thought in observing that the Soviet Union would prefer to dominate the world—not by fighting wars and occupying countries—but by forcing acquiescence to its policies through intimidation.[22]

The apprehension over the erosion of U.S. naval power expressed by Moorer, Zumwalt, and their Pentagon colleagues failed to sway the administration, single-mindedly sensitive to domestic pressures for more generous social programs that forced reductions in defense budgets. Congressional and presidential candidates campaigning in the 1972 elections could not win if they disregarded public chagrin over the debacle in Vietnam, resentment over inflation, and opposition to the military. Fresh in White House memory was the attempt in May 1971 by thousands of antiwar demonstrators to close down Washington by rioting in the streets.[23]

Any hopes that Admiral Zumwalt entertained for stronger support from the people and the Congress were blighted by Nixon's determination not to publicize in Congress any impairment of U.S. naval strength. Rather, the president chose first to nail down strategic arms negotiations with the Soviets and to pull all troops out of the Indochina war. Only then would he go to the people for greater defense outlays. As events turned out, that possibility was overturned by the Watergate scandal that forced Nixon from office.

In his first month as CNO, Zumwalt correctly predicted to the president that in light of America's lack of concern with its Navy, the Soviets would be tempted to take greater risks with their warships.[24] That is to say, sensing that the U.S. Navy did not constitute an adequate political-military force, their Navy would act more aggressively in "naval presence" and sea-control situations.

Certainly, the Soviet Navy's subsequent willingness to make a show of force during the Cuban landings in Angola (1975) and in South Yemen and Cuba (1979) was indicative of Russia's militancy in establishing bases on the strategic oil lifelines to Europe, America, and the Far East.[25] Another reason for concern stemmed from the appearance, beginning in 1968, of Soviet Navy ships in the Indian Ocean in ever increasing numbers. The Kremlin's interest in the strategic value of that ocean area had become too obvious.

The Rise of the Soviet Fleet

Any comparison of the U.S. and Soviet navies must first take into account their basic missions. As U.S. naval officers perceived the issue, the basic task of the Soviet Navy was to deny the use of the oceans to the United States and its allies. Conversely, the responsibility of the U.S. Navy was to keep the sea-lanes open by destroying Soviet ships and aircraft.[26] Different national missions accounted for the different structure of the two fleets. Fleets can be measured by tonnage as well as by actual numbers of vessels. With this caveat in mind, let us consider the numerical comparison of major ships in the two fleets.[27] In 1968 the Soviet Navy had 790 major ships to 574 in the U.S. Navy. In 1972 the ratio was 820 to 447; and in 1978, 740 to 289, a startling difference of 451 ships.

Numbers alone do not highlight the vast changes in the structure of each fleet. Thus in 1958 the U.S. Navy was far ahead in carriers, destroyers, and amphibious ships. But by 1968 the number of American surface combat ships had dropped from 428 to 217, a cut of almost 50 percent, while the Soviets possessed 454 ships. Another startling fact: in 1968 the U.S. Navy could deploy 31 carriers (attack, ASW, and amphibious assault helicopter); the Soviets had none. In 1979 the United States had 13 attack carriers (plus a carrier used for training purposes) and 8 amphibious assault ships. But the Soviet Navy had deployed 2 helicopter carriers and 2 vertical short takeoff and landing (VSTOL) carriers.

As for submarines, in 1960 the Soviets had 399 submarines to 113 in the U.S. Navy. By 1978 the number of Russian boats numbered 294 to 119 for the United States, still a sizable difference. But the Russians in 1979 had 142 nuclear boats to 109 for the U.S. Navy. In 1968 the Soviets had only 49 nuclear submarines, evidence of their remarkable advances in shipbuilding. In sum, by 1978 the Russian Navy outnumbered the U.S. fleet by a factor of 2.5 to 1.

Before the reader perceives too gloomy a picture, one should note that in total tonnage the U.S. Navy approached almost 4 million tons compared with 2.3 million for the Soviet fleet. This American superiority stemmed largely from its thirteen big carriers, some of which were becoming obsolescent. But the enormous investment represented by these huge ships impelled some civilian and naval analysts to oppose their replacement on the grounds that they were fat, juicy targets whose time was drawing to a close.

We should remember too that the U.S. Navy, in all likelihood, would not stand alone against the Soviets. The allied navies constituted a substantial threat to Moscow's maritime force. Britain and France boasted nuclear missile submarines. The French fleet included aircraft carriers. Western European fleets collectively operated a formidable number of ASW vessels and aircraft. In the Far East Japan's so-called maritime self-defense force was small but growing. Presumably some, but certainly not all, of these ships and aircraft would fight the Soviet Navy in the event of World War III.

The other side of the coin revealed that nations had different strategic requirements. That is to say, they structured their respective fleets to meet their own particular needs, which were not necessarily congruent with those of the United States. For example, Italian ships built for service in the Mediterranean did not have the built-in cruising range of similar U.S. warships. Moreover, there were national differences in communication systems, gun and ammunition calibers, and engine fuel requirements that presented difficulties in joint combat operations despite efforts to overcome them.

Last, the sober truth remained that one ally will support another only when it is in its national interest to do so. Some Washington policymakers could remember the melancholy experience of World War II when the French Navy split into two factions, one supporting the Vichy puppet government and the other, a fugitive squadron of small ships loyal to the Free French headed by General Charles de Gaulle in London. Years later this same proud, aloof Frenchman, who as president, pulled France out of NATO, proved again that coalitions are ever vulnerable to national self-interest.

The High-Low Controversy

Admiral Zumwalt was disturbed to discover that U.S. national strategy seemed defective in that it constituted merely current reactions to ongoing problems. Nowhere was there a comprehensive national security strategic plan that spelled out tasks for long-range goals.[28] Thus, according to Zumwalt, naval planners were forced to rely partly on guesswork in their formulation of fleet strength.

By April 10, 1971, when it was apparent that the Navy's budget (together with those of the other services) would be cut, Zumwalt informed the chairman of the JCS that the United States, faced with many competing programs in support of its armed forces, had three alternatives. First, the nation could uphold its international commitments by allocating sufficient funds and personnel. Second, it could fix the maximum amount of national resources for defense and reduce U.S. commitments proportionally. And, third, the nation could "continue the present facade of keeping the commitments without providing the forces to sustain them." But, he cautioned, if the United States made this third choice, it should "be ready to back down when our bluff is called [presumably by the Soviets]." [29]

Zumwalt's tough stand for a stronger fleet did not imply that he advocated more expensive carriers and their supporting ships. On the contrary, he foresaw that the budget slashes would force the Navy to make a hard choice. No longer could the Navy "go first class" in its selection of ships. The service should scale down its appetite for high-performance ships and acquire more moderate-performance (and cheaper) vessels. This latter choice, declared Zumwalt, would allow the fleet to have enough ships to be "in enough places at the same time to get the job done." [30] Zumwalt suggested that the Navy would have to acquire a larger percentage of low-performance ships if it were to operate effectively within the penny-pinching budgets ordained by the White House and the Congress.

Zumwalt's concept, known as High-Low, was a compromise, a mix of a few high-performance ships and many smaller, relatively low performance ships. Such a fleet would avoid a budget-breaking program for high-cost warships but not expose the nation to the risk represented by a fleet of low-cost, ineffective vessels that could meet certain combat threats. A High-Low fleet appealed to many in Congress when they learned that a nuclear-powered missile frigate cost 2.5 times more than a conventional destroyer and 4 times more than a small patrol frigate.

The basic question was: Given a High-Low fleet, could the Navy carry out its global missions? According to retired Vice Admiral John T. Hayward, the weakness of High-Low became obvious when one recognized that Zumwalt's Low was set so far down that his Low ships could not compete with those of the enemy. [31]

A second broadside was fired by retired Vice Admiral Gerald E. Miller, a naval aviator. He agreed with Zumwalt that asymmetries (a Pentagon term for differences) existed between the Soviet and U.S. navies simply because their respective naval requirements differed.

But Zumwalt veered off course, said Miller, when he proposed to meet the challenge of the growing Soviet fleet "by building lots of ships, many with weapons systems in the mirror image of the Soviets." [32] The main appeal of this idea was its relatively low cost, but, argued Miller, High-Low was defensive in nature and was better suited to the Soviet Navy's goal of denying access to certain sea areas. High-Low would serve admirably the needs of the Greeks and the Turks in the Aegean Sea, or the Norwegian Navy in its fjords. The U.S. fleet could employ High-Low ships profitably in denying the Russian Navy entrance to Chesapeake Bay, the Caribbean, or Puget Sound. But the advantages ended there. A number of senior naval officers argued that High-Low was not an acceptable concept for the U.S. Navy chiefly because the U.S. Navy's mission was offensive—not defensive. Miller reasoned that a fleet that must dominate selected sea-lanes in the North and South Atlantic and the Indian Ocean and also guarantee the security of the Middle East could not rely on warships consisting largely of Low ships. Unlike the Soviet Union, a land power that needed a defensive navy to prevent access to sea areas near Russia, the United States needed a fleet capable of sustained, power-projection operations far from home.

Rather than a navy weighted to the Low side, Admiral Miller, a former Sixth Fleet commander, contended that the greatest mistake the nation could make would be to stress the Low end of the High-Low mix. Because of the strategic demands imposed by geography (the United States must guard the world sea-lanes to guarantee the flow of materials and men between itself and its allies), the United States needed to build a fleet on the High side to defeat the Soviets' defensively oriented navy. Such a goal would not be attained until U.S. public opinion was persuaded that national defense was relatively more important to the country's survival than social benefit projects.[33] Despite the words of the popular song, the best things in life (such as national security) were not free.

In the meantime the downward trend in U.S. naval fighting abilities received a major test during the Yom Kippur war in the Middle East. The episode highlighted the growing Soviet disposition to stand up to the U.S. Navy in time of crisis.

Maritime Friction in the Mediterranean

To the United States and its NATO allies, the Soviet fleet signaled its ascension to major naval status by its buildup in the Mediterranean. Starting slowly in 1964 with five ships, the Soviets by 1970 had expanded their *eskhadra* (squadron) to a virtual fleet whose presence had become permanent.

So unawed were Soviet skippers by the Sixth Fleet that during the 1967 Arab-Israeli Six Day war, they conned their ships alongside U.S. naval vessels in reckless demonstrations of cockiness, but not of good sea manners. Soviet and U.S. warships had been engaging in this hazardous game of "chicken" for some years. Perhaps the Soviets assumed that since the U.S. Navy was already heavily committed in Vietnam, it was not prepared for a second crisis in the Mediterranean.[34] Again, in 1969 in a challenge to U.S. naval dominance, Soviet ships sailed in close to the Libyan coast during Colonel Muammar Qadhafi's takeover of that oil-rich country. Qadhafi, the erratic, anti-American supporter of international terrorist groups, was a leader whom the Kremlin wished to cultivate. And the Soviet naval presence was an intimidating means of conveying this announcement to the world.

Admiral Isaac C. Kidd, commander of the Sixth Fleet during the Jordanian crisis of September 1970, watched through narrowed eyes the aggressive movements of Soviet ships interspersing themselves in U.S. tactical formations.[35] Soviet captains, acting on orders from Moscow, were in effect, warning the Americans that Russian ships were a force to be reckoned with. Specifically, as Kidd saw it, the Soviets were cautioning Washington to think twice before landing the Marines to aid King Hussein in his fight against Arab commandos backed by the anti-Israeli Yassir Arafat. During the flare-up it became common practice for Soviet ships, armed with cruise missiles, to trail such high-value U.S. ships as carriers in a tactic obviously designed to inform the Sixth Fleet commander that Soviet missile ships would fire on the flattops the instant that combat action commenced. In a game of tit-for-tat, smaller U.S. ships, ready for action, trailed the Soviet trailers.[36]

In another new development, twelve Russian submarines were on patrol in the Mediterranean. Ironically, Admiral Kidd noted that his fleet lacked an ASW carrier because in the interests of economy the U.S. Navy had been forced to cut back on this category of ship. This patent vulnerability to Russian submarines led Kidd to declare that the United States could no longer with any confidence allow its oilers and other logistics ships to steam unescorted during times of tension. And, he pointed out, if the maritime pipeline from U.S. ports to the Mediterranean were ever severed (as German U-boats almost succeeded in doing in World War II), then Sixth Fleet operations would come to an abrupt halt.

Moreover, the threat of Soviet aircraft based in the Black Sea area probably contributed to the conclusion that U.S. naval lines of communication were stretched to a near breaking point in the Middle East. Nevertheless, as Henry Kissinger observed, the Sixth Fleet had helped to mold events without ever approaching closer to the Middle East shore than 200 miles.[37] The dramatic buildup of U.S. naval strength, he felt, was a "crucial signal" of U.S. determination not to allow the Jordanian crisis to get out of hand.

The Yom Kippur War

On October 6, 1973, Arab forces equipped with Soviet planes, tanks, and heavy guns suddenly struck Israel on two fronts in an effort to recapture Arab lands lost in the Six-Day war of 1967. Reacting late to the Syrian and Egyptian onslaughts, the Israelis shortly found themselves facing imminent disaster. To prevent America's ally from being overrun in tank battles that rivaled those of World War II in scope and intensity, President Nixon ordered a giant airlift of U.S. equipment to Tel Aviv. The Kremlin directed a similar resupply of the Arab armies. In an amazing reversal of events, the Israeli forces surged across the Suez Canal to threaten the enemy's rear. By October 22 the Egyptian Third Army was encircled.

The fragile nature of alliances was brutally brought home to the U.S. Navy and Air Force when they sought the use of allied airfields to refuel the airlift planes bound for Israel. In supporting Tel Aviv, Washington ignored the possibility that its NATO allies and Spain might not perceive aid to this tiny nation as being in their national interests. Thus only a reluctant Portugal was persuaded to allow U.S. planes flying tanks to Israel to refuel (at Lajes in the Azores). Greece and Italy, however, allowed use of their ports. Other NATO countries dependent on Arab oil were not about to jeopardize their industrial economies by offending the likes of Saudi Arabia and Libya. A weakened Turkey, under the Soviet gun, authorized Soviet airlift planes headed for Egypt and Syria to overfly its territory, a warning sign of the erosion of the once strong U.S.-Turkish military ties. The entire episode confirmed the old military adage: Never depend on allies; they may not be there when you need them.

White House instructions to the Sixth Fleet (48 ships), probably initiated by Secretary of State Kissinger, who was also the president's national security advisor, were to maintain a low-key approach to the war.[38] Following orders, Vice Admiral Daniel Murphy initially positioned a carrier task group in the eastern Mediterranean.

Interestingly enough, during the crisis President Nixon reportedly did not attend a single formal meeting on the war, for the very good reason that his administration was foundering.[39] Vice-President Spiro Agnew, accused of taking bribes, had just resigned, and more trouble, the so-called Saturday Night Massacre, lay ahead. For the Navy the absence of the president from the scene meant that Secretary Kissinger "almost certainly" was issuing White House directives for Sixth Fleet actions, even specifying latitude and longitude limits that severely restricted Admiral Murphy's maneuvers.[40]

Meanwhile, Moscow had ordered heavy reinforcements to its Mediterranean fleet. Ten Soviet submarines were identified in the area. Two Soviet cruisers, a destroyer, and a submarine tender trailed the U.S. carrier group near Crete. Back in Washington, Admiral Moorer, chairman of the JCS, on several occasions requested authority from the White House to move the Sixth Fleet closer to the battle to be in position for the possible evacuation of Americans. Each request was turned down, reportedly by Kissinger.[41]

Another Cuban missile crisis loomed when the White House learned on October 24, 1973, that the Soviets planned to send airborne troops to Suez to rescue the beleaguered Egyptians. President Nixon responded by alerting all U.S. strategic forces. A U.S. carrier task group in the Atlantic and a destroyer group in the Baltic steamed into the Mediterranean to join the Sixth Fleet, bringing its carrier strength to three.

The Soviet Mediterranean fleet, also reinforced, numbered 80 ships including sixteen submarines on October 26, 1973.[42] Three days later the number rose to 96 vessels. Admiral Murphy declared that the Sixth Fleet and its adversary were "sitting in a pond," setting the stage for an unlikely "war at sea" scenario. Both fleets were ready for action, but neither knew what to expect.

The Psychological Value of the Sixth Fleet

The naval confrontation in the Yom Kippur war proved to be no repetition of the Cuban episode of 1962. Zumwalt saw the massive display of Soviet naval strength as a bold move to save Egypt from a military debacle. He regretted that "in the crunch we lacked either the military strength or the stable domestic leadership" to muster enough force to support the Israelis. Zumwalt noted that "we [the U.S.] had no choice, and because we had no choice, the Soviets derived great benefits from the war." The admiral had in mind the Soviets' attainment of their goal of reopening the Suez Canal, vital to their warship transits to and from the Indian Ocean. Yet the U.S. Sixth Fleet continued to symbolize American resolve to maintain stability in the area. Nixon's order to reinforce the fleet provided it with the opportunity once more to demonstrate the complex psychological value of its presence to diplomacy.

The shooting ended in an uncertain truce when Washington, and Moscow, and the U.N. Security Council effected a cease-fire. By the beginning of November 1973, both fleets began to disperse.

However, once the truce was in effect, the Arab oil nations, angry at Washington's support of Tel Aviv, decreed an oil embargo against all nations supporting Israel. Any satisfaction felt by Americans when the Arabs lifted the embargo after five months was quickly dissipated by skyrocketing price increases in oil that guaranteed a constant energy crisis for the United States, Western Europe, and Japan for years to come.

Equally grave, the oil crisis suddenly made Americans aware of the vulnerability of the oil lifelines from the Persian Gulf through the narrow Strait of Hormuz into the Indian Ocean. The more frequent presence of Soviet naval ships in those waters signified clearly the Kremlin's intention to challenge the U.S. Navy for control of this strategic sea area. In contrast, the U.S. Congress proved singularly slow in recognizing the value of Diego Garcia as an Indian Ocean base for the U.S. Navy, as Zumwalt and his successor learned.[43] A decade later Pacific Fleet staff officers were extremely grateful to Admiral Zumwalt for his persistence in pushing Congress to allot funds for the improvement of this tiny but important facility.

From Containment to Détente

In an effort to reduce nuclear weapons rivalry, President Nixon chose a policy of détente with Moscow. A French term signifying a relaxation of tensions, détente soon came into common usage.

Not surprisingly, this new policy had an immediate effect on national security policy, specifically the Navy's budget. It was Kissinger's contention that if the Soviets were persuaded to join in a series of cooperative enterprises, then benefits for the Soviets could be linked to a web of treaty commitments. No Soviet cooperation meant no benefits. As a first step, in May 1972 Nixon, once one of the sternest anticommunists, journeyed to Moscow. There he signed the first Strategic Arms Limitation Treaty (SALT I), the terms of which were designed to limit the chances of a nuclear war by according the Soviets parity in nuclear weapons. Theoretically at least, U.S. national security would be assured for the next five years and a missile-building contest avoided.[44]

In addition to these arguments there were others that fostered a U.S. move toward détente. To begin with, both nations desired a breathing spell from the tensions of a long cold war. Aerospace and weapons programs were soaking up billions of rubles and dollars. The Soviets needed American technology, particularly computers, to keep pace with the West in armaments and aerospace. Meager Russian harvests of grain could be offset by huge imports of U.S. wheat and corn. Finally, détente seemed in the air. Relations between West Germany and Russia had improved to the point where the two powers were about to sign a nonaggression treaty, which they did in June 1972. Even the festering problem of access to and from Berlin was resolved on the same day by a Four-Power accord signed by Britain, France, Russia, and the United States. Clearly, all signs appeared to favor Nixon's move.

If the defenders of détente pleaded for low-key restraint in dealing with Moscow to ''inspire'' similar sentiment by the Soviets, critics of the policy quoted the words of Foreign Minister Andrei Gromyko:

> The Communist Party subordinates all of its theoretical and practical activity in the sphere of international relations to the task of strengthening the positions of socialism, and the interests of further developing and deepening the world revolutionary process. Directed towards strengthening peace and the security of the peoples, imbued with a spirit of solidarity with revolutionary, progressive forces throughout the world, Soviet foreign policy constitutes one of the chief factors of the class struggle in the international arena.[45]

Lest there be any doubt in anyone's mind, Robert Conquest, the eminent British sovietologist, points to the 1976 words of another high Soviet functionary. Said Minister of Defense Dmitri Ustinov, ''Détente does not mean any Soviet abandonment of full support for revolutionary movements in the non-communist world.''[46] Ustinov's words confirmed the belief of many U.S. naval officers that the Kremlin was preparing for a protracted conflict with its superpower rival, the United States. Understandably, they expressed little agreement with champions of détente who foresaw new ''options'' for the United States if only Washington could reach a peaceful modus vivendi with the Soviet Union. In the collective mind of many naval critics, advocates of détente, who sought by pious sentiments and naive diplomacy to induce the Soviets to abandon their aggressive ways, were living in a fool's paradise.

Any hope that the Nixon administration may have held that, henceforth, improved Soviet behavior would justify Washington's new policy proved ephemeral. Détente in no way hindered the Kremlin from transporting Cuban and East German troops or technical advisors into Africa to establish Soviet-sponsored regimes. Of special concern to the U.S. Navy was the Russian naval presence off west Africa. In 1971 these vessels had racked up a total of 661 ship days, about one-third of all Atlantic operations of Soviet surface combat ships.[47] These stepped-up operations pointedly illustrated the fact that the Soviet Navy meant business in establishing its presence from the South Atlantic to the Indian Ocean. But the unanswered question was: Did Washington policymakers and the American public recognize this ominous fact?

The Ford Transition

Following the resignation in disgrace of Vice-President Spiro Agnew in 1973, President Nixon chose the House minority leader, Congressman Gerald R. Ford, as his successor. Less than a year later upon the resignation of Nixon, Ford became president. An outgoing man, universally liked in the Congress, Ford was a World War II naval veteran who had attained the rank of lieutenant commander. As president, Ford had the depressing task of witnessing on television the headlong flight of thousands of Vietnamese (plus the U.S. Embassy staff) from Saigon as North Vietnamese armies overran the area in March 1975. Ships of the Seventh Fleet rescued hundreds by boat and helicopter from almost certain death or imprisonment.

Mention must be made also of Ford's forthright decision in May 1975, only six weeks after the chaotic events in Saigon, to rescue a U.S. merchant ship in the Gulf of Siam. The *Mayaguez*, a 10,000-ton container ship, was sixty miles off the Cambodian mainland on May 12 when it was captured, along with its crew of 39, by Cambodian communists. Diplomatic approaches to China and the United Nations proved futile. Faced with the prospect of another ignominious *Pueblo* affair, Ford directed a naval-Marine task unit, aided by Air Force helicopters, to recapture the ship and rescue the crew.

The lost ship was sighted at Tang Island, 34 miles off the mainland. In a coordinated attack, planes from the carrier *Coral Sea* bombed a Cambodian base on the mainland, destroying seventeen aircraft, a runway, and a hangar. They also sank three gunboats at a naval base. Meanwhile Marines on board a destroyer escort steamed toward the *Mayaguez*, but on boarding it found the ship abandoned. At the same time a force of Marines was landed by helicopter on Tang Island where a brisk firefight with 150 Khmer Rouge troops broke out, causing casualties on both sides.

In short order the 39 U.S. crewmen were picked up on a fishing boat not far from Tang Island. The Marines were evacuated by helicopter as two destroyers and carrier aircraft laid down a protective fire. Unfortunately, the White House, in the manner of the Kennedy-Johnson era, hampered the carrier task group commander on the scene by demanding minute-by-minute reports on the operation, once again raising doubts about Washington's proclivity to control combat situations thousands of miles away. Tragically the operation cost the lives of 41 servicemen, but Ford's action was cheered by Republicans and Democrats alike as a reaffirmation of the American fighting spirit after the humiliating episode at Saigon.

Despite later claims in 1980 by Carter administration officials that Ford had neglected defense programs, Ford's proponents contended that his defense budgets actually were cut by Carter, who had pledged, as a candidate, that he would slash defense programs by $5 billion. Ford's five-year shipbuilding program called for 157 ships, which Carter had dropped to 67. By late 1979, after the budget cutters had become born-again big-navy men, the figure was boosted to 95 ships. To accuse Ford of neglecting the Navy was blatant historical revisionism in an election year, charged angry Republicans.[48]

Six

WHAT KIND OF NAVY?
THE UNCERTAIN SEVENTIES

If we open up a quarrel between the past and the
present, we shall find we have lost the future.

WINSTON S. CHURCHILL
Speech, House of Commons, June 18, 1940

An Annapolis Man as Commander-in-Chief

FORMER GOVERNOR OF GEORGIA Jimmy Carter won the presidency from the
incumbent Gerald R. Ford in 1976 by a relatively narrow margin. Capitalizing on
his status as a Washington outsider and winning the hearts of many with his
ingenuous smile, he pledged to rid the nation's capital of an overstaffed bureau-
cracy and bring the budget under control despite a rapidly inflating economy. His
plain-folks manner and disarming Southern accent helped him to attract 51 percent
of the popular vote as against 48 percent for Ford.

Interestingly, Carter, as a presidential candidate, received strong support from
the Trilateral Commission, an impressive group comprising leaders and opinion
makers on the American scene. Founded with the help of David Rockefeller, its
members included Harold Brown, Cyrus Vance, and Zbigniew Brzezinski, all of
whom were subsequently named to high positions by President Carter. (The
Trilateral Commission was dedicated to the development of close relations among
the leaders of North America, Western Europe, and Japan in order to foster
economic expansion for the benefit of all. Because of its worldwide connections, it
was described as an ''old boy'' network among the world's industrialized nations.)
Rightly or wrongly, because of the prominence of Trilateralists among Carter's
foreign policy advisors, commission members were reputed to be concerned more
with international goals than with U.S. national interests.

Carter, a member of the class of 1947 of the U.S. Naval Academy, was commissioned as an ensign and subsequently was selected for the submarine service.[1] In 1953 he resigned his lieutenant's commission in order to manage a family-owned peanut farm and warehouse at Plains, Georgia.

Because he was an Annapolis alumnus and a former officer, many Navy advocates predicted that Carter would be predisposed to the sea service. They were doomed to disappointment. The new president, although seemingly well qualified to deal with domestic social issues, had no experience in handling foreign affairs or strategic problems. Nevertheless, his inclination toward diplomatic matters equaled, if not exceeded, his interest in internal politics. Moreover, as a self-professed born-again Christian, he evinced a humanitarian—some said utopian—approach to world problems, notably in his insistence on the observance of human rights on a global scale. His critics made the point that Carter's consummate faith in his ability to sway foreign leaders predisposed him to believe that he could resolve major diplomatic issues mainly by persuasion and without a superior navy to back up his diplomatic moves.

Carter took office at a time when the national mood was one of revulsion against the Indochina debacle and growing public apprehension over Washington's inability to control the budget and the inflated economy. Many politicians assumed that they would not remain long in office by pushing for a big defense budget. Inevitably efforts by senior naval officers to persuade the White House and the Congress to redress the growing imbalance between the Soviet and U.S. fleets met resistance.

Continued cutbacks in military spending meant a drop of 20 percent in the funds allocated to combat forces from 1964 to 1975. At the same time the Soviet's overall military budget rose by 40 percent, clear evidence that by all available measures, American power, both in absolute and in relative terms, was declining while Soviet power was rising.[2] Table 1 illustrates the trend in U.S. defense budgets.

Arms Reduction and the "Good Example" Syndrome

Various reasons have been ascribed to the Carter administration's decision to hold back on programs designed to strengthen the services. The hawks charged that the administration's leaders mistakenly took comfort in the assumption that if the United States provided a good example by limiting its defense spending, the Soviets would do likewise. But according to a study commissioned by the U.S. Air Force, there was little question that Soviet military and naval spending during the preceding decade represented a "fairly steady pace of increase," while U.S. military expenditures declined.[3] Particularly noticeable was the improvement of Moscow's already formidable strategic missile forces, including submarines.

TABLE 1
DEFENSE SPENDING
(Billions of Fiscal Year 1976 Dollars)

Year	1970	1971	1972	1973	1974	1975	1976
Total Obligational Authority	115.7	105.6	104.4	101.9	100.8	99.5	104.7

Source: Lawrence J. Korb, "The Defense Budget and Detente," *Naval War College Review*, Summer 1975. p. 21.

Additionally, the Soviets had produced a new long-range naval reconnaissance plane. The Backfire, described as the world's most powerful long-range aircraft armed with bombs or missiles, had a range of 5,000 miles or more, depending on its payload and midair refueling by a tanker-plane. The authoritative journal, *Aviation Week*, reported that the Russians had under development an even more potent bomber capable of flying two to three times the speed of sound, with a range of 7,300 miles.[4] Ironically, the new aircraft reportedly resembled the aborted U.S. B-1.

American policymakers who seriously argued that the Soviet Union's defense buildup would cease if the United States reduced its own military forces received a jolt in 1979 when reports of a new Soviet super nuclear submarine appeared in the press.[5] With a hull built of titanium, the new boat reputedly could dive to 2,000 feet and cruise submerged at 43 knots, a speed that apparently exceeded that of allied submarines. Conceivably, such a submarine that could outdive and outrun enemy vessels would test U.S. and allied ASW ships beyond the limits of their capabilities to seek and destroy it. The new titanium boat, dubbed the Typhoon class by allied navies, reportedly carried advanced strategic missiles. Development of the Typhoon, said the hawks, was Moscow's latest move in its steady march toward naval superiority.

Russia's political adventures abroad kept pace with its advances in modern weaponry. Soviet sponsorship of Cuban troops in Angola and Ethiopia in 1978–1979 was followed by support of the Vietnamese in Cambodia. Soviet aid to local communist groups led to their seizure of the governments of Afghanistan and South Yemen. Saudi Arabia, the most powerful of the Arab oil states, represented the richest prize of the Middle East, a plum that the Soviets yearned to pick. In short, contended the hawks, it was foolish for Washington to ignore the obvious actions of an adversary who threatened America's vital interests. Roundly rejecting the chimera of alleged Soviet imitativeness of U.S. arms reduction, Senator Daniel Patrick Moynihan of New York accused President Carter of downgrading and diverting attention from the "central political struggle of our time—that of liberal democracy and totalitarian communism."[6]

Why was the administration reluctant to allocate more funds for defense, specifically a costly shipbuilding program? One reason stemmed from a belief that the Soviets were active but not unfriendly rivals of the United States in world affairs. Thus Secretary of State Vance earnestly observed that President Carter and Soviet President Brezhnev have "similar dreams and aspirations" for the world.[7] Extending this pacific thought, President Carter, on February 20, 1979, in what was billed as a major foreign policy address in Atlanta, described the U.S. relationship with the Soviet Union as a "mixture of cooperation and competition."[8] Critics averred that this characterization was an unduly charitable interpretation of Moscow-directed aggressions and hardly sufficient justification for paring the defense budget.

Harold Brown Returns to the Pentagon

Carter selected as his secretary of defense, Harold Brown, a 49-year-old veteran of government service. A onetime prodigy, Brown had graduated from Columbia University at 18 and earned a doctorate in physics at 22. After teaching at several universities and serving on the staff of the Livermore (California) Radiation Laboratory, he joined the McNamara team at the Pentagon in 1961 as director of defense research and engineering. Recognized as one of McNamara's so-called whiz kids, Brown was promoted in 1965 to secretary of the air force. With the election of Carter, he was called from his post as president of the California Institute of Technology to return to the Pentagon's E-ring.[9]

Brown did not join those administration spokesmen who looked on the bright side of U.S.-Soviet interchanges. In testimony before congressional budget committees on February 21, 1979, he announced that the president was determined to "begin countering the Soviet military buildup that has been underway for over 15 years." Accordingly, he asked for an additional $2.2 billion to supplement the 1979 fiscal year defense budget of $125.8 billion.[10]

Brown then went on to describe the steady downward trends in U.S. military and naval strength in contrast to major Soviet increases in arms. In the United States the overall trends since 1964 reflected a reduction in military manpower of 24 percent; a reduction in active Navy ships of 43 percent; a cut in active military aircraft of 40 percent; and a reduction in sealift (ship-transport) and airlift (military air transport) of 30 percent. In contrast, the Soviet armed services had exhibited constant growth since 1960. Brown disclosed that since the early 1960s, Soviet investment in new military hardware had increased twofold and was "more than twice ours today." Moveover, there was every indication that the Soviet trend would continue. He acknowledged that the trends, if not changed, would place the Soviet Union clearly ahead militarily, warning that each yearly imbalance increased the U.S. shortcoming and "in many measures of capability [for example, submarines]" the disparity grew progressively worse.

Speaking of the exorbitant rate of Soviet military spending, Brown observed that the Soviet Union "has shown no response to U.S. restraint—when we build, they build; when we cut, they build."[11] His words were confirmed by Rand Corporation experts who revealed that the Soviets since 1973 had expended some $100 billion (or its equivalent in rubles) more than the United States on military procurement and construction.[12] This sum approached the average yearly defense budget of the United States. Brown was well qualified to judge Soviet actions, having served as a U.S. delegate to the SALT talks, in addition to his various Pentagon responsibilities.

A Georgetown University scholar predicted that the enormous Soviet outlays for defense would give Russia military dominance over the United States by about 1985. According to Dr. Edward Luttwak, the danger was that the Kremlin's leaders would be tempted to exploit their military advantage by attacking the West in the mid-1980s when Russian forces were in the full flood of power.[13] The bleak alternative for aggressive Soviet hawks was to let the opportunity slip by and face the grim future of the 1990s. Why grim? Luttwak pointed to gloomy forecasts of economic lag, the shakiness of the Soviet Union's quasi-imperial grip on Eastern Europe (dramatized by the pope's triumphal visit to Poland in 1979), unrest among the varied ethnic and religous groups in Soviet Russia, and the specter of China along its eastern frontier.

Two charts (see Figures 3 and 4) prepared by the Rand Corporation, the government-supported research center at Santa Monica, California, dramatized the slump in defense spending. Beginning in 1967 the Pentagon budget peaked at $170 billion, the start of a steady decline. In contrast, nondefense outlays soared, the Department of Health, Education and Welfare alone expending almost $200 billion by 1979. Apparently the American people either had not been impressed by the expansion of the Soviet armed forces or, more likely, were not fully aware of its significance. The popular mood was shared by President Carter, who brushed aside claims that America was falling behind in its competition with the Soviet Union.

President Carter Lauds U.S. Power

Speaking at the graduation exercises of his alma mater, the U.S. Naval Academy, on June 7, 1978, President Carter hammered on Soviet weaknesses and extolled American power. No one doubted the president's descriptions of Soviet economic growth, which was "slowing greatly," and Soviet agriculture, which was so primitive that Moscow was forced to import grain from the United States

FIGURE 3
FEDERAL OUTLAYS

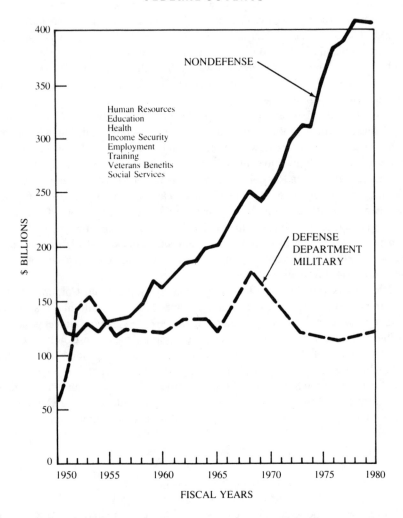

Source: U.S., Congress, House, Committee on Armed Services, *Hearings: Military Posture,* Report no. 96–5, 96th Cong., 1st sess., Part 1, pp. 10, 12.

FIGURE 4

COMPARISON OF U.S. DEFENSE OUTLAYS AND
ESTIMATED DOLLAR COSTS OF SOVIET DEFENSE PROGRAMS
(Billions of Constant Fiscal Year 1980 Dollars)

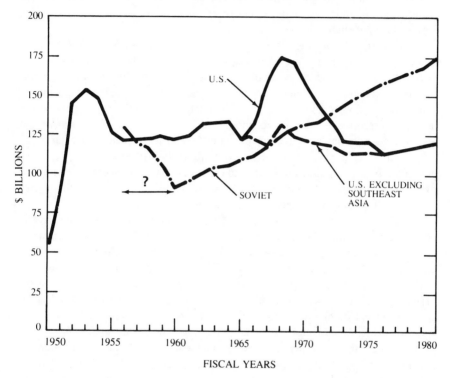

FISCAL YEARS

Source: See Fig. 3.

and other nations. The United States, in contrast, was in a much more favorable position. "Our industrial base and our productivity are unmatched. Our scientific and technological capability is superior to all others. Our alliances with other free nations are strong and growing stronger, and our military capability is now and will be second to none," he proclaimed.

Carter was correct, but only to a degree. How did one square his bold words with the cancellation of the B-1 bomber, the MX missile delay, the refusal to build a nuclear carrier, and tacit acceptance of Cuban-Soviet takeovers in Africa and Russian moves in South Yemen, Afghanistan, and Cuba? Administration opponents asserted that Carter and his supporters were relying too heavily on the assumption that U.S. economic and technical superiority would guarantee victory in a prolonged confrontation.

As if in answer to these charges, the president assured his audience that America "need not be overly concerned" or show any "cause for alarm" regarding competition with the Russians. In the president's eyes mammoth Soviet economic troubles, coupled with a low standard of living, made it inevitable that American economic productivity and technology would overwhelm the Soviet Union should it challenge the United States.

In criticizing the president's forensic logic, a *Wall Street Journal* commentator noted that paradoxically President Carter, in deploring the military might employed by Moscow, which used military power and military assistance as the best means of expanding its influence abroad, had thereby refuted the very thesis that he sought to develop. Unwittingly, Carter had underlined that sheer military power usually overcomes economic, technological, or political advantages, asserted Kenneth L. Adelman,[14] who pointed out that history was replete with instances of barbarians overrunning more advanced civilizations. If comforting optimism, generated by unwarranted confidence in the superior U.S. economy and technology, leads Americans to cut back on strategic and naval programs, the consequences will be perilous indeed, concluded Adelman.[15]

Administration proponents countered that Carter's assessment was correct, citing seemingly impressive statistics as proof. The United States had a per capita gross national product of around $9,000, while the Soviet Union's was below $3,000. The United States was the world's largest exporter of agricultural products. It possessed the largest coal reserves in the world. Of the last 22 Nobel prizes in science, 16 were awarded to Americans. Finally, the United States, in spite of current problems of inflation, energy, and falling productivity, was still superior to the Soviet Union and would remain so, said Carter supporters.

Taking another tack, administration opponents charged that the president's infinite confidence in U.S. economic and industrial strength implied an unwarranted conviction: The Soviets were so conscious of U.S. superiority that they would "rationally" rule out any major war with America. If Americans nurtured such a belief, said critics, they should recall that in the 1930s a similarly exaggerated mindset regarding Japan had prevailed in Washington. American pride in its war-making and industrial prowess had inclined the nation to an unspoken belief that the Japanese would never be so foolish as to wage a major war against the continental United States and Hawaii. There would be attacks, perhaps in Southeast Asia, but never against Pearl Harbor.

Almost forty years later another generation of Americans, in predicting Moscow's future actions, argued that the Russians would avoid major confrontations with the United States. Instead, they would rely on the salami-slicing technique used so effectively by Hitler in his pre–World War II territorial grabs of the Rhineland, Austria, and the Sudetenland. According to this line of reasoning, the Soviets, like Hitler, would continue to nibble away with the aid of proxies at foreign territory while the United States continued to protest.

The Navy's Right to Fight

The chronicle of the U.S. Navy in the 1970s is the story of a service in crisis, fending off forays on its budget by systems analysts zealously tailoring the structure of the fleet to fit a shrinking budget. As Robert Conquest suggests, systems analysis could be applied to both space-age hardware and other less tangible problems (for example, naval strategic needs), but the inputs in each case were vastly different. In an engineered system the components were substantive, the variables controlled, and the outputs identifiable. In naval system analysis, the principal elements were difficult to identify and the variables occasionally not controllable. Moreover, a space hardware system could be tested for results, but testing the effectiveness of a naval battle group and its weaponry implied actual combat.[16]

Time magazine described the battle between the naval professionals and the administration bureaucrats as "perhaps the nastiest battle on the banks of the Potomac in decades." Civilian officials in Defense Secretary Brown's office were so incensed at the Navy's spirited opposition, reported *Time*, that they referred to its officials as "bastards," who were "stupid, narrow and anachronistic."[17] Naval officers, for their part, were convinced that they were literally struggling for the right to fight future wars on even terms with the most likely opponent.

Brown's efforts to bring the huge defense budget under tight rein came at a time when the White House had decided as a matter of priority to strengthen U.S. participation in NATO forces, both army and air, by reducing the Navy's role (and budget). This startling development stemmed from the administration's concern over the growing threat posed by Warsaw Pact forces on the Central European front. The decision surfaced in early 1978 in an official Defense Department document that, the Navy properly assumed, had the concurrence of Secretary Brown and the White House. Identified as the author of the paper was Russell Murray, an Army Air Forces veteran of World War II and an MIT-trained aeronautical engineer, who in the 1960s had served in the Defense Department as a systems analyst with Harold Brown in Alain Enthoven's office.[18] In 1977 Murray returned as assistant secretary for program analysis and evaluation under his old colleague, now the defense secretary.

Briefly, Murray (and presumably the administration) announced that the short-term objective of the Defense Department was to ensure that NATO would not be overwhelmed in the first few weeks of a blitzkrieg war. Consequently, he wrote, "we will spend our [defense] resources to that end." He advised that the naval service should concern itself with localized contingencies beyond Europe.

Navy Secretary W. Graham Claytor, thoroughly aroused, protested that Secretary Brown and Murray had prescribed a "fundamental change in national strategy." In brief, naval supporters perceived that the administration had chopped $1 billion from the Navy's shipbuilding funds in order to fund the buildup of

NATO land-based forces. To justify this action by concluding that the nation's
strategic needs could be met by a reduced Navy was not good logic, declared
Claytor.[19]

Patiently the Navy once more made its case. If the Navy's role were shrunk to
one dealing only with "localized contingencies outside Europe," it would be
unable to defend (through power projection) the maritime flanks of NATO Europe
in the North Atlantic and Mediterranean. These tasks currently were the responsibility of the Second and Sixth fleets. Additionally, the Navy was responsible for

FIGURE 5

NORTH ATLANTIC

The critical G-I-UK (Greenland, Iceland, United Kingdom) gap through which
Soviet submarines and ships must pass. This nautical bottleneck is under electronic and visual surveillance by NATO countries.

Source: "Planning U.S. General Purpose Forces: The Navy," Congressional Budget
Office, 1976.

"sea control," a mission that was particularly relevant to U.S. support of allies in Europe and elsewhere by ship convoys. News accounts reported that Claytor had informed Brown that cutting the Navy back would virtually concede the Norwegian Sea to the Soviets. Moreover, naval officers predicted that a stunted fleet would mean virtual abandonment of Norway, Greece, and Turkey, all on the flanks of NATO, and of Japan, separated only by the Sea of Japan from Asian Russia. While the CNO's staff was pleading its case in the Pentagon, the Navy encountered problems with its public image.

Difficulties with Public Regard

The Navy's decline in fighting strength during the 1970s was aggravated by stories that placed it in an unfavorable light. In administering its procurement programs the Navy was stung by charges of inefficient management of contracts for ships and weaponry. Unhappily too, an impression gained currency that the service suffered from disunity and poor organization, which weakened its efforts to win congressional and public approval for more ships, more planes, and more research money.

A discordant parochialism was perceived by congressional and administrative critics, who alleged that three so-called unions existed in the Navy, representing respectively naval aviators, submariners, and surface-ship officers. To some it appeared that the aviators, who had dominated the most senior command assignments, had not maintained a balanced outlook because of their presumed devotion to a carrier task force concept of war. Such talk prompted various journalists and Washington officials to conclude that intraservice squabbles had made suspect certain shipbuilding programs presented to the defense secretary or to the Congress.

The public's perception of a wrangling navy was not enhanced by the presence of the able but contentious Admiral Hyman G. Rickover, who has headed the Navy's nuclear propulsion program for some two decades. The aging Rickover, rightly credited with being the "father of the nuclear navy," was still on active duty in 1980, although, amazingly enough, he was in his eightieth year. His combative, single-minded zeal for building expensive nuclear ships, coupled with the high regard accorded him by influential members of Congress, caused successive CNOs to abandon any attempt to place him on inactive status. So powerful were his connections on Capitol Hill that even the imperious President Johnson had given up on retiring him. Inevitably the disagreements between the CNOs and the outspoken Rickover stirred public misgivings that the service did not speak with a single voice.

Furthermore, suspicious voters, who still retained bitter memories of Vietnam, were disposed to believe charges that the Navy in its desire to "go first class" had escalated the price of ships and weapons by adding multiple changes to the original contract design. Such gold plating, said Capitol Hill critics (with some justification), caused delays in delivery dates as well as huge cost overruns. Provable or not, those accusations served to portray the Navy as a careless spender of public monies.

It is also true that antimilitary politicians and journalists did not always accord similar attention to civilian shipbuilders and aerospace contractors, some of whom were guilty of poor management practices, thus contributing to higher costs. Moreover, much of the public's confusion about the Navy's requirements derived from the very complexity of current naval weapons and operations. Terms like SLOC, ASW, sea control, power projection, and electronic surveillance were too technical or too complicated for the public or even many in the Congress to grasp. And much of this information was secret. Not surprisingly, the Navy had difficulty in selling its programs to already skeptical congressmen who were prepared to believe that the services had not always spent defense funds wisely. Part of the Navy's public reputation was nurtured by newsmen on the lookout for colorful stories in which the press sometimes failed to obtain the Navy's side. For example, on February 27, 1980, the headline on a United Press dispatch read "Navy to Retire Ship It Just Overhauled," leaving the reader with a sense of outrage at the lack of foresight of naval officers in squandering millions of dollars. This story, attributed to a Virginia congressman, implied that vigilant public servants were on guard against the Navy's wasteful ways. Had the press or the congressman checked with the Navy beforehand, they would have found that the obsolescent ship had been in overhaul to extend its service life for two years, after which it was to be sold to a friendly foreign nation in late 1981. Thus was the Navy's image sometimes damaged by unthinking journalists and headline-hunting politicians who broadcast stories that belittled the Navy and had the effect of downgrading the importance of U.S. sea power and of encouraging cuts in the fleet.

Suspicions of a Military-Industrial-Congressional Complex

An additional charge voiced over the years implied that senior military officers, on retiring from active service, accepted well-paying jobs in defense industries, thus creating a secret network between the Pentagon and business tycoons eager for billion-dollar contracts. Reports of this unholy alliance had been bruited about ever since President Eisenhower's administration. Yet few voters looked at the other side of the coin and perceived that, overall, the nation's defense production benefited from the contributions of retired officers with user experience.

The unwelcome notoriety growing out of such publicity was matched by similar reports involving naval-congressional dealings. Powerful members of Congress, it was alleged, saw no reason why their constituencies should not benefit from naval contracts even if the awarding of such contracts could be challenged on grounds of suitability. One "horrible example" was portrayed by a popular national television program, which devoted some time to a large naval medical center built in New Orleans, leaving the impression of a facility that was grossly overbuilt at taxpayers' expense and with the Navy's approval. Congressman F. Edward Hébert, chairman of the House Armed Services Committee, was from New Orleans, which added substance to the charge. True or not, the report was detrimental to the Navy.

Public Opinion and the Shipbuilding Program

In March 1978, before an assembly of the nation's business leaders, academicians, military officers, and senior bureaucrats, Admiral Robert Long, the vice-chief of naval operations, set forth the Navy's position for more ships, a view that won him no kudos from Defense Department officials. Long, obviously reflecting the CNO's views, took as his basic assumption that U.S. foreign policy since 1898 called for the Navy to keep war far away from the continental United States.

In the 1970s, Long explained, this policy, now known as forward strategy, meant that the Navy continued to station the Sixth and Seventh fleets thousands of miles from home. Forward strategy also meant that, first, the sea lines of communication (SLOC) linking the nation with its allies and suppliers of critical materials be protected and, second, the Polaris/Poseidon/Trident submarine force be kept at sea for strategic nuclear deterrence.

Long found a disturbing tide of opinion, probably based on ignorance, running against the Navy's quest for more ships. How many U.S. citizens appreciated that the United States would always remain an island nation dependent, at least in the foreseeable future, on raw material from abroad and on foreign buyers for its exports? How many voters understood that the U.S. national acceptance of moral responsibilities, global in scope, depended in large measure on the Navy? Finally, did the American people sense that for the remaining years of this century and possibly beyond, the United States and the Soviet Union would continue to confront each other much as Britain and France had in the eighteenth and early nineteenth centuries?

Admiral Long contended with reason that these basic considerations were obscured in the current debate on the Navy. Unless the Navy got its message through to the public, then the economic well-being and survival of the United States and its allies would be jeopardized. He expressed understandable concern over the 250 torpedo-carrying Soviet submarines, many of them nuclear powered. These undersea marauders posed a very real threat to allied sea-lanes. Not only could they decimate allied convoys by firing torpedoes, but many of the boats could launch antiship cruise missiles at very long ranges from the target. Although

Long did not say so, other naval spokesmen, notably Admiral Kidd, now the commander-in-chief of the Atlantic Fleet, had warned that a lack of U.S. and allied escort ships signaled the likelihood of appalling losses of merchant ships from Soviet submarine attacks during the first few weeks of any future war.[20]

Submarines represented only part of the threat. Soviet surface ships and naval aircraft were cause for equal alarm. As an example, Long described the Backfire reconnaissance plane, which constituted a major menace to allied shipping. Reportedly, Moscow had allocated half of its new Backfires to the growing naval air arm.

Worst-Case Scenarios and Trident Submarines

As to how the U.S. Navy could combat this ominous threat, Long supplied an answer: build a balanced force of different types of ships with offensive and defensive weapons systems. But the cost, seen as exorbitant by many, made it difficult for some congressmen, administration officials, and the public at large to accept the high price. The U.S. public apparently was hard put to comprehend that the cost of ships, like those of automobiles and houses, had risen at a dizzying pace, but, unlike cars and houses, warships were some insurance against an uncertain future.

Admiral Long, one of a handful of senior naval officers charged with maintaining U.S. superiority at sea, voiced his strong suspicion of arms-control pacts with Moscow and their long-range benefits to the United States. America, he declared, had no choice but to serve as the counterweight to Soviet ambitions, "which for the most part run counter to our own." So long as "the Soviets continue to deploy more capable strategic offensive systems," the "chief danger would remain a possible nuclear attack against the United States itself." No matter how improbable such an attack might seem, its possibility was ever present in Pentagon defense planning.

Long expressed some doubt concerning the popular view of "essential equivalence" in nuclear weapons, a concept basic to U.S. arms control philosophy. Such equivalence was by no means static. So rapid was the rate of improvement in Soviet missiles that the 1,000 U.S. land-based Minuteman missiles might become vulnerable to a Soviet attack as early as 1984.

Where did the Navy fit into this worst-case scenario? The self-evident answer was that the U.S. strategic missile submarines were the most survivable of the so-called Triad forces and as such represented the strongest insurance to protect the nation against the danger represented by obsolescent land-based missiles.[21] Yet, the 41 Polaris/Poseidon boats would eventually require replacement by Trident submarines. In the interim, the Navy planned to install Trident I missiles in existing Poseidon boats as a stopgap. Thus the Trident I missile, by virtue of its longer range (estimated at 4,000 miles), would improve the Poseidon's survivability by greatly expanding its launch range.

As for the Trident class submarine, this faster, quieter cruising boat could more easily evade Soviet hunter-killer ASW forces. For the next 25 years the Navy counted on the Trident boats (to be modernized periodically) to form the backbone of the U.S. strategic deterrent. Without mincing words, Long declared that the Navy would be shortsighted and irresponsible if it procured anything less than the most survivable and flexible sea-based deterrent that U.S. technology could provide. In other words, with national survival at stake, cost should not be the major consideration. He undoubtedly had in mind the $1 billion price tag of the Trident class boat, a monster 560 feet in length, carrying 24 ballistic missiles.[22] Because of the great range of its missiles, these submarines needed no overseas bases, unlike the Polaris boats.

Long then pointed out a plain fact sometimes ignored by those who placed too much faith in nuclear arms agreements. Since Hiroshima, history has demonstrated that nuclear deterrence can fail in many ways as an instrument of foreign policy (that is, short of a nuclear incineration no one wants). The postwar years had also demonstrated that an absolute requirement for national security was a "conventional" deterrent force, which provided a range of swift responses commensurate with the provocation. Obviously, this essential, conventional force was the Navy. Only the future would tell whether Long's warnings would be heeded by the American people and the Congress in facing up to new and unwanted dangers.

The Navy as a Reflection of the National Sprit

The Navy's problems occurred in an era when the U.S. economy was foundering. A long-predicted recession was in the offing. The cost of living was rising alarmingly. The *Wall Street Journal* described the nation's economy as a victim of years of neglect for which there was no quick cure.[23] The economy would not improve, according to a Columbia University scholar, unless Americans made a long-term commitment to rebuilding the country's industrial base, to developing new sources of energy, to increasing basic research and development, and to erecting modern plants equipped with the most effective technology that money could buy.

These recommendations could be applied equally well to the future of the shipbuilding program. The Navy's problems, along with those related to a sagging economy, could be resolved only if the American public determined as a national policy that the rebuilding of the nation's industries, rather than quality-of-life programs, should receive top priority.

Treasury Secretary W. Michael Blumenthal bluntly advised Americans to forgo consumption and make sizable, short-term sacrifices to build up the nation's industrial base.[24] Blumenthal, a successful businessman (Bendix Corporation) and a Princeton Ph.D. (economics), understood that while his recommendation was technically sound, it had one flaw—the American people, the most consumption-oriented in the world, were not likely to accept the new gospel quickly or at all unless the economy suffered catastrophically. He noted wryly that ''tomorrow has no political constituency in our political system.'' A British military expert expressed the same thought in a way that unmistakably described the defense posture of the United States in the 1970s: ''What a society gets in its armed services is exactly what it asks for, no more and no less. What it asks for tends to be a reflection of what it is. When a country looks at its fighting forces it is looking in a mirror: if the mirror is a true one, the face it sees there will be its own.''[25]

One Pentagon naval planner, a vice admiral speaking to a limited group, attributed much of the Navy's trouble to an excess of hobbyists and self-styled experts on naval matters in the ranks of the media, the Congress, Defense Department staffs, and the executive branch, many of whom created confusion within the system. Long-range naval planning was uncertain at best. No one knew where a future war would start or how much warning time would be granted to the U.S. Navy. Therefore, he asked, could the country prudently refuse to expend funds on more ships and materiel? The service, for its part, had the responsibility, first, to operate a global fleet, characterized by striking power, endurance, and mobility; and, second, to develop new types of ships that could meet these criteria but still be affordable. The admiral believed that the American people were too complacent about the combat readiness of the Navy, now and for the future. Ever since the Spanish-American War, the U.S. public had taken it for granted that the Navy and Marines always would be the first on the scene of action, a legend that because of a lack of ships was increasingly open to question. He concluded that the naval service had failed to focus the attention of the Congress or the people on its serious plight.

Navy Secretary Claytor struck a similar note in testimony before the Senate Armed Services Committee in February 1978.[26] He conceded that the U.S. Navy had earned an image as a powerful fighting force. However, the American people should not delude themselves that the military power symbolized by its Navy could decline ''without an appreciable effect upon [foreign] perceptions and attitudes, both regional and worldwide.'' Claytor warned that if the U.S. public expected to continue to enjoy the benefits of a Navy with both war-fighting ability and an aura of strength, then it must furnish it with sufficient ships and aircraft to accomplish its missions and to counter the Soviet Navy whenever necessary.

A Trust in Arms Limitation

In the 1970s U.S. policymakers who advocated arms limitation pacts with the Soviets disturbed many members of the Congress and the press. Students of history will note that these same Washington treaty negotiators followed a well-worn path in U.S. diplomacy first trod by the Harding administration during the Washington disarmament conference of 1921−22. Despite a notable lack of enduring success, the concept of armament limitation continued to inspire a number of U.S. political leaders to believe religiously in it as an instrument of peace. That is to say, they contended that the fewer armaments nations possess, the greater the chances of a tranquil world.

The list of post−World War I peace pacts includes the Washington naval treaty of 1922, the demilitarization of the Rhineland, the Kellogg-Briand agreement of 1928 permitting defensive combat but rejecting war (and hence, weapons) as "an instrument of national policy," and the London naval conference of 1930. It must be acknowledged that in the short term these pacts eased international tensions by restricting, temporarily at least, the international naval race. Free of huge naval budgets, shattered Europe was aided in its economic recovery from the ravages of war.

Tragically, these agreements, as Professor Eugene V. Rostow of Yale points out, hastened World War II simply because they reinforced "the blind and willful optimism" of many in the English-speaking world who strongly resisted any defense program aimed at building up the armed forces of the United States and the British Commonwealth.[27] Their insistence on living in a world of good intentions and prayerful hopes inhibited military preparedness (save in the Axis nations) and scuttled the diplomatic measures that, if backed up by force, could have deterred World War II.

Rostow's words found favor with naval officers trained in the tradition of buttressing U.S. diplomatic moves by bringing support at precise points whenever required. They feared with good reason that by the mid-1980s the Navy would be forced to meet a seemingly endless list of commitments abroad with an inadequate fleet.[28] The ugly consequence would be the most dangerous yet to confront the nation in future limited confrontations where the use of nuclear arms was clearly unsuitable. Thus the Soviets would continue to win a series of small successes that in the aggregate would accomplish their political goals. Cold war veterans were reminded of the words Walter Bedell Smith uttered in 1954 when he was under secretary of state: "It's well to remember that diplomacy has rarely been able to gain at the conference table what cannot be gained or held on the battlefield."[29] One who did not share this view as Ronald V. Dellums, a prominent congressman from California, who described himself as a former social planner and director of community programs.[30]

Congressman Dellums, a Democrat and a perennial champion of programs for the disadvantaged, damned defense spending as a measure to "divert needed resources from human needs, while spending billions on unnecessary military projects." It reflected, he said, "the 'wants' of the military brass" and not "a reasoned policy."[31]

Dellums scoffed at so-called "panic stories of 'the Russians are coming.' " He noted that the "overall balance between the U.S.A. and USSR remains stable." It was not important that the Soviets had increased their defense budgets over the past fifteen years. They were "clearly behind when the increase started and clearly they have not surpassed us." Both nations could destroy each other "many times over" and "the world's problems are not solvable by U.S. arms." Dellums urged that the United States be noninterventionist but strong enough "to defend the United States and our vital interests." Neither should the nation be a world police officer or intervenor in the Third World. "Clearly we must disengage," he proclaimed.

As for the Navy, Dellums gave it short shrift. U.S. naval policy was "based on yesterday's war," he said, apparently referring to long-range missiles that, he assumed, would sink distant aircraft carriers. "It is not rational to expect our Navy to conduct extended conventional surface warfare with the Soviet Navy in any future war," he argued. He contended that the Navy had more than enough forces to meet contingencies "across the world" and that the "desires of the Admirals" for "a nuclear carrier and cruiser construction" were without logic or justification. Defense hard-liners observed that Dellums' naive belief in no more conventional naval wars coincided with the sincere but unrealistic dreams of well-meaning advocates of strategic arms limitation treaties who placed their faith in nuclear parity. But the hawks asserted that the influence of Dellums and like-minded colleagues, coupled with the desire of economy-minded taxpayers not to pay for a superior navy, resulted in a U.S. fleet of the late 1970s that was below the level required to meet the needs of U.S. security.

Senate Hawks Sound the Alarm

In May 1979 Senator Sam Nunn, a Democrat from the president's home state of Georgia recognized as a leading arms expert in the Congress, advocated an immediate buildup in the Navy.[32] Nunn was apprehensive that unless this step were taken, the Soviet Union would achieve a clear military superiority in the 1980s. To reverse the ten-year decline (since 1969) of the fleet, he demanded that the construction of war vessels be accelerated. A greater investment was required in submarine-launched strategic missiles (more Trident boats), chiefly because the United States was being forced to find ways of reducing the vulnerability of its land-based intercontinental ballistic missiles from a Soviet first strike, he said.

A real increase in U.S. defense spending, particularly in research and development of new weapons, was a matter of first priority, for only in this way could the United States demonstrate to its adversaries that it possessed the necessary resolve to defend itself in the absence of arms control. Like a latter-day Churchill spurring Parliament in 1938 to recognize the alarming weakness of British defense forces, Nunn warned that until the United States and its allies were prepared to compete effectively with the Soviet Union in the military arena, they could expect arms control agreements ''to do little more than ratify an emerging Soviet military superiority.'' But public opinion had not yet jelled to the point where the man in the street was convinced that U.S. security, as embodied in a powerful navy, must be a prerequisite to any arms limitations pact—nuclear or conventional. Within the government itself, different voices called for different directions in U.S. defense, a condition that dampened public perception that the Soviet Navy was a growing threat.

It was curious, according to Daniel Patrick Moynihan, the colorful senator from New York, that the steady downward slide in naval and defense budgets and the upward climb of social service funds was perceived in public discourse as just the opposite.[33] Why was this so? And to what extent did it affect the Navy's long-range mission? Moynihan was a former Harvard professor of government, ambassador successively to India and the United Nations, and advisor to Presidents Kennedy, Johnson, and Nixon. While ambassador to the U.N., he was noted for his puckish wit in debate and his unconcealed impatience with the U.S. policy of benign tolerance of barbs hurled by representatives of Third World nations.

Moynihan observed that the public perception of excessive defense funding was in direct contradiction to the decline in the U.S. defense budget for the period 1969–1979. His explanation of the Navy's lean budgets went as follows. On the one hand, Nixon and his political supporters feared that he, as the champion of prudent Republican budgets, would be blamed for the vast increases in social spending. On the other hand, Democratic politicians feared that Nixon would be given credit for such programs as unemployment benefits, medicare, and old-age benefits, all categories for which Democrats long had adopted a proprietary stance.

So commenced what Moynihan labeled a ''conspiracy of inversion'' to which public spokesmen of each party contributed. Thus every time President Nixon increased the social budget, he heard with satisfaction his political opponents contend that he had reduced it. And when he cut the defense budget, he would hear that he had increased it beyond essential limits. The statistics are illuminating. In 1960 national defense made up about half (49 percent) of the government's expenditures. Nondefense outlays, most of which originated in social programs, accounted for the remainder. In contrast, by 1980 the defense budget was reduced by half, to some 23 percent, yet the public seemed unaware of this drastic drop.

The ignorance of the average citizen on defense matters was revealed by a public opinion poll conducted in March 1979 and cited by Moynihan. The respondents were asked: ''What percentage of this country's total economic output do you think now goes for national defense?'' (The correct answer is 4.9 percent.) More than half said that it was over 25 percent. A quarter said that it was more than 35 percent. Only 9.8 percent of those quizzed correctly answered, ''5 percent or less.''[34]

In commenting on the public's startling failure to appreciate the shrinking of the defense (and the Navy's) budget in terms of the gross national product, Moynihan noted that this lack of knowledge apparently extended to high-ranking statesmen such as the former governor of Georgia, Jimmy Carter. Campaigning as a presidential candidate in 1976, he urged a cut in defense spending. Shortly thereafter the Democratic party platform pledged to do so. And when candidate Carter became president, defense reductions included the cruise missile delay, the nuclear carrier cancellation of 1978, the shutdown of the B-1 bomber program, the halt on the emotively named neutron bomb, and the agreement to a Soviet request in the SALT II talks to restrict the range of the cruise missile.

The "Greek Tragedy" Theory of Vietnam

Paradoxically, as the U.S. armed forces sagged in strength, administration spokesmen announced that U.S. military forces had been too powerful in recent years, an invidious condition that had led us into the habit of intervention. Apparently the Carter administration believed that the U.S. presence in Vietnam had originated because our military power, coupled with fear of communism, had induced the nation to intervene wrongly in an Asian civil war. As the reasoning went, had we not been so powerful, we would not have succumed to the temptation. President Carter touched on this theme at Atlanta, Georgia, when he declared that "the United States cannot control events within other nations"—a statement that no one would dispute.[35] Almost two years before, at the University of Notre Dame at South Bend, Indiana, Carter had proclaimed that Americans were now "free" of the "inordinate fear of communism," a dreadful misconception that had lured the nation into war. Said the president: "For too many years we have been willing to adopt the flawed principles and tactics of our adversaries, sometimes abandoning our values for theirs . . . this approach failed, with Vietnam the best example of its intellectual and moral poverty."[36]

Vice-President Mondale reinforced this self-critical concept. On February 25, 1979, he responded to a reporter's question on the slipping posture of the United States as a world leader by castigating the U.S. custom of "intervening in other nations, ordering them around, bludgeoning them, intimidating them." Was there a rational explanation to this charge? Senator Moynihan offered this theory: the debacle of Southeast Asia required a credible explanation by Democrats to account for the involvement of two Democratic administrations in the Vietnam war.

Thus originated the so-called Greek tragedy theory of America's defeat in Vietnam. America's downfall came about because it was "too powerful." And so the gods had punished the United States for its reckless arrogance and cavalier disregard of the moral rights of others. Moynihan suggested that Lord Acton's "dubious axiom has made its way into our thinking as if it were a codicil to the Constitution itself."[37] The senator explained that proponents of the theory assumed that America had become a danger to the world and to itself, but the nation could redress this sin simply by becoming less powerful. How? By bringing U.S. troops home from Korea, by negotiating arms reductions and a SALT II pact, by cutting back on the armed services, and by restraining the American predilection to intervene in world affairs.

Observers of the Carter administration were mystified by the contrast between the evangelistic call to grace sounded by the Greek tragedy school and the depressing view of Defense Secretary Brown. "We are limited in the numerical reductions [in defense] we can stand. We must face contingencies of a global nature, and a [Soviet] threat increasing in sophistication and size."[38] This clash of views on national security within the administration helped to explain its inclination to vacillate or defer judgment on strengthening the U.S. defense budget.

Inevitably, after the trauma of the "no-good" war in Vietnam, the American people displayed a notable lack of interest in building up the Navy. Meanwhile, the growing obsolescence of warships, aircraft, weapons, and other equipment (which was reflected in increasing materiel breakdowns and a lack of replacements) assumed serious proportions.

Seven

THE BATTLE OVER
ROLES AND MISSIONS

Crises, Carriers, and Sea Control

THE CARRIER DEBATE, which first flared up in 1976, turned on the question of whether carriers were really essential or even suitable as warships in the modern world of missiles. Naval aviators argued that the big flattops represented the *only* weapons systems—both strategic and tactical—that gave the United States an enormous advantage over the Soviet Navy. In the past three decades carrier task forces had formed the spearhead of the U.S. fleets in the Mediterranean and Far East. In fact, "calling out the carriers" had become a byword in Washington whenever a show of U.S. naval strength might stabilize international discord.

Former Secretary of State Kissinger acknowledged as much when he told a Naval War College audience: "In the crises in which I was involved, the use of naval power, particularly the carrier, turned out to be almost invariably the crucial element." The reason, of course, was that carriers could steam at 25 knots or faster to reach trouble spots and usually, by their very presence, resolve any broils. A nuclear carrier task force was self-sustaining and needed no bases.[1] A conventional task force, provided naval tankers were available for refueling, was equally self-sustaining. No other type of military unit—army, air force, or navy—could equal the mobility and fighting force of a carrier battle group with some ninety planes.

Administration reluctance in 1978 to authorize a fifth nuclear carrier resulted in part from the awesome cost, which had soared to over $2 billion for a *Nimitz* class nuclear ship. Cheeseparing planners reasoned that if the Navy's carriers did not need immediate replacement, new construction could be deferred. Politically such a decision appealed to many voters who had shown every sign that once clear of the Asian quagmire, they wanted no part of costly defense spending that would heat up the cost of living.

To gain public support for an admittedly expensive shipbuilding program, Navy spokesmen repeatedly explained that the frenetic pace of naval operations during the 1960–1978 period had taken its inevitable toll on ships, many of which were built during World War II. Of the thirteen carriers operating in the fleet (not counting the training ship at Pensacola, Florida), only four were less than 25 years old.[2] As a stopgap measure, the careers of some of these aging ships were extended by a costly refit program. Unfortunately, while certain improvements could be made, the basic dimensions of the ships could not be modified, thus preventing in many cases the installation of modern weaponry and communication systems. As with all make-do programs the Navy ended up with ships of lesser fighting effectiveness, and possibly at a higher cost than if new ships had been constructed.

Chief among the naval advocates for big carriers and more ships was Admiral James L. Holloway, III, the CNO between 1974 and 1978. The son of a noted flag officer and a naval aviator himself, Holloway, in testimony before a congressional panel in July 1976, used the occasion to explain the differences between sea power and sea control.[3] It is safe to say that the CNO wished to dispel any confusion on these terms that might lead to budget cuts, particularly for carriers.

Sea power was a general term meaning command of the seas. Sea control was an element of sea power and was defined as the use of naval and air power to keep open a specified sea area for military and commercial sea traffic against a challenge by the enemy. Sea control, as a fundamental function of the Navy, meant that the fleet would control selected areas when and where needed.

Sea control was, first of all, a prerequisite for most naval operations. For example, if a sea area were not first made secure, then a planned amphibious operation or carrier air strike against an enemy might be jeopardized. Sea control of selected areas could make possible strategic operations to destroy hostile forces far distant from the sea area to be protected. Such operations might include carrier air attacks on maritime choke points on the enemy's access routes from his bases to the open sea (such as from Murmansk to the Atlantic). Similarly, in a tactical sense, sea control was clearly a prerequisite in operations such as close naval support of convoy operations or underway replenishment (an operation in which combat ships were refueled or resupplied by other ships cruising close alongside while under way on the high seas).[4] As matters turned out, Holloway's desire to remove any ambiguity about the Navy's interpretation of sea control and power projection evidently fell on deaf ears in the Congressional Budget Office (CBO).

Budget Analysts as Strategists

To assist federal lawmakers in understanding the Navy's program, civilian analysts in the CBO brought the Navy's budget under gimlet-eyed scrutiny. If the CBO's motives of achieving cost-effectiveness were laudable, one could reasonably assume that its collective understanding of long-range strategy and naval warfare was relatively limited. Nevertheless, in December 1976, CBO analysts produced a formal assessment of where and how naval forces could be employed under certain war conditions. Surprisingly, the CBO concluded that changes should be made in the Navy's basic missions, a finding that apparently justified its conclusion that a sharp reduction in the Navy budget would mean a savings of millions of defense dollars, especially in limiting the role of carriers.

When the CBO study reached Florida Congressman Charles E. Bennett of the Sea Power Subcommittee, he promptly sent it to Admiral Holloway.[5] The Navy's blunt rebuttal, contained in a point-by-point critique of the study, revealed the traps ensnaring those who had ventured into the unknown. Holloway found the CBO study completely unacceptable, mainly because its authors, in failing to comprehend the nation's basic need for naval and Marine forces, had made dubious assumptions about the nature of sea warfare. Surprisingly, the study sought to confine the Navy to a specialized sea control force that would commit the fleet to an "inflexible and potentially disastrous future while greatly enhancing the opportunities of the enemy."[6]

In forwarding the Navy's comments to Chairman Melvin Price of the House Armed Services Committee, Admiral Holloway expressed sympathy for the plight of the CBO analysts in trying to come to grips with their assignment. Obviously, they had been hard pressed to develop new and less costly naval strategic alternatives that directly contradicted the Navy's "balanced force" concept that best served U.S. national security. According to the CNO, the CBO experts had drawn conclusions that could not be supported by facts. Holloway's response constituted a basic primer on current naval strategy and merits brief discussion.

Over the years the Navy, the staff of the defense secretary, and the Congress had continued to consult on the nature of what Admiral Holloway described as the "threat" to U.S. national security, that is to say, problems such as those posed by the Soviet Navy, Middle Eastern rulers unfriendly to Washington, Warsaw Pact nations, and the structure of the Navy itself. As Holloway explained, it was the responsibility of the CNO, the defense secretary, and members of Congress to decide on ways to meet the threat and to examine various scenarios in order to forecast and hedge against future risks.[7] Only then could U.S. naval forces be shaped to control these dangers over a broad range of contingencies.

However, the CBO analysts had chosen to disregard the judgment of naval strategic experts and had instead proposed the formation of "specialized naval forces" for tasks envisioned in selected war plans. Unfortunately, the CBO's study was rendered inadmissible, in Holloway's eyes, because of its spurious conjectures regarding the strategic naval factors involved. Left unsaid was the fact that the CBO experts did not, in the Navy's eyes, understand the differences between sea power and sea control. Nor did they fully comprehend the role of power projection in the exercise of sea power.

To enlighten the congressmen, Holloway explained the use of power projection by naval carrier forces in order to gain sea control (that is, the continued safe use of certain ocean areas in wartime). For example, power projection by long-range (more than 500 miles) carrier air strikes against enemy warships in port or while en route to their patrol areas meant that the Navy could eliminate these predators before they destroyed or damaged U.S. ships. Similarly, Marine amphibious forces, supported by carrier air and naval gunfire, could be "projected" ashore to seize and hold land areas, thus denying key bases to the enemy who would use them for interdiction of allied sea lines of communication. Moreover, once these land areas were in American hands, U.S. forces could exploit them as advance bases to attack enemy forces.

Fixation on a NATO Land War

According to the Navy, the CBO analysts were under a delusion when they argued that power projection missions for the Navy's general purpose force could include air attacks on the European heartland against Soviet and East European targets.[8] In rebuttal, the Navy pointed out that this task was properly an Air Force mission. A more likely Navy power projection role in a general war would be one in support of Marine amphibious forces. But such a Navy role first required that the fleet establish sea (and air) control of the beach landing areas.

The CBO assumption that carriers and their support ships existed solely to strike land-based military objectives was false, asserted the Navy analysts. Rather, carriers and their air groups represented defense in depth in areas of highest threat, where Soviet forces could be concentrated—for example, the European port areas, the Mediterranean, and the Sea of Japan.

Neither did the authors of the CBO study understand that the degree of difficulty of projection attacks in either the Mediterranean or Atlantic depended on the target. Although there were other possible targets, the CBO study focused on strikes against the Soviet Union. Pointing out the obvious, the Navy indicated that if U.S. power projection in the Mediterranean called for air strikes against Bulgaria or an amphibious operation to reinforce the Dardanelles or Thrace, then less opposition would be encountered than during carrier air strikes against the Soviet Crimea in the Black Sea area.

Naval experts described as questionable the CBO scenario that the inevitable use of tactical nuclear weapons would mean a short Central European war. The script sought to demonstrate that the war would be of short duration, and consequently the U.S. Navy would have no opportunity to exercise either sea control or power projection. On the contrary, naval staff officers contended, some studies on a future Central European war revealed that the use of tactical nuclear weapons would determine neither the outcome nor the duration of the land battle, but only

FIGURE 6
THE TURKISH STRAITS

The Soviet Black Sea Fleet's only channel to the Mediterranean is through the Bosporus-Dardanelles chokepoint, a distance of 192 potentially dangerous miles.

Source: Lawrence Griswold, "The Chokepoint War," *Sea Power* (September 1973). Reprinted with permission.

the intensity of the conflict in, what could turn out to be, a long drawn-out struggle where an allied victory turned on the outcome of the war at sea.

In the CBO description of sea control, the analysts also fell into error when they assumed that the Navy's role was one of ensuring the "relatively unimpeded transit of friendly shipping across selected sea-lanes" in the Atlantic. In effecting sea control, they added that the Navy must "reduce enemy submarine activity and prevent enemy ships and air forces from significantly disrupting" allied shipping.

Naval critics judged this description as totally unreal, inasmuch as it painted a picture of an "almost . . . benign environment" or, at the very least, an environment where the threat level was considerably lower than the Navy's studies and analyses had predicted. On the contrary, given the grave importance of the need to reinforce Europe in a war involving NATO nations, the Navy quite reasonably expected that a determined Soviet Navy would mount attacks equal to or exceeding in ferocity those of German U-boats and the Luftwaffe on allied convoys during World War II. To count on "relatively unimpeded transits" would be reckless and irresponsible, said naval planners. After all, the Soviets had a huge submarine fleet deployable to the Atlantic or Asian-African waters.

Without a strong projection force, asserted the Navy, it was most doubtful that the fleet could exercise sea control in the Atlantic or elsewhere. For example, a war with the Warsaw Pact in Europe inevitably would be part of a worldwide confrontation with the Soviets. If the U.S. Navy was not prepared to defend its interests in areas other than NATO Europe, the Soviets would soon take advantage of such weakness.

A land war on a Central European front with heavy attrition on both sides would mean that a successful U.S. resupply of allied forces was crucial and could determine the eventual outcome of the war. Recognizing the preponderance of Warsaw Pact land and air forces and their strong logistic advantage, the Navy argued that it would be absurd to dismiss the need for swift, well-escorted convoys to Europe. To gamble that allied sea control over a prolonged time was not a vital requirement would condemn the United States and its allies to defeat from the outset. Glaring deficiencies in U.S. sea control forces would be obvious to the Soviets and would invite conflict.

Moreover, the U.S. Navy had no intention (as implied in the CBO study)[9] of operating carriers in the Baltic in the face of massive Soviet opposition. True, the Navy recognized that one of its missions was to mine the Baltic exits and to prevent the Warsaw Pact forces from controlling the Danish Straits. Here again naval power projection supported sea control, for example, by U.S. naval bombardment and air strikes followed by an amphibious landing in Norway. To the pessimistic observation that NATO defense of Norway and close air support of the European land battle would be very difficult, the Navy replied that so are most tasks in war. The idea that in war (as in peace) there would be opportunities as well as risks in combat operations never seemed to occur to the CBO.

On the other hand, one could not deny the CBO contention that U.S. naval support for Norway and close air support in Central Europe would be less difficult than strikes, say, against the Kola Peninsula and the huge port of Murmansk in arctic Russia. Navy analysts noted that the CBO had presented "two very worthwhile and credible projection missions" (NATO defense of Norway and close air support in land battles), but the CBO destroyed the effect either by lumping them with the more difficult anti-USSR strikes or by failing to examine them as arguments for a stronger U.S. Navy.

Surprisingly, the significance of the Navy's weapons system, Aegis (Greek for shield), failed to impress the CBO. Scheduled for fleet operation in late 1982, Aegis was a total, integrated combat system designed to launch multiple missiles at swarms of incoming enemy missiles and aircraft. The system also could fire at surface ships and submarines. Erroneously, the CBO study focused on the role of Aegis only as it pertained to the defense of aircraft carriers. The Navy emphasized that Aegis also could perform its air defense role in other types of ships as well. Aegis, fitted in destroyers and cruisers, as well as carriers, ensured that U.S. ships could operate in a high-threat environment, for example, one within range of Soviet naval aircraft. Without Aegis, the opposite was true, according to naval strategists. In brief, it was inaccurate to imply (as did the CBO) that a sea control navy might not need this defense system. If the survivability of carriers depended on Aegis, it was equally true that the weapon would give to any battle group the ability to detect and destroy incoming missiles, particularly the shorter-range submarine-launched missiles.

In sum, as Admiral Holloway informed Congressman Bennett, the CBO study unintentionally confirmed the Navy's case that a balanced force (and its capacity for flexible response) was "the most rational option" open to the nation's decision makers in the light of budget restrictions, political aims, and the Soviet threat. There was a great temptation to "specialize the Navy for one set of circumstances" such as a NATO war on the Central European front, but to do so would create a navy lacking the flexibility needed for future U.S. security. Moreover, some naval ships took from six to eight years to build. Therefore the Congress should be mindful that the ships to be authorized and funded in these times would determine the balance and the relevance of U.S. naval forces well into the next century.

During the 1960−1980 era the sustained criticism of the Navy's structure by civilian experts required an inordinate amount of effort and time by naval staff officers in preparing rebuttals. Had the CBO analysts had some degree of command experience in naval matters, their proposals for a smaller (and weaker) fleet would have been more convincing. Yet one cannot escape the conclusion that many congressmen were swayed by their views. No one doubted that these latter-day prophets were sincere in their beliefs. Unhappily, in the eyes of the

Navy, their dollar-mindedness and their promotion of unsound doctrine helped to weaken the fleet of the future.

The Carrier and the Battleship: A Historical Parallel

Opponents of the large attack carrier pounced on its allegedly outmoded battle effectiveness in a world of long-range cruise missiles and sophisticated torpedos. Representative of the arguments made against the carrier was an article in *Foreign Affairs* by Michael Krepon, a congressional staff member. [10] Krepon compared the inevitable decline of the aircraft carrier to the earlier demise of the battleship. Because this journal was widely read and highly regarded by many opinion makers, politicians, and government officials, his views presumably carried considerable impact. The historically minded recognized that the ongoing campaign against the carrier, exemplified by Krepon's arguments, provided interesting parallels to the crusade against the battleship a half century before.

Krepon took as his theme the general inability of senior naval officers of any given era to comprehend that new technologies make current weaponry obsolete. According to Krepon, the carrier proponents of the 1970s were guilty of the same lack of foresight exhibited by the battleship champions of the 1920s. In his view, today's "tunnel-visioned supporters" of the "obsolescent carrier," who placed continued and exclusive reliance on this type of ship, were courting disaster.

Recalling the destruction at Hampton Roads, Virginia, of an "unsinkable" battleship in July 1921 by Army planes commanded by General Billy Mitchell, Krepon criticized the subsequent refusal of "the Navy brass" to replace the battleship with the carrier as the backbone of the fleet. [11] He then concluded that the sinkings of capital ships by aircraft at Pearl Harbor and in the battles of Midway and the Coral Sea "finally proved General Mitchell's point beyond refutation." Only then, he said, did the Navy redirect its shipbuilding efforts toward the carrier, with each ship "growing more expensive with each succeeding design."

Similarly, in 1978, it was the height of folly for the Navy to build a technically obsolescent $2 billion nuclear carrier for service in the late twentieth century, Krepon contended. Myopic admirals adamant in their refusal to give up the expensive and outmoded warships, in Krepon's view, were stubborn, old sea dogs. But there was a side to the debate that differed from the Krepon version.

The Billy Mitchell controversy erupted at a time when the art of naval warfare was changing. The affair is well known from the movie starring Gary Cooper and from exhaustive analyses in military literature. Mitchell, a career Army officer and a confirmed stormy petrel, was a disciple of the Italian strategist, General Guilio Douhet. It was Douhet who first theorized that land-based aircraft could win wars by bombing enemy targets into rubble, thus immobilizing the opposing armies and navies by denying them logistic support. Drawing freely from accounts in biographies sympathetic to Mitchell, Krepon depicted senior naval officers as hopelessly blind to the threat of aviation bombing to the fleet. A more objective appraisal of the battleship was made by naval historian Clark Reynolds who ascribed the slow obsolescence of the battleship to new technology and to the naval treaty limitations that were a hallmark of international politics in the years between the world wars.[12]

Mitchell's campaign to convince the Harding administration, the Congress, and the public that air power was supreme failed; the Navy remained the first line of defense. Spurred on by the Mitchell affair, the Navy Department lost no time in building carriers and integrating the naval air arm into the forces afloat.[13] The late Samuel Eliot Morison, the country's foremost naval historian, summed up Mitchell's battle with the Navy as unsoundly based and conducted by people wholly incompetent to evaluate the impact of aviation on naval power. Nonetheless, their lobbying was most effective in its use of a proved technique of proverbial crusading, that is, leveling sensational charges against someone or something—in this case, the Navy's so-called warmongering "mossback" battleship admirals. "Unquestionably," concluded Morison, "he substantially weakened the Navy which was destined to begin World War II."[14]

In judging the decline of the fleet during the period between the world wars, one also must take into account the emotional atmosphere of disarmament or, to use a more accurate and modern term, arms control. Morison has suggested that in the 1920s and 1930s a flood of distorted and misleading propaganda for "disarmament by example" caused America's emotions to overwhelm its reason. Undoubtedly the activities of the fervent pacifists and disarmament champions of the 1920s did nothing to slow the coming of World War II. As Morison put it: "Ardor for righteousness must be amply tinctured with rational judgment if constructive results are to be achieved."[15]

Power Projection and the Carrier

Naval warfare develops by evolution, not revolution. So long as the major sea powers of the post–World War I era, such as Britain, Japan, France, and Italy, put their faith in the battleship, it was expecting too much for U.S. flag officers to renounce it in favor of the carrier.[16] True, there were a few shortsighted senior officers who frowned on aircraft engine turn-ups because the engines leaked oil on spotless teak decks, but the Navy as a whole looked with pride on its growing air arm and its giant carriers, *Lexington* and *Saratoga*, commissioned in 1927.

In the early days of naval aviation senior officers saw the role of aircraft as scouts to locate the enemy and as aerial spotters for the fall of shot fired by warships. Gradually these tasks were expanded to include dive-bombing and torpedo attack, in other words, power projection.[17] During the 1930s lessons learned from the Navy's annual maneuvers and individual ship or air squadron operations led to the evolution of the task force with carriers, battleships, cruisers, and destroyers. The concept of supporting fast carriers and their escorts with underway replenishment by oilers, ammunition ships, and supply vessels was a direct result of peacetime war games. Prophetically, in the 1938 fleet exercises, planes from carriers 100 miles at sea struck Pearl Harbor in a successful mock attack, a move successfully duplicated by the Japanese just three years later. To ignore, as Krepon does, the alertness of the prewar Navy to the advantages of naval aviation in an era when the battleship had not yet been replaced as a major weapons system is to misread the historical evidence.

In short, despite the myths spread during the Billy Mitchell crusade, the battleship was not rendered useless by the advent of aircraft or submarines. During the Vietnam war the battleship *New Jersey*, an anachronism in the jet age, was recommissioned and sailed to Indochina where U.S. land forces were grateful for the heavy offshore bombardment of enemy targets delivered by the old ship. Whether heavy ships could operate close to enemy shores depended on which antagonist established sea control of a selected ocean area. As in World War II and Korea, the battleship with its heavy guns possessed a unique combat capability because it alone could deliver heavy firepower on enemy shores and withstand enemy fire, something critics failed to sense. Arrestingly, in March 1980, the press reported that the Navy had requested authority to take four battleships out of mothballs to meet fleet needs in the Indian Ocean. Three of these old ships would be fitted with cruise missiles with a range of 200 miles. Special situations in war—hot or cold—sometimes call for the use of special ships and weapons systems.

The dawn of the missile age, according to opponents of naval air power, heralded the imminent death of the carrier. In their reasoning, the carrier, like the battleship, became another sitting duck, vulnerable to destruction by a submarine torpedo or a cruise missile. Soviet ships could launch missiles at targets from twenty to fifty miles away, an ability to which they gave great weight. But they were unimpressed by the Navy's F-14 fighter aircraft, which could fire a burst of Phoenix antimissile missiles to counter an enemy missile attack many miles away from the target.[18] American naval destroyer—type ships were equipped with SAMs. In addition, ships such as the new DDG-47 class of destroyer fitted with Aegis were scheduled to join the fleet soon. Yet critics suggested that this new air-defense missile system might be outmoded before it became operational.

Pentagon officers privately scoffed at attempts to downgrade the Navy's mission of power projection.[19] Land-minded dissenters wrongly assumed that the Navy's main mission was sea control. As Krepon, for example, perceived it, this was the ability to resupply troops, to support allies, and to allow ''the Navy to carry out its secondary mission, which is the projection of power ashore in support of combat operations.'' His view clashed directly with the Navy's concept that sea control and power projection were interrelated and that considering them as two separate missions was fatuous.[20]

To the Navy, sea control and power projection always have been and would continue to be mutually supportive. Power projection (and the carrier) was necessary for sea control; the converse was also true, and it was sometimes difficult to know where one category began and the other ended. If the Navy did not possess carriers, it would lose its ability to project power. And the Soviet Navy would be the first to exploit such weakness by wresting sea control from U.S. forces.

Defense in Depth and Untested Theories

Naval officers reasoned that carriers and their supporting ships could achieve sea control by establishing a defense in depth in sea areas of highest threat where Soviet naval and air forces could be concentrated, as, for example, in the North Sea and eastern Atlantic. Rather than being helplessly exposed to Soviet submarines or missile attacks, the Navy counted on its powerful ASW force, its air arm, and its deadly antiair defenses to protect its forces operating in such zones. If necessary, U.S. naval battle groups could launch air strikes (that is, project power) to regain control of maritime choke points such as the Barents Sea or to launch amphibious landings on territory (such as Norway) needed for the maintenance of sea control.

As for the sitting duck argument, the Navy responded that, in addition to its antimissile weaponry, the fleet could counter missile attacks by electronic jamming, deception, and higher ship speeds. In others words, to imply that the Navy's carriers constituted a costly and dangerous imbalance for national security was not only wrong but based on a misunderstanding of the nature of naval warfare.

Admittedly, since the end of World War II the Navy had encountered little or no threat to U.S. sea control and consequently could use its carriers unremittingly for power projection, as it did in Korea and Indochina. But the uninformed took little note that in the past 35 years the carrier had repeatedly proved its versatility in crisis situations short of major war. In the next twenty years there was every expectation that the carriers and their supporting ships would continue to be called.

Criticism that sea control and power projection by carrier task forces would be difficult and costly was met by the Navy's rejoinder that potential difficulty in planning and executing combat operations was not a valid criterion in reaching a decision. Most wartime operations essential to victory are tough to handle, but this seldom constitutes sufficient reason to abandon a plan. No thinking officer denied that in a conventional war with the USSR the Navy would meet heavy opposition from enemy forces. But if it were to emerge a victor in the battle for sea control in the next three decades, the Navy had no doubt that it would need *carrier* battle groups.

While staving off the criticisms of latter-day Billy Mitchells, most naval officers understood that only through the development of new technologies and combat tactics could the Navy advance. Under Holloway and his successor, Admiral Thomas B. Hayward, the Navy continued to oppose any actions to dilute the naval air arm and its large carriers in favor of untried ideas conceived by academic theorists unschooled in naval warfare.

Large or Small Carriers

Faced with the possibility in 1979 that President Carter would veto the construction of a large carrier, the Navy searched for possible alternatives. To measure the respective benefits and shortcomings of large and small carriers, the Center for Naval Analysis (CNA), a Navy Department—supported research center, studied the problem under conditions that simulated wartime operating restrictions as closely as possible. The study was projected to show the results to be expected from both systems in twenty or thirty years. To be of any value, a study of this nature requires accurate assumptions about factors that are at best uncertain. For example, what missions would the Navy face in the year 2000?[21] Would technology be available to develop the vertical short takeoff and landing (VSTOL) aircraft? What about the plane's future speed, endurance, and payload?[22]

Other assumptions included a series of five typical carrier warfare situations: establishment of an antiair barrier (against enemy planes and missiles), defense of ship convoys, a preemptive enemy strike on U.S. ships, a battle on the high seas, and a U.S. naval attack on shore targets. The issue boiled down to the type of carrier forces the Navy should plan to acquire for the next thirty years.

One discouraging element in the calculations was that in the late 1970s a combat-capable VSTOL plane did not exist and progress was slow. The Harrier aircraft was still under development by the Marine Corps for close-in support of its amphibious troops once they were landed on beaches. Unhappily, the Harrier still suffered from low speed and a relatively short range, even though it needed no catapult or arresting gear for ship takeoffs and landings. If the plane's engine could be perfected to provide more thrust with less fuel consumption, then the Harrier might provide a partial answer to the Navy's big-carrier question. That day, however, was long in the future, according to naval aviators. One reason for governmental foot-dragging on the Harrier was the frightening price of any development effort. Inasmuch as in 1978 the Navy had twelve operating carriers in the fleet, there was a distinct tendency in the Congress to delay a full development program for the VSTOL until the national economic situation improved. Ironically, the longer the legislators waited, the more costly the price became.

Opponents insisted that the carrier was not the solution to the Navy's goal for maritime superiority. Some even cited Galbraith's law of social policy, "the available remedy drives the diagnosis," as pertinent to the Navy's dilemma.[23] That is to say, when faced with a problem, officials are prone to diagnose it and to prescribe its cure in terms of the available medicine. Thus the Navy's carrier champions demanded more big carriers; its opponents argued that other remedies yet to be uncovered were the answer, and therefore research and development funds should be spent on other programs yet to be explored. But if carried to extremes, this argument, contended the carrier supporters, would mean the eventual loss of the U.S. carrier force; in effect, throwing out the baby with the bathwater.

As a yardstick to gauge costs, the CNA experts estimated that if the Navy were to purchase the type of carrier forces that currently operated in the late 1970s (carriers, aircraft, destroyer escorts, oilers, supply ships,), the total bill would be a mind-boggling $217 billion, of which over 6 percent would be for aircraft.

To measure the relative costs of the most battle-effective mix for each system (big carriers and cheaper VSTOL carriers), the CNA assumed that in any future war the Navy should be prepared to operate in five combat theaters: The Greenland–Iceland–United Kingdom Straits, the Mediterranean Sea, the Far East, the Indian Ocean, and in the Atlantic for convoy operations to Europe. They also forecast that no one type of naval force (for example, a large-carrier battle group, a VSTOL ship battle group, or a mix of the two types) would be ideal for all five theaters.[24] However, in the context of a conventional war, the study revealed that the large carrier could sustain more damage and was far less vulnerable than smaller naval ships. One reason for its relative invulnerability lay in its heavily armored magazines, as well as in its hull, which was well protected against underwater torpedo explosions. Because the smaller ships equipped for VSTOL operations were considerably more vulnerable to enemy attack, one could conclude that the demise of the large carrier was not yet at hand.

Carriers as Mobile Air Bases

As part of Navy Secretary Claytor's educational process to persuade Brown, his staff, and the public of the rightness of the Navy's position, the secretary stressed that if the number of carriers were reduced during the next quarter century, the ability of any U.S. president to respond swiftly to foreign flare-ups would correspondingly suffer. For example, he said that if the Navy were forced to cut back its presence in the Mediterranean, the Indian Ocean, and the Western Pacific, then the resulting vacuum would be quickly filled by Soviet naval forces, with grave consequences for global stability. Evidently Defense Secretary Brown was impressed, for he gave assurances that the administration did not advocate abandoning the flanks of NATO, as had been implied in the so-called Murray directive aimed at buttressing NATO forces at the expense of the Navy.[25]

Surprisingly, Senator Gary Hart of Colorado, an implacable foe of the nuclear carrier, came to the defense of carrier-minded officers. Hart pointed out that the United States could be evicted from foreign air bases by a change of government (as happened some months later in Iran) or might not be permitted to operate from allied airfields even in support of a NATO nation (as had happened when America's NATO allies shrank from granting the U.S. Air Force fueling privileges for flights to and from Israel during the Yom Kippur war of 1973).[26] As floating air bases, carriers were immune to foreign political pressures. Time and again the Navy's spokesmen hammered on the carrier's twin roles of sea control and power projection. Without the ships and aircraft to carry out these two wartime missions, the fleet had little hope of keeping the sea-lanes open to Europe, the Middle East, or elsewhere.

Newly appointed as CNO in the summer of 1978 was Admiral Hayward, who most recently had served as commander-in-chief, Pacific Fleet. A slim, handsome officer of marked intellectual force, he had been a combat pilot in the Korean War, commanded the Seventh Fleet during the Vietnam conflict, and served as a senior Pentagon staff officer. Hayward's fight for the big carrier derived from his belief that in the foreseeable future the margin of difference at sea between the United States and Soviets rested on the U.S. Navy's carrier-based offensive punch.

To those who dismissed the carrier as useless in combat, Hayward replied: "Compared to what?" Could there be any rational question about which would be harder to locate and attack: a fixed, shore-based airfield or a carrier at sea; an ammunition depot or a mobile carrier force? "The carrier wins, hands down, in any such comparison," he declared.[27]

As for the allegations by uninformed critics about the helplessness of the carrier, Hayward asserted that "between one category of [naval] ship and another, there can be no question but that the carrier is the *least* vulnerable of all ship types [emphasis supplied]." Although it was true that the carrier's large silhouette made it more detectable by radar, it was also true that enemy radars could be "spoofed and misled" by electronic deception.

Hayward then related an account of a major accident on board the nuclear carrier *Enterprise* in 1969 when nine 500-pound bombs exploded on the flight deck. The explosion was the equivalent to that caused by six Soviet cruise missiles. "*Enterprise* could have commenced flight operations within hours had the situation demanded," said the CNO. But, as with the stories perpetuated by Billy Mitchell's supporters in the 1920s concerning the battleship, Hayward learned that such myths died hard, particularly in the office of the secretary of defense.

Carter Cancels the Nuclear Carrier

To the Navy's surprise President Carter displayed a rocklike resistance to costly Navy programs, such as the nuclear carrier (CVN) and an expanded five-year shipbuilding program.[28] However, there were enough congressional supporters of the CVN to press for a tentative compromise in the fiscal year 1978 budget that presumably would grant congressional approval for a CVN (*Nimitz* class) provided that the Navy would agree to three conditions: first, the conversion of two LPHs (helicopter ships for landing Marines ashore) to VSTOL support ships (VSSs); second, the building of an LHA (a ship that can accommodate helicopters and landing craft); and third, the funding of eighteen VSTOL aircraft (improved Harriers).

But compromises were not enough to save the CVN, for President Carter vetoed the 1979 fiscal year defense authorization bill after both houses of Congress had passed it. His principal target in the bill was the nuclear carrier. An economy-minded House sustained the veto by a vote of 191 ayes (to override the veto) to 206 nays. In his veto message, the president pledged that he would include a small carrier (CVV) in the next year's budget, a promise that gave cold comfort to the CVN proponents.

One of these supporters was Congressman Melvin Price, chairman of the House Armed Services Committee. Price disagreed with the president's assertion that spending $2 billion (the cost of a CVN) "would weaken our national security in certain critical areas and waste scarce defense dollars."[29] The chairman was disturbed because the president had implied that funding a CVN required that $2 billion be cut in other needed defense programs, a measure that the Congress had not taken.

Price, then 75 years old, had served 38 years in the House. Ordinarily one to avoid political donnybrooks, he lashed back that the president's charge was "most grievous" to him. He found offensive the burden of the president's message that the congressional role in defense policymaking was one of rubber stamping the recommendations of the executive branch. On the contrary, he believed that the Congress deserved respect "as a partner in defense decision making, not as a poor relation."

Senator John C. Stennis, chairman of the Senate Armed Services Committee, took a similar position, notifying the president that he "strongly defended" the vetoed bill and rejecting charges by the president that it was deficient for national defense needs. Stennis actively supported the CVN, which he described as 50 percent more combat-effective than the Carter-sponsored CVV. Last, the senator scored the White House argument that the CVV was $1 billion cheaper than the nuclear flattop. Stennis, in contradiction, asserted that when the cost of a thirteen-year supply of fuel oil for the CVV was added to its construction price, the two ships were of equal cost.

Naval proponents said that the president's veto was a result of his decision to obtain more funds for the support of U.S. forces in NATO. Such an increase, amounting to 3 percent, was evident from a pledge by the administration to NATO to beef up U.S. funding in exchange for similar pledges by NATO's other members to equal or surpass the 3 percent figure in their respective defense budgets. In any event, the White House hoped that the Congress would accept the less costly (but less effective) CVV substitute, despite the Navy's strong objections to it.

In spite of all the oratory the battle for the CVN was over. A week later the House leadership introduced a new bill that deleted the nuclear carrier. The bill was passed in both houses. So ended, for the time being, the great carrier debate. For the Navy the signs were clear that its hopes for a fifth nuclear carrier were dim. Under ideal conditions of a booming economy and no inflation, no politician would have opposed the idea that the nation and the Navy required the CVN. But in the Washington arena of 1978 and 1979 many interests jockeyed for federal funds. It was not enough that the Navy believed that loss of the CVN endangered its ability to carry out its responsibilities. There were other powerful voices that argued that the nation's economic health and social goals would be strongly damaged by an excessive defense budget.

Unexpectedly, events in the Middle East and Cuba and their impact on the Congress caused the president to change his stand. On November 6, 1979, the Senate joined the House in voting to substitute the CVN for the president's recommended cheaper, smaller, and slower CVV carrier. Reluctantly, the president went along.[30]

Eight

STRATEGISTS AND BUDGET CHOPPERS

The Budget Drives Strategy in Peacetime

THE NAVY'S public controversy with Defense Secretary Brown's aides focused attention on an issue fundamental to U.S. security. Should the people tacitly accept a navy made obsolescent by virtue of a costly war? Or should actions be taken to rebuild the naval forces to their former levels of strength, taking advantage of technological developments? Admittedly, the costs would be great and would call for cuts in social programs. But did the people and their government have any real alternative? Historically, the U.S. public resents large defense expenditures unless national security is in peril. In fact, the appropriation of public monies for poorly understood defense programs, the effect of which will not be apparent for ten or even twenty years, is not the hallmark of a successful politician. Thus American leaders had been prone to put off expensive defense programs if a reassuring rationale could be developed. One Washington wit wryly remarked that their motto was "Don't prepare until you see the whites of their eyes."

Seldom has a peacetime president argued that our national security goals should be the driving force behind the budget. Rather, incumbent officials prefer to extol U.S. strength and the military power represented by our alliances. Since President Jefferson's day, the American people have preferred to assume that their security is guaranteed by international law, by neutrality proclamations, or by disarmament (actually arms control) agreements, all reasons that have been used, rightly or wrongly, to justify relatively small defense budgets. Jefferson chose cheap and ineffective gunboats over costly frigates while the British Navy boarded helpless U.S. merchant ships and brutally impressed thousands of luckless seamen. Prior to America's entrance in World War I, Woodrow Wilson relied unsuccessfully on American neutrality and the clouded sanctity of international law to protect American vessels and citizens on the high seas.

Similarly, in the late 1930s, while Japanese forces invaded China, and European dictators were on the march, an isolationist-minded Congress placed its trust in a series of neutrality acts to prevent U.S. involvement in foreign wars such as those being waged in Spain and Ethiopia. Meanwhile throughout the 1920s and 1930s inadequate funding and Washington treaty restrictions on ship types contributed to the Navy's inability to carry out its mission for control of the Pacific even though after World War I, a conflict with Japan was its prime concern.

With these historical precedents in mind, critics of the Carter administration contended that although the White House could achieve immediate savings (and evoke public cheers) by deleting funds for ships to be commissioned in the far-off future, it was also true that the resultant penalty, the erosion of U.S. naval power, would be all too apparent in the mid-1980s. But the Navy Department was not without blame.

The disagreeable truth was that the Navy, during the preceding decade, had flawed its record of efficient management in ship and aircraft construction, a fact its critics were quick to turn against it as a plausible reason to delay, drastically modify, or cancel outright certain major projects. As a result, the charge of mismanagement may have indirectly produced a hidden impact on the Navy's roles and missions that would be visible only some years later when the Navy's flexibility to meet its worldwide commitments would be on the decline.

In the late 1960s the Navy began to make up for the virtual shutdown of new ship construction during the Vietnam war. Unhappily the flood of new contracts came at a time when inflation, labor problems, and the entrance of conglomerates (such as Litton Industries) new to shipbuilding created vexing problems. Inevitably, all these factors, when tied to a long-term fixed-price contract, placed the shipbuilders in a squeeze that produced uncontrolled cost overruns. Thus, in 1969 Ingalls Yard (owned by Litton) at Pascagoula, Mississippi, won a contract for nine LHAs, which was later cut to five because the yard fell sixteen months behind schedule. In a second instance, the Grumman Aerospace Corporation, longtime builder of crack naval aircraft, was awarded a contract for the F-14 fighter. Because of unforeseen design and production problems, the program generated a huge overrun, the cost of a single plane rising from $11.5 million to $16.8 million. The contractors blamed higher wages and material costs plus expensive changes demanded by the Navy.

In other cases the Electric Boat Company, a division of General Dynamics, at Groton, Connecticut, charged that the Navy had ordered some 40,000 modifications during the construction of the *Los Angeles* class of nuclear attack submarines. The Newport News Shipbuilding and Dry Dock Company (Tenneco) at Hampton Roads, Virginia, voiced similar complaints. By 1978 various shipbuilders claimed $2.7 billion as reimbursement for cost overruns. Naval representatives retorted that the shipbuilders had condoned worker inefficiency, excessive delivery times on equipment, and unwise capital investments in modernizing their plants. Neutral observers opined that there was blame enough to go around for all concerned. Almost everyone agreed that the public wrangling and litigation, all aired in the press, had battered the Navy's plans for a future fleet. Fortunately for the Navy, Assistant Secretary of the Navy Edward Hidalgo and the contractors eventually achieved settlements satisfactory to almost all concerned.

Systems Analysis and Subjective Judgment

Administration dissatisfaction with the Navy's alleged mismanagement of shipbuilding contracts surfaced at Newport, Rhode Island, in March 1978, at a current strategy forum. Edward Jayne, an associate director in the Office of Management and Budget, told a Naval War College audience that in his view "President Carter chose not to accelerate Navy ship purchases in the 1979 budget" because the service had not resolved its management problems.[1] In blunt terms he warned the Navy to set more realistic priorities, to cease its demands for more funds, to end the friction within the Navy on ship types, and instead seek out reasonable choices to limit the Navy's future role.

Stony-faced naval officers listened to Jayne's injunctions: "What the Navy needs to do is to understand itself, its highest and lowest priorities, and be able to tailor forces accordingly within a budget share reasonably consistent with those of the past."[2] Some weeks later, Jayne denied that he was a Svengali who exercised great influence on the administration's policies. The Navy simply had to understand that it was just not possible to fit into the budget the "very large [naval] program that some in the Navy have viewed as absolutely essential." Commenting on his Newport speech, Jayne said, "I just wanted to say the Navy does need to get its act together."[3]

It is safe to assume that Jayne's stinging admonitions reflected instructions previously given to him in the Oval Office. Clearly, the Carter administration was adamant on two points: (1) limiting the defense budget to a figure near $126 billion (of which about one-third would go to the Navy) and (2) bolstering NATO for a land war on the Central European front.

The administration's warning did little to answer the Navy's question of how to cope some years hence with a Soviet capability to deny the use of the oceans to the United States and its allies. Naval officers in the Pentagon wondered aloud if the civilian analysts (irreverently referred to as the "field marshals on the fourth floor") really understood that the Soviet Union, in contrast to the United States, was 90 percent self-sufficient in raw materials and did not need the sea-lanes for its economic well-being or, indeed, its actual survival. The administration's fixation on a land war in Europe, with the Navy relegated to a secondary role in what inevitably would be a global war, was gravely in error, they declared. Since World War II, the U.S. Navy had not encountered such a triple threat to U.S. sea control and projection of power as that posed by Soviet submarines, carrier air units, and surface combat ships.

Jayne's critical speech at Newport came a day after Navy Secretary W. Graham Claytor had addressed the same audience. Claytor, a destroyer skipper in World War II and one-time president of Southern Railway, took aim on Defense Secretary Brown's systems analysts, asserting, "One of the most frustrating things I have encountered in this job has been a tendency on the part of some staff people to use systems analysis as a cover for what is really subjective judgment."[4] Claytor, in a direct jab at statistics-obsessed officials, said that it was easy to argue against personal opinion, but "if it can be hidden behind hard numbers, an unsophisticated opponent can be overwhelmed." Claytor apparently referred to the suspicion that Brown's chief analyst, Assistant Secretary Russell Murray, was shaping naval policy by making decisions in favor of programs such as the smaller, cheaper carrier, a move that would reduce the Navy to a mere "police force."

Claytor identified the crux of the problem when he stated that the current Defense Department plans for the Navy were shortsighted because they failed to consider the year 2000 and beyond. "But we must think of that time frame now, or our citizens of that era will judge us harshly, and with good reason." Drawing on history, the secretary said that "we must plan as Lewis and Clark did—to take along whatever we will need for a whole range of unforeseen contingencies." He solemnly warned that "we must, as Americans did in the past, make some tough decisions and some sacrifices to benefit those who follow us."[5]

Admiral Holloway, in conversation with the author, observed that he had publicly stated several times that the fate of the Navy rested with the American public: "If they don't want to keep the leadership in the world, then we can change our strategy." Historical precedent suggests that the U.S. public wakes up to danger only when struck by a catastrophe such as a Pearl Harbor or a Cuban missile crisis. But in the 1970s doubt existed whether, in the event of a future crisis, the country would be afforded the necessary time to gear up operations against its most probable adversary, who by then might control the sea. So the controversy between the professional Navy and civilian strategists continued to boil.

Ringing Declarations and Naval Skepticism

The shrinking size of the Navy (from over 900 ships in 1970 to about 460 vessels in 1978) alarmed Chairman Price of the House Armed Services Committee.[6] In responding to Price's queries, Defense Secretary Harold Brown, circumspect and assured, argued at some length before a doubtful House Sea Power Subcommittee that he did not intend to "alter the traditional roles and missions of the Navy." He went further and assured the congressmen that the "commitments" of the Carter administration "require that we maintain a two-ocean

Navy." Brown even spelled out the Navy's specific missions. In addition to the strategic nuclear deterrence provided by the 41 *Polaris/Poseidon* submarines, the missions comprised the following:

> 1. To protect the sea-lanes by multipurpose aircraft carriers, nuclear-powered attack submarines, patrol aircraft, mines, surface combat ships, and surveillance systems (such as SOSUS) of the Navy.[7]
>
> 2. To protect U.S. power with sea-based strike aircraft (that is, carrier planes) and missiles, and the amphibious assault forces of the Navy.
>
> 3. To retain the ability of the Navy to establish a peacetime presence worldwide.

Specifically, Brown stressed that the administration wanted the Navy to be able to operate in relatively high threat areas such as the northern (Atlantic) and southern (Mediterranean) flanks of NATO. Finally, Brown asserted that U.S. sea-lanes were so important, that "we want them protected regardless of whether future wars are likely to be long or short." Clearly, Brown's words reflected a new desire to support the Navy's superiority at sea.[8]

Chairman Price doubted that Brown's resounding affirmation of naval power satisfied naval professionals. Only a short time before Brown's appearance before this panel, Price noted that Admiral Holloway had declared, "I do not think that size of the Navy today, the 459 ships, realistically represents a two-ocean Navy."[9] In other words, it was a one-ocean navy, precariously overextended to cover two oceans.

Why were senior naval officers at odds with the resolute declarations of the secretary of defense? In their view, Brown's words expressed bold intentions that did not square with the cheerless intelligence collected by the Navy on the Soviet fleet. Holloway predicted that although the U.S. Navy currently held a margin of superiority over the Soviets in some categories, it was a slim advantage.

The CNO was not reluctant to give reasons for his sobering assessment, claiming that in the event of war, the United States could probably retain control of the North Atlantic sea-lanes to Europe but at the expense of serious losses to allied shipping in the early stages (as in World War II). As for the eastern Mediterranean, the Navy's ability to operate in an area so close to Soviet bases would be "uncertain at best."

The picture in the Pacific was even more unsatisfactory, as Holloway described it. If a NATO conflict required that air squadrons and ships of the Pacific Fleet be shifted to the European theater, the CNO estimated that remaining ships could be counted on to protect only the sea-lanes from U.S. west coast ports to Hawaii and Alaska. He held out no similar promise for the sea-lanes to U.S. allies in the Western Pacific because the Navy would only have sufficient strength to protect the military lines of communication.

As Holloway peered into the murky future, he did not like what he saw. He observed that in the mid-1960s the United States was far and away the dominant naval power in the world, but in 1978 the Soviet Navy had "the capability to challenge the U.S. Navy in many areas." Confronted with this serious situation, the CNO predicted that if the downward trends that had brought about "this major change" were allowed to continue, then by 1988 the balance of maritime superiority could tip in favor of the Soviets. Implicit in his warning was the adage, "Eternal vigilance is the price of liberty," and, one might add, of what good were social programs (Russia providing a ready example) when liberty was gone.

Holloway's solution for this dangerous predicament lay in more shipbuilding and a buildup of the fleet. The CNO's meaning was clear; the United States would ignore at its peril his warning that it must begin now to build the ships and planes needed to retain its slender superiority. The admiral's words conveyed unmistakable opposition to those who expressed strong affirmation, but fell short on actions, for an adequate ship construction program.

A Clamor in the Congress

During the congressional debate in 1978, defense-budget choppers were vigorously opposed by Congressman Lawrence McDonald of Georgia. McDonald, a conservative Democrat and a naval veteran, lashed out at those who persisted in cutting the essentials of defense to the bone in order to fund social engineering projects. Charging colossal waste in such federally supported programs, he urged economy-minded doves to search for "fat" by monitoring the $7 billion "which dripped unheeded into unauthorized pockets from the HEW [Health, Education and Welfare] budget" in 1977.[10]

The spirited Georgian declared that the devaluation of U.S. strategic policy was obvious in the national decline from a clear superiority in strategic nuclear weapons to a mild "essential equivalence" in the mid-1970s. He protested that even though U.S. command of the sea had become an empty phrase, the Carter administration attacked "the heart of the Navy's task forces, the large nuclear powered carriers."

Congressman McDonald demanded more nuclear-powered ships and a speedup in the Aegis air defense system for the fleet. There was much to be done if the Navy was to carry out its functions, he said, contending that the Congress should not permit "the admittedly blameworthy cost reasons to halt [ship and aircraft] construction programs that are already proceeding too slowly."

Insisting that "our lotus-eating days are fast coming to a close, one way or another," McDonald condemned the Congress for "failing again to provide for the common defense." What was lacking, he concluded, was leadership and strong will.[11]

A second congressman who believed his colleagues had placed too much faith in a limited defense budget was John R. Breckinridge of Kentucky. Quoting Winston Churchill's warning to a prewar appeasement-minded England that "virtuous motives, trammeled by inertia and timidity, are no match for armed and resolute [Nazi] wickedness," Breckinridge spurred his colleagues to wake up lest the failure to pay heed to the warning lead "relentlessly" to a repetition of World War II and the burying [of] a reported 30−50 millions of people."[12]

Breckinridge, who had fought in Europe during World War II, rising to the rank of colonel, asserted that the Western world was becoming imperiled by the continued trend toward a military imbalance. He was profoundly disturbed that the estimated percentage of the Soviet gross national product spent on defense was 8 percent in 1958, 12 percent in 1970, 15 percent in 1975, and a projected 18 percent in 1980.[13] He insisted that if the United States had invested the same percentages of the gross national product for defense as the Soviet Union, the U.S. defense budget for fiscal year 1978 would have been between $250 and $300 billion (instead of less than half that figure). These figures were reflected in the 50 percent reduction of the U.S. fleet since 1968, while the Soviet Navy registered the biggest gain in its history. Plainly the American people were not yet prepared to accept the financial burden of building a stronger fleet.

Compelling evidence of the shift in the balance of global political power, said Breckinridge, was clear from the Soviet Navy's "out of area" operations, which had grown at an annual rate of 25 percent between 1965 and 1973. Breckinridge referred to Russian naval incursions into the Caribbean, the Indian and Pacific Oceans, and other distant seas. Soviet naval ships in the Middle East, Southeast Asia, and Africa had supported military land operations in those areas. Breckinridge pinpointed the new Soviet supersonic bomber, the Backfire, as a new threat to "the vital sea-lanes of the North Atlantic and Mediterranean." It was even capable of operating against the United States (with nuclear missiles). Thirty-six to fifty Backfires, he disclosed, were being built every year. By 1980 the Soviet Union would have some four hundred operable.

Moreover, the Soviet naval Backfires could be used for antiship attacks using stand-off (long-range) missiles. In this role they conceivably could represent a greater menace to the West's shipping than invisible Soviet submarines. Although Moscow denied that the Backfire was a strategic bomber and thus should not be included in the SALT negotiations,[14] there was no doubt that it could fly to the continental United States and refuel en route in other countries friendly to Moscow. The plane could also be staged and refueled from arctic bases for missions against targets in the United States or against allied shipping.

Breckinridge predicted that the Soviets and their newfound allies, aided by the newly established string of Soviet bases throughout the Mediterranean and Indian Ocean, unless arrested, would make the United States a secondary strategic power. The continuing trend toward U.S. military and naval inferiority was intolerable, he continued, and would be "tantamount to a conscious decision by the American people" to become militarily inferior to the Soviets. He recommended a minimum $15 billion increase in the defense budget, plus a 10 percent annual increase in real 1978 dollars over the next decade. The efforts of Congressman Breckinridge to arouse his colleagues to the dangers of a deteriorating naval and defense balance were not immediately successful. As we shall see, not until news of a Soviet armored brigade in Cuba was broadcast in August 1979, coupled with the capture of the U.S. Embassy in Tehran and the brazen Soviet takeover of Afghanistan in December 1979, did the White House, Congress, and public opinion swing overwhelmingly toward a stronger defense.

Soothing Words from Brown and Vance

The pessimistic long-range outlook broadcast by the Navy's leaders did not please Defense Secretary Harold Brown. Strong-willed, hardworking, impatient with those of lesser intellect, Brown quickly made clear that the Pentagon would present a united front on defense policy matters. Specifically he directed that no uniformed member of the Defense Department should conduct informal "liaison" with members of Congress. Brown's attempt to suppress this long-standing custom caused an immediate uproar on Capitol Hill, where Republicans condemned it as a muzzling of the military.

By shutting off this informal pipeline of information, particularly to legislators who took their constitutional mandate to "provide for the common Defence" and "to provide and maintain a Navy" seriously, the defense secretary apparently hoped to calm the controversy over the naval budget. But Brown had no such control over retired officers. Evidently nettled by the public statements of individuals such as Admirals Thomas Moorer, U. S. Grant Sharp, Elmo Zumwalt, and Gerald Miller, the defense secretary, in a speech delivered at San Francisco, tried to dispel the public concern over naval rivalry with Moscow.[15]

In broad generalities Brown assured his audience that the United States and its allies possessed the armed might needed to thwart the Soviet buildup and to deter any surprise attack. Placing the utmost confidence in U.S. nuclear strategic weapons, he prophesied that we were powerful enough to wreak "catastrophic damage" on the Soviet Union. He rejected the suggestion that the United States and its allies should match the Soviets in personnel and weaponry, a concept that to him made no sense. Rather, the American people should take heart in the power, determination, and stability of the United States as a competitor and in the visible cohesion of U.S. alliances. These were the elements that would influence Soviet behavior, he emphasized. Therefore the nation should build only those weapons systems that would protect its interests and deter conflict.

Brown's confidence in U.S. military power was echoed by Secretary of State

Cyrus Vance, a cautious lawyer, trained to search for negotiated solutions. In a speech at Chicago, he declared that U.S. military strength was formidable. Noting that no responsible U.S. military official would exchange our strategic position for that of any other nation, he described the ''strong and reliable security relationships'' that reinforced the West's overall military strength. He spoke approvingly of U.S. strategic, nuclear submarines, of cruise missiles for B-52 bombers, and the decision to commit real increases of 3 percent in defense funds to modernize NATO forces. No one should doubt that we would use our forces in Europe or elsewhere if our vital interests or those of allies were threatened, said the mild-mannered Vance in an indirect warning to Moscow.[16]

Critics labeled the bland assurances of the two Cabinet members as obvious cosmetics that ignored the point made by Navy Secretary Claytor: unless the declining trend of the Navy's budget were reversed, it would be well-nigh impossible to maintain control of vital sea areas twenty years hence.

A second official who took exception to the optimistic outlook of the administration was Under Secretary of the Navy R. James Woolsey.[17] In a talk at the Naval War College, Woolsey reminded his listeners that ''planners'' (systems analysts) could not predict the crises the Navy would face in the future. Consequently, their efforts to limit the Navy's fighting abilities constituted a hazard to national security.

For example, Woolsey said, who in the audience could have foreseen in 1946 that in 1978 the country would need naval forces to ensure the safety of Israel and the protection of the sea-lanes to the Persian Gulf? Similarly, who in 1946 could have predicted a split between Communist China and the Soviet Union and the U.S.-Soviet parity in strategic weapons? Woolsey questioned the judgment of systems analysts whose decisions could restrict the traditional flexibility and mobility of the naval service. ''What makes anyone even remotely confident that the national security problems of the early 21st century are any clearer to us today than the forces that drive naval planning in 1978 were clear in 1946?'' he asked. To these pointed questions, the answers were self-evident.[18]

Charting the Navy's Future

For years it has been the responsibility of the CNO and his staff to draft long-range plans extending for five and ten years. These plans, based on the threats the Navy might face in the future, were translated into goals to be achieved in shipbuilding programs, personnel training, materiel procurement, contract procedures, and the like. In short, the CNO staff searched for answers to three questions: What should the national strategy be? What were the proper roles for the Navy to carry out such strategy? And what kind of ships should be built for these roles?

The Navy's sensitivity to its alleged dilemma over its roles and missions in 1977 undoubtedly prompted it to conduct—in collaboration with the Marine Corps and the Department of Defense—a major assessment of naval forces. Entitled Sea Plan 2000, the study was ready in March 1978.[19] One of the principal contributors to the section on the Navy's general purpose forces was Francis West, a faculty member at the Naval War College in Newport, Rhode Island. A Princeton-educated political scientist, West had served as a Marine combat officer in Vietnam. Later he had been an assistant to Secretary of Defense James Schlesinger during the Ford administration.

Assistant Defense Secretary Murray had alarmed the Navy by his faultfinding analysis that sought to limit the fleet to a sea control mission, which the CNO considered rashly unrealistic. Designed to refute and overturn the Murray study, Sea Plan 2000 came to grips with the problem of building a fleet in terms of time, money, and public support. The study produced by the West group was in effect a basic handbook for legislators and policymakers on the use of naval power and the program choices open to them.

At the outset the study spelled out warnings of potential troublespots where U.S. naval power would be needed. The list was familiar and included these broad tasks:

1. To maintain stability by forward deployment of carrier battle groups and Marines in such sensitive areas as the Mediterranean, Northeast Asia, Southeast Asia, and the Indian Ocean;

2. To contain crises by U.S. superiority at sea and by the deployment of air and assault (Marine) forces that can put on a demonstration of force without being committed;

3. To deter a major war (a) by defending the sea-lanes; (b) by reinforcing U.S. allies on the flanks of the Soviet Union (Norway, Greece, Turkey, Japan); (c) by retaining the ability to put pressure on certain Soviet forces; and (d) by providing naval forces to the policymakers as a hedge against an uncertain future.

Dangers loomed. It was a safe assumption that in the next twenty years the Soviets would improve their nuclear attack submarines (as differentiated from their strategic missile boats), build more long-range Backfire (missile-carrying) bombers for their naval strike force and increase the number of VSTOL aircraft carriers.

From the U.S. Navy's vantage point, the future would not be more secure than the past, reason enough for the sea service to retain its superior, offensive fighting character. But could this be done when the fleet seemed destined to become more vulnerable year by year? The authors of Sea Plan 2000 asserted that a bright spot in the picture was U.S. technological improvements in antimissile and ASW defenses. Fortunately these favorable developments came at a time when Soviet antiship missiles, launched from ships, submarines, and bombers constituted a major threat to U.S. surface ships.

The significance of the U.S. capability to counter such missiles carried considerable import for the nation's policymakers. We need only recall that the sheer superiority of U.S. naval strength influenced the conduct of a young President Kennedy in the Cuban missile crisis and of President Nixon during the Yom Kippur war of 1973. The Sea Plan 2000 strategists made one telling point: only to the extent that America's allies on the flanks of Russia recognized the survivability and fighting potential of the U.S. Navy would they be reassured and act accordingly.

A Balanced Fleet as National Insurance

Sea Plan 2000 offered three options, each representing a balanced fleet but in graduated order of strength. Each was designed to support, on a declining scale, three basic national security goals: maintenance of stability, containment of crises, and deterrence of wars. By way of persuading Washington policymakers that Sea Plan 2000 was a suitable framework for a future shipbuilding plan, the Navy planners emphasized that U.S. naval forces could keep pace with technology, but at a price. To convince doubters, they likened the situation to a trust fund set up for one's heirs. "A balanced portfolio [fleet] provides the optimum insurance against uncertainty." One does not divest blue-chip stocks (carriers) that have demonstrated a good return on investment without a reasonable certainty of a better investment (VSTOL carriers?). New stocks or bond issues (new missiles, surface-effect ships, etc.) are samples as possible blue chips of the future.

Admittedly there were any number of alternate plans for building ships as insurance for the future. The danger lay, as Sea Plan 2000 pointed out, in decisions to unbalance the structure of the fleet and so run an ominous risk in one mission area by an effort to reduce the dangers in another. With budget funds as a controlling factor, Sea Plan 2000 sought to minimize this pitfall in its three illustrative options for the fleet of the year 2000. Option 1, 439 ships, was a cheap but high-risk choice marked by minimal fleet capability, requiring only an annual 1 percent real growth in the naval budget. Option 2, 535 ships, would impose a minimum acceptable risk while allowing the fleet to maintain a selective superiority at sea. Its price was an annual 3 percent real growth. Option 3, 585 ships, would assure a lower risk and provide hedges and options for the Navy's missions. Table 2 depicts the makeup of the respective fleets for each option.

How did the Navy measure these three options in terms of the Navy's missions? Table 3 depicts the three main national objectives and the naval mission associated

TABLE 2
ILLUSTRATIVE FLEET OPTIONS FOR YEAR 2000

Ships	Option 1 1 Percent Real Growth	Option 2 3 Percent Real Growth	Option 3 4 Percent Real Growth
SSBN[a]	25	25	25
CV[b]	10	12	14
SSN[c]	80	94	98
Aegis ships[d]	10	24	28
Surface combatants	210	252	272
Amphibious ships	52	66	78
Other	52	62	70
Total	439	535	585

[a] Ballistic missile nuclear submarine.
[b] Aircraft carrier.
[c] Nuclear attack submarine.
[d] Vessels equipped with the powerful surface-to-air antimissile system Aegis.

TABLE 3
OBJECTIVES AND MISSIONS

Security Objective	Naval Mission
Maintenance of stability	Forward deployments to the Far East, Indian Ocean, Mediterranean, etc.
Containment of crises	Calibrated use of force against the shore Superiority at sea in a crisis setting
Deterrence of a global war	Defense of sea lines of communication (SLOC) Reinforcement of allies Pressure on the Soviets Hedge against uncertainties of the distant future

with each. None of these three security objectives had priority over any other. All were tightly interwoven with current international politics and economics. One example was the Organization of Petroleum Exporting Countries oil price hikes beginning in 1973 in which the Arab oil nations, unawed by U.S. power, placed the United States and other nations on the receiving end of the oil squeeze. In these and similar cases, the relative strength of the U.S. Navy became an important element in the protection of future oil shipments from abroad.

The Sea Plan 2000 panel argued that it was imperative that the United States not lose control—or give the appearance of losing control—of events at the crisis level. Without a strong navy, no U.S. president would have the flexibility of force to contain critical situations on the rimlands of the world's oceans. And, in the event of a war within Europe, nothing was more essential to U.S. interests than the Navy's ability to support American allies across the Atlantic.

Specifically, the Navy estimated that the least desirable Option 1 would mean a pullback of ships from the Mediterranean and Far East. Moreover, any U.S. wartime naval reinforcement of allies situated close to Russia would be in doubt.

American policymakers would have more confidence in handling crises if Option 2 were chosen. According to Sea Plan 2000 a fleet of 535 ships, including Aegis antimissile ships, would protect the carriers and permit the formation of surface action groups (SAGs) designed as supplementary ship units for carrier battle groups. Acting independently, SAGs could be counted on to overwhelm Soviet surface combatants. In the event of a major war, Option 2 would give the Navy the potential to move into areas near the Soviet Union, such as the waters around Norway, Greece, Israel, or Japan.

Option 3, with 585 ships, provided by far the strongest choice. Current ship deployments would continue. Foreign perception of U.S. power would be strengthened by the all-round superiority of the fleet. Option 3 also would provide hedges against ship losses, which Option 2 could not give. Such was the Sea Plan 2000 group's reasoning in urging the administration and the Congress to maintain a fleet that could support the nation's security objectives in the years ahead.

The Message of Sea Plan 2000

The Sea Plan 2000 panel harbored no illusions about the efficacy of détente, and the authors emphasized that Americans should expect the unexpected. If the past was a valid guide, there was every reason for the administration to place its trust in the Navy's actual combat capabilities to handle unexpected crises rather than in scenarios based on questionable assumptions. The nation would be better served by a fleet capable of a wide range of measures in support of U.S. foreign policy rather than by a "dominant force" of strategic nuclear missiles capable only of wreaking wholesale incineration. Optimistic reliance on a weapon that the United States never would use first was tantamount to having no weapon at all. In sum, Sea Plan 2000 held that the Navy must retain a balanced fleet, a goal that could be best achieved by a 3 percent real growth in shipbuilding funds.

As for new technologies, admittedly the Soviets had made substantial gains. However, the U.S. Navy had achieved breakthroughs in cruise missiles and antimissile systems; ASW defenses were being improved, as were electronic jamming and decoys. True, while the U.S. Navy was occupied with the war in Indochina, the Soviets had developed deadly antiship missiles. But by the early 1980s the Navy planned to have new weapons to counter them.

The U.S. public, in the meantime, had not yet grasped the possibility that the Navy was approaching the point where it might be forced to concede maritime superiority to the Russians. Continued reductions in U.S. naval forces might mean that the Navy in the 1980s could no longer exhibit the strength evident off Cuba in 1962, Jordan in 1970, and the Middle East in 1973. The American people likewise were slow to sense that Soviet adventurism in Africa, the Caribbean, and Asia had not been thwarted by any U.S. superiority in nuclear weapons. Rather, in most cases during the past five years the White House, when it had reacted, had summoned the conventional forces of the Navy to dampen Soviet moves.

Sea Plan 2000 signaled that the nation should realize that conventional forces were just as essential as nuclear weaponry. The mission was clear: to maintain the power to destroy the Soviet fleet and to deny Russian ships access to any ocean; and, in conjunction with allied navies and land-based air forces, to maintain maritime superiority over the Soviet forces in the key strategic areas of the world.

The Threshold of Vulnerability

The authors of Sea Plan 2000 were keenly aware that ships could not be churned out in a fashion similar to automobiles. The days of World War II when Henry Kaiser's yards took only months to build naval vessels were gone forever. The complex technology of the space age, mirrored in the fighting ships of the 1970s, meant that lengthy construction periods were unavoidable. Consequently, the United States no longer could rely on its legendary industrial magic to create combat ships virtually overnight in event of war. The harsh truth, as Sea Plan 2000 made clear, was that the no-growth naval policies of the preceding decade were reflected in a dangerously overextended Navy, which could not be suddenly increased as had happened in the past.

Without resorting to alarmist rhetoric, naval proponents urged the nation's policymakers to abandon their tightfisted policy and realize that time was against them. Short-term, year-to-year shipbuilding appropriations constituted a sure road to military inferiority. Decisions made in 1978 would determine the strength of the Navy in 1988. More important, these decisions would profoundly affect the nature of U.S. power and diplomacy. Simply put, if the United States had more ships in the 1980s, it would have proportionally greater clout in its diplomatic dealings around the world. Conversely, if the fleet were weaker, Americans would be forced to accept less naval flexibility and diminished expectations in foreign affairs. This was the unpalatable choice facing the administration in the interpretation of practical-minded naval officials responsible for contending with future crises at the scene of action.

Sea Plan 2000's unvarnished conclusions helped to focus the attention of the Congress and the Carter administration on the need for a bigger naval budget. Nevertheless, many lawmakers hopefully believed that the SALT II talks would lead to treaty limits on nuclear weapons (''strategic equivalence'' or ''parity'') that would cool the military competition with Russia. Others were unwilling to intensify an escalating inflation by voting for bigger naval appropriations. Still others were heedful of the need to court certain advocacy groups such as the underprivileged, labor, and the elderly by showering federal funds on them. If the Sea Plan 2000 authors shook the complacency of various legislators, the voting public did not yet sense that U.S. sea power had sagged to a stage that might be most difficult to redress in the hazardous years ahead. Paradoxically, the Soviet naval commander-in-chief unwittingly was doing his best to alert Americans to that possibility.

Nine

SOVIET RUSSIA AS
A MAJOR NAVAL POWER

The Postwar Renascence

A BATTERED SOVIET UNION emerged from World War II with a loss of twenty million souls and one-third of its territory ravaged by German invaders. At war's end the Soviet Navy, considered something of a step-child by the Soviet land-minded hierarchy, consisted of a motley collection of captured German and Japanese ships, submarines, and aging prewar surface ships, all assigned a mission of coastal defense. Submarines dominated the fleet, partly because Soviet submarine-building yards had never been overrun by German forces.

Stalin's unlamented death in 1953 led to the assumption of power by the bellicose and unpredictable Nikita Khrushchev. The new premier, who had served as a political commissar with the Red Army during the war, knew next to nothing of naval affairs. However, he must be credited with good judgment in approving to the appointment of Admiral Sergei G. Gorshkov as naval commander-in-chief, a post Gorshkov still held as of 1980.

In selecting Gorshkov, Khrushchev chose a career officer who early on had been marked as an outstanding leader. Promoted to rear admiral at the young age of 31, Gorshkov had fought the Germans in the Black Sea, led Soviet seamen in the defense of Stalingrad, and later chased the enemy out of his native Ukraine, as well as out of Romania, Bulgaria, and Hungary. His record as a loyal party man and a tested combat leader was matched by his later success in persuading Kremlin decision makers of the crucial importance of the Soviet Navy for their plans to advance the "correlation of [anti-American, communist] forces" worldwide.

For the next quarter century this competent and resourceful officer was unremitting in his efforts to convince his superiors of the appalling threat represented by missile-launching U.S. submarines and carrier attack planes.[1] Gorshkov emphasized that unless the Soviet Navy were expanded and strengthened, the Kremlin's grand plans for defense and for global strategy would be for naught.

Because he was forced to compete for funds with the Missile Force, the Air Defense Force, the Long-range Bombing Command, and Army Ground Forces, his ability to win the approval of his Kremlin masters for a growing fleet was a tribute to his professional stature and bureaucratic skill.

During the post-Stalin era the Kremlin authorized the construction of missile submarines, the first of which, the *Golf* class, went to sea in 1958. Concurrently, the Soviets developed shipboard missiles for surface vessels, thus equipping their Navy with an offensive power that it had lacked. Keeping pace with U.S. naval technology, the Soviets, in the early 1950s, made the decision to design and build a nuclear-powered submarine.[2] In 1955 the U.S. Navy's first nuclear boat, the USS *Nautilus*, joined the fleet. By 1961 the Soviet Navy not only had commissioned its first nuclear submarine but had fitted air-to-surface missiles to its long-range patrol bombers. Clearly, Gorshkov had made good his pledge that his forces could threaten any U.S. carrier task force that ventured within a thousand-mile range of Russian shores.

Gorshkov's satisfaction with the development of missile ships doubtless was dampened by the Kremlin's decision to shift hundreds of land-based naval aircraft to the Air Defense Force, a move that must have been resented by proud Russian naval officers. During the Eisenhower adminstration the so-called policy of massive retaliation by long-range U.S. bombers and carrier planes had created apprehension in Moscow over the deficiencies of its air and sea defenses. The Soviet Navy might have been more distressed had it known that Khrushchev had considered (but not carried out) the transfer of naval ships to the Missile Force, in effect further diluting the sea service.[3] On the other hand, during the 1950s Khrushchev and Marshal Georgii Zhukov, the defense minister, agreed to the transfer to Naval Aviation of several hundred medium-size land-based bombers to be used to seek out and attack enemy shipping.[4]

Khrushchev Learns about Sea Power

The Kremlin's obsession with an essentially defensive navy revealed an embarrassing weakness in 1956 during the Suez crisis and again in 1958 when the U.S. Sixth Fleet landed Marines in Lebanon. On each occasion U.S. warships had provided awesome leverage to U.S. diplomatic moves. Conversely, Soviet leaders were limited to loud but unproductive protests in U.N. forums. The lesson was not lost on Khrushchev, who seemed finally to sense that until he could muster an imposing surface fleet, the Soviet Union was not qualified to engage in power politics in the Middle East or elsewhere. In short, Soviet submarines, no matter how numerous, were not the equal of surface warships in establishing a naval presence.

About this time, to no one's surprise, Gorshkov was authorized to push ahead with the building of a fleet of modern warships. The missile-minded premier, who previously had scoffed at large combat ships as unnecessary,[5] now publicly acclaimed the Navy and tacitly accepted the new building program.[6]

Any Soviet doubts about the value of a naval task force in support of diplomatic adventures were dispelled completely during the Cuban missile crisis of 1962, an ignominious experience that subsequently led to Khrushchev's banishment from public life. We may easily imagine a postmortem scene where Kremlin leaders asked Admiral Gorshkov why the Soviet Navy had been of so little use in foiling the U.S. blockade. He may well have responded that he lacked sufficient surface ships to put on an effective show of force. Indeed, even if he has possessed such ships, he still would have lacked vital logistic support vessels. And most important of all, he would have needed carriers to provide air cover. He may also have pointed out that Russia had no naval or air bases in Cuba or the Caribbean to carry out maritime operations so far from home. Gorshkov could have added that, lacking all of these naval assets, Russia inevitably was forced to cave in to Kennedy's demands. One can picture the Russian admiral tactfully explaining to his dejected superiors that until he was given a fleet strong enough to carry out its missions, the Kremlin should be prepared for similar retreats when opposed by the Americans. It is reasonable to assume that Gorshkov made the most of this diplomatic setback in pressing his civilian masters for funds to build a truly ocean-going fleet to surpass that of the United States.

FIGURE 7

THE FOUR SOVIET FLEETS

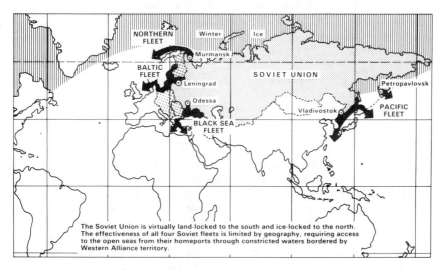

The Soviet Union is virtually land-locked to the south and ice-locked to the north. The effectiveness of all four Soviet fleets is limited by geography, requiring access to the open seas from their homeports through constricted waters bordered by Western Alliance territory.

Source: Paul H. Nitze, Leonard Sullivan, Jr., and the Atlantic Council Working Group on Securing the Seas, *Securing the Seas*. Used with the kind permission of the Atlantic Council of the United States.

Gorshkov, the Soviet Mahan

Like his American precursor, Rear Admiral Alfred T. Mahan,[7] Admiral Gorshkov wrote books and articles to publicize his new global doctrine. American readers first became aware of his writings in 1974 when the U.S. Naval Institute published a collection of his writing entitled *Red Star Rising at Sea*. A second book, *The Sea Power of the State*, appeared in the United States in 1979.[8]

If Gorshkov had a particular concern, it was the problem of protecting his strategic missile submarines against enemy antisubmarine forces. In *The Sea Power of the State* he drew an interesting parallel between the future defense of Soviet missile submarines and the allied ASW campaign of World War II. Actually, by late 1944 the U.S. and British navies, using hunter-killer teams of carriers and destroyers, had virtually eliminated the Nazi submarine force.

In analyzing the failure of the U-boats, the admiral condemned Hitler for not allocating more of his surface warships and aircraft to protect his submarines against allied sub killers on patrol in the dangerous waters of the eastern Atlantic. Gorshkov created the distinct impression that, faced with a similar situation, he would try to destroy enemy ASW assets (that is, bases, ships, and aircraft), thus allowing Soviet boats more immunity from enemy hunter-killer teams. How else can his concentration on Soviet attack submarines, powerful missile-firing ships, the *Kiev* class carriers, and long-range missile-firing aircraft be explained? These ships and planes, aided by satellite surveillance, would constitute a lethal punch against the enemy.

In a similar vein the plainspoken Soviet admiral made it clear that his missile submarines should be used to strike enemy shore targets such as ports, staging areas, and industrial plants, thus exerting a very considerable and perhaps decisive influence on the course of the future war.[9] As Gorshkov put it:

> . . . while earlier the crux of the efforts of a fleet was directed against the enemy fleet, now the chief goal of a fleet is becoming that of . . . action against enemy ground objectives and the protection of one's enemy from the strikes of his fleet.[10]

Gorshkov continued:

> Today, *a fleet operating against the shore* [emphasis supplied] is able not only to solve the tasks connected with territorial changes but to directly influence the course and even outcome of a war . . . The operations of a fleet against the shore have assumed paramount importance in armed conflict at sea, governing the technical policy of building a fleet and in the development of naval art. Confirmation of this is that in the USA atomic-powered missile submarines are assigned to the strategic forces and all other ships to the general-purpose forces . . . These operations are now the most constituent part of the efforts of a fleet, aimed at undermining the military potential of the enemy.[11]

Gorshkov stressed that (if his counsel were heeded) in an all-out war his fleet would be prepared to strike enemy shore targets, an action designed to deprive ships of their bases. Without logistic support these isolated vessels would soon exhaust their fuel and supplies, leaving control of the seas to the Soviets by default. Gorshkov's utter confidence in his missile boats is confirmed by one sovietologist's assertion that the one high-value unit in the Russian fleet is the SSBN, the strategic nuclear missile submarine.[12]

Strategy for the Duel at Sea

Gorshkov's acquisition of long-range (4,200 miles) ballistic missiles in the early 1970s enormously increased the striking range of his strategic submarines. By positioning these boats in home waters for the launching of their missiles, Soviet submarines henceforth were spared the danger of transiting those maritime bottlenecks that for centuries have been the bane of Russian warships. No longer would a strategic submarine skipper en route to the Atlantic be forced to pass through the tortuous Danish Straits or the well-guarded Greenland-Iceland-United Kingdom gap. Instead he could find sanctuary in areas such as the Barents Sea, turning a high-seas handicap into a geographic advantage.[13]

Meanwhile the Soviet ASW forces were committed to the baffling task of searching globally for the U.S. Navy's strategic boats. Could this mutually imposed, strategic submarine threat be considered a standoff by each side? In one sense the answer was yes, but only if the Soviet ASW units failed to discover ways to overcome the *Poseidon* and *Trident* boats.[14] Otherwise U.S. strategic submarines would remain invincible.

To sum up, the effectiveness of Gorshkov's future fleet turned on (1) a strategic submarine force to destroy continental targets or to discourage potential enemies from escalating conventional combat operations; (2) a surface and attack submarine fleet to protect his strategic missile boats by destruction of enemy sea forces; (3) an attack submarine force and Backfire reconnaissance bombers to be used in conjunction with Soviet spy satellites to launch long-range missiles at allied ships or battle groups; and (4) a Marine assault force for amphibious operations.

The U.S. Navy could judge the battle efficiency of Gorshkov's global navy by examining the successful world-wide maritime exercises, OKEAN (ocean) in 1970 and 1975, in which the technology of space-age satellites and instant communications enabled Moscow to direct most effectively the movements of four fleets against ''enemy'' shipping lanes and land targets. The impressive OKEAN exercises were proof that in the short space of three decades the coastal defense navy of 1950 had been transformed into a force designed to deny use of the seas to its enemy.[15]

The first of the U.S. *Polaris* submarines, *George Washington*, nuclear-powered and capable of firing sixteen missiles with a thousand-mile range, was commissioned in 1959. Advance news (probably in the late 1950s) of its appearance prompted Gorshkov's planners to design a new type of ship to meet this menace. The result was the *Moskva* class of antisubmarine helicopter carriers, two of which were commissioned in 1967 and 1968. As the first "aircraft-operating" ships in the Soviet Navy, these 8,000-ton ships, similar to cruisers when viewed from ahead, were easily identified by their after-section, which essentially was a large helicopter flight deck. Each ship carried eighteen ASW aircraft fitted with submarine detection equipment as well as with bombs and torpedos.[16]

According to intelligence sources, the Soviets learned from maneuvers at sea that the *Moskva*s, because of their low freeboard, were not suitable for service in the stormy North Atlantic and North Pacific.[17] Not surprisingly, the Russians soon produced the *Kiev* class multipurpose carrier, which displaced some 40,000 tons and was equipped with helicopters and the VSTOL fixed-wing planes known as Forgers.[18] Two of these ships were operational in 1979, and a third *Kiev*, plus a huge nuclear carrier, reportedly were being built at the Nicolayev and Severodvinsk shipyards.[19] The trend toward large aircraft carriers signaled a portentous pattern in Soviet naval strategy.

The appearance of the *Kiev*s was proof that the Russians were building up an effective naval air arm. As part of a coordinated submarine-aircraft force, this air arm ultimately would constitute the prime attack team to counter allied (chiefly U.S.) battle groups.[20] Too, the Russians were well aware that Soviet surface vessels required air cover for defense against enemy tactical aircraft, whether carrier- or land-based.[21]

With their strong ASW helicopter squadrons operating in conjunction with destroyers and attack submarines, the *Kiev*s conceivably could seek out and destroy allied missile submarines. Finally, the *Kiev* ships, armed with missiles and antimissiles and operating with Forger strafing planes, could venture into areas where both air defense and air striking power were essential. By deploying squadrons far from home waters, the Soviets unmistakably had broadened their ability to support so-called wars of liberation and their challenge of open warfare to the U.S. fleet.

An Expanding Naval Presence

Aware of the political value of a so-called naval presence, the Kremlin directed in the late 1960s that Soviet naval vessels appear frequently in Indian Ocean ports. In 1968 Premier Aleksei Kosygin, accompanied by Admiral Gorshkov, paid an official visit to New Delhi. Shortly thereafter, India received Soviet ships, with naval instructors assigned to Indian sailors. By such aid agreements Gorshkov paved the way for future logistic support in an area new to his vessels.[22]

As members of the big-navy club, warships of the Soviet fleet were seen at ports in the Arabian Sea, the Persian Gulf, and the South Atlantic. Demonstrating that the Soviet Navy could be used for more than showing the flag, Soviet warships by their presence in the Gulf of Guinea in 1968 helped to persuade Ghana to free impounded Soviet fishing vessels. In 1970 Gorshkov established a naval patrol off Guinea, ostensibly to discourage any Portuguese attacks on the leftist government at Conakry.[23] Other instances of Soviet gunboat diplomacy took place in 1970 at Mogadiscio, the chief port of Somalia, and at Freetown, Sierra Leone.

Castro's role as Moscow's man in Havana and his 1968 trade agreement with Russia guaranteed that Soviet warships would be welcome at the Cuban capital and at Cienfuegos on the south coast.[24] Moscow clearly was saying that if Washington could maintain the Sixth Fleet in Russia's backyard, then Soviet ships could intrude in America's front yard with equal impunity.

In 1970 the Soviets, in a test of U.S. acquiescence in their naval presence, established a nuclear submarine support facility at Cienfuegos in the short time of three weeks. In September of that year, a Soviet submarine tender and two barges (shipped from Polyarny, the naval base twenty miles from Murmansk) appeared in Cienfuegos Bay. Such barges could be used for the storage of radioactive material peculiar to nuclear submarines. In addition, U.S. intelligence reported a task group of Soviet ships sailing toward Cuba. The group comprised a cruiser, a destroyer, a submarine tender, a salvage tug, a salvage ship, an oiler, and an amphibious ship.[25] Photographs made by U-2 pilots on daily flights gave evidence of Soviet communication towers, submarine crew quarters, and antiaircraft (missile launching?) sites at Cienfuegos. To cap it off, a Soviet missile submarine was identified in the area. By replenishing in Cuba these submarines could extend their time-on-station by one-third, a tremendous advantage if their home base was at Polyarny, 4000 miles away.[26]

When the Nixon administration warned Moscow that any Cuban base for strategic submarines was unacceptable, the Soviets backed down and withdrew their ships. The matter presumably ended in October 1970 with the understanding that the Russians would observe the Kennedy-Khrushchev pact of 1962 that prohibited the introduction of offensive weaponry into Cuba. Ostensibly, the Kremlin agreed (with its fingers crossed) that the repair and resupply of submarines in Cuban ports were no longer sanctioned. Nine years later, as we shall see, the problem of the Cienfuegos sub base flared up again, proof that the Soviets never ceased to test situations that, if not met by U.S. firmness, would gain them a strategic advantage.

Russian Naval Limitations

Gorshkov's success in building four large fleets headquartered respectively in the Barents Sea at Murmansk, the Baltic at Baltisk, the Black Sea at Sevastopol, and in the northern Pacific at Vladivostok was not without its limitations. As Rear Admiral Sumner Shapiro, director of U.S. naval intelligence, disclosed in 1977, the Soviet Navy was vulnerable in several important areas. To begin with, its long-range reconnaissance planes, flying well beyond the range of fighter protection, were open to attack by U.S. aircraft.[27]

Next, in the field of mobile logistic support the Soviet Navy, unlike the U.S. Navy, suffered from grave inadequacies. Operating far from home bases, Russian warships lacked sufficient supply ships, ammunition ships, tenders, and fleet oilers to sustain them on long deployments. But Gorshkov had made a small start in building support ships, notably four fleet replenishment ships capable of underway transfer of fuel, ammunition, and supplies to warships steaming alongside. Furthermore, the Kremlin-controlled Soviet merchant fleet provided a ready means of supplying naval ships. Mooring in ports of friendly nations such as Syria, Cuba, Yugoslavia, Tunisia, Guinea, Angola,[28] and South Yemen, Soviet fleet units routinely were serviced by the merchant marine. In spite of these strenuous efforts, the Soviet Navy fell far behind the U.S. Navy in logistic strength.[29] Whether this deficiency would continue was another question.

Other glaring weaknesses stemmed from a lack of tactical air power. Soviet advances in this field, exemplified by the relatively small carriers of the *Moskva* and *Kiev* classes, paled when compared with the U.S. naval air arm. If the Soviets suffered from a low capability in open-ocean ASW, they were not deficient in modern shipboard ordnance. Their advanced SAMs for close-in defense against enemy planes and missiles suggested that they were ahead of the Americans in this type of missilery.[30]

To the geographic penalty imposed on Russia by virtue of its lack of ready access to open oceans must be added the handicap of protecting some 8100 miles of Arctic coastline and 6,100 miles of Pacific coast, compared with 11,000 miles for the United States.

Despite these burdens, by the early 1980s the Soviet fleet was edging into superiority over the U.S. Navy, according to Pentagon trend watchers. Admiral Hayward gave substance to this possibility when he declared in May 1979: ''I guarantee the threat will get worse.''[31] Perhaps mindful of his nonpolitical status, he left unsaid the conclusion that ultimately only an aroused U.S. public would determine what kind of U.S. fleet would face the Soviet Navy in the next five years.

Brigades and Bases in Cuba

The security of the Caribbean sea-lanes, over which thousands of ships have sailed to and from the Panama Canal, historically has preoccupied the U.S. Navy. To protect these waters the fleet has long relied on its bases at Guantanamo,

FIGURE 8

U.S./USSR COMBATANT DEPLOYMENTS

(Average calendar years 1966 and 1976)

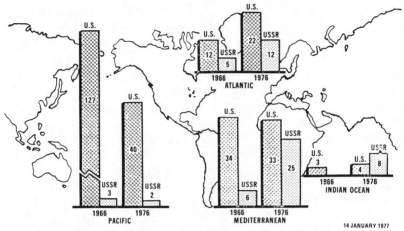

* INCLUDES AIRCRAFT CARRIERS, GENERAL PURPOSE SUBMARINES, MAJOR SURFACE COM-
BATANTS, MINOR SURFACE COMBATANTS, AMPHIBIOUS SHIPS, AND MINE WARFARE SHIPS.

Source: Department of Defense

Cuba,[32] and Roosevelt Roads, Puerto Rico, to support patrol aircraft and ships for U.S. surveillance and control of the Caribbean and the approaches to the canal.

As President Nixon had demonstrated, from a U.S. strategic viewpoint it has been taken for granted that a Soviet naval base in Cuba would never be acceptable. Consequently Washington's reaction was immediate when Soviet naval activity in Cuba was revealed in September 1979 by the construction at Cienfuegos of a large pier and maintenance shops. Senator Richard Stone of Florida described it as a "major expansion of facilities."[33]

Other intelligence reports confirmed that in February 1979 the Soviets were operating a diesel submarine out of Cienfuegos.[34] In May the U.S. press reported that Cuba had "received" a second submarine.[35] In addition, Cuba in 1978 had received thirteen MiG-23 attack aircraft capable of carrying nuclear weapons. Moscow's attempts to allay Washington's concern with assurances that the planes and the submarines were solely for defensive use were received with skepticism.

Not until the news broke in September 1979 that a Soviet combat brigade of some two to three thousand troops, with 40 tanks plus artillery, had been stationed in Cuba apparently for several years did the U.S. government react sharply, announcing that the "status quo" was unacceptable, in effect, virtually demanding that Moscow withdraw the brigade.

The combat brigade's presence was but one of a host of developments in Cuba that occupied the attention of the CNO, Admiral Hayward. The press reported variously that Soviet pilots were flying air defense patrols around Cuba, presumably to replace Cuban aviators on duty in Africa, and that a squadron of Soviet military transport aircraft was being delivered to Castro. Other reports estimated that 10,000 Russian military and civilian technicians and professionals were advising the Cubans and that Soviet electronic intelligence equipment was monitoring U.S. space and defense communications.[36] *Time* reported that National Security Council officials held evidence that the Kremlin's department of mischief making was fishing in troubled Caribbean waters.[37] Moscow, by expanding its forces in Cuba, was again testing Washington's mettle.

On October 1, 1979, a grim-faced President Carter delivered a televised address to the nation. Among the countermeasures that he announced was an increase in the U.S. naval forces in the Caribbean. Coincidentally a force of 1,500 Marines sailed from east coast ports to conduct amphibious exercises at Guantanamo, the U.S. naval base on the southeast Cuban coast. In a bizarre sidelight, the exercise was monitored by a nearby Soviet intelligence collection ship.[38] American air surveillance of Cuba was intensified, a change from the administration's cancellation in 1977 of U.S. spy plane flights (a move taken at the time to foster better relations with Castro). A joint Caribbean task force headquarters of some seventy people set up offices at the Naval Air Station, Key West, in order "to respond rapidly to any attempted [Soviet] military encroachment in this region."[39] Critics saw this latter action as of little import, asserting that the Atlantic Fleet staff at Norfolk, Virginia, was perfectly capable of handling Caribbean emergencies, as it had proved during the missile crisis of 1962.

What implications did this turn of events hold for the U.S. Navy with regard to its responsibility to protect the sea-lanes and its allies in the Americas? Unlike the missile crisis of 1962, when President Kennedy at one stroke clamped a naval blockade around Cuba, President Carter chose to protest—futilely as it turned out. The Soviets indignantly rejected Washington's allegations, declaring that the troops were in Cuba for training Cubans, that they had been there for some time, and that they would continue their mission, as indeed they did.[40]

Hawks cried out that all of Latin America had been put on notice that Russia was capable of staring down the United States, that the entire world was now aware that Moscow's military forces could operate even in nearby Cuba, and that Washington's apparent inability to take a strong stand conveyed a lack of resolve and a posture of passivity.

In October 1979 *Time* magazine announced that the Caribbean could no longer be considered an "American lake." *Time*'s writer drew this conclusion from the evidence of "a new mood of anti-imperialism in the Caribbean directed against the big brother to the north." The tremors included the Soviet combat brigade in Cuba; the Cuban-backed revolution that forced Nicaraguan President Anastasio Somoza to flee to Miami; the left-wing revolt in Grenada in March 1970; the turmoil in El Salvador and Guatemala; the anti-American noises in Panama despite the treaties of 1978 giving eventual control of the Canal Zone to Panama; and finally Castro's expanding influence in Jamaica, Guyana, St. Lucia, and Grenada. State Department officials reportedly had information that Moscow, using Cuba as its proxy, was behind much of the ferment in the Caribbean.[41]

Varied Views in Washington

It was beyond cavil that other nations would interpret Carter's October 1 speech as evidence that the United States no longer could protect its interests in the Western hemisphere. Senator Sam Nunn of Georgia, one of the most knowledgeable members of the Armed Services Committee, accused the administration of not drawing "a clear line on the continued buildup of [Soviet] forces in Cuba." Nunn had in mind not only the brigade, but coastal missile boats, the SAMs, and the buildup of the Soviet naval base at Cienfuegos. But Senator Edward Zorinsky, a Democrat from Nebraska, ridiculed those who criticized the president. "The long and short of it is that, yes, the last several weeks 'Chicken Little' has been loose in Washington. But, no, the sky is not falling."[42] Administration opponents immediately responded that Zorinsky forgot to add the final word "yet."

No sensible person in Washington believed that the brigade would invade Florida, but disagreement arose over the long-term significance of the trend of Soviet activities. Obviously, Latin American nations were being conditioned to accept a permanent Soviet presence in Cuba. And, clearly, the Russian Navy was sufficiently powerful in 1979 that the Kremlin could safely risk a move that in 1962 would have exposed the Soviets to humiliation and international loss of face.

Senator Nunn may have had the last word when he remarked: "Historians of the future will be hard pressed to explain how it was that the United States in the 1970s permitted a tiny hostile nation 90 miles from its own shore to assume the role of superpower."[43]

Cuba was but one place in 1979 where the Soviets had exhibited a pattern of increasing willingness to challenge the United States and its allies. In the southern Kuriles off Japan, the Russians, evidently worried over a growing Japanese-Chinese relationship, strengthened their garrison from a brigade to a division. Japanese diplomatic protests, according to the press, were not even accepted by Moscow. These new Soviet moves inevitably caused staff officers of the hard-pressed U.S. Pacific Fleet to reflect again on the difficulties of maintaining a naval presence from the Indian Ocean to the Sea of Japan some 4,500 miles distant. Similarly, Atlantic Fleet officers must have pondered how they could rearrange fleet employment schedules to increase patrol operations in the Caribbean to deal with increased Soviet naval activity.

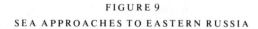

FIGURE 9

SEA APPROACHES TO EASTERN RUSSIA

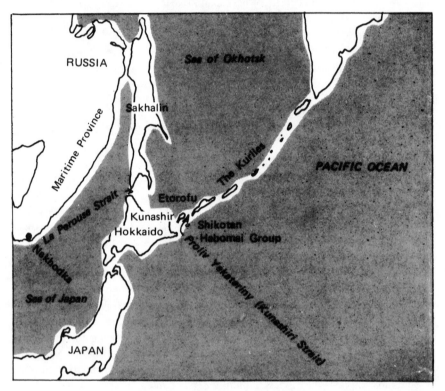

The constricted sea approaches to eastern Russia. Moscow sees Japan's growing maritime force as a threat to Soviet access to its Pacific bases.

Source: Lawrence Griswold, "The Chokepoint War," *Sea Power* (July 1973). Reprinted with permission.

Brezhnev's decision to enlarge the base at Cienfuegos suggested that (with Admiral Gorshkov's concurrence) he believed Soviet military strength was sufficiently intimidating to persuade the Americans to condone, reluctantly, this new submarine facility. We may assume that Soviet strategists based their actions in Cuba on perceptions of a fading U.S. disposition to take strong stands and, very possibly, on a comparison of Soviet and U.S. naval power. Any sign of U.S. hesitancy only reinforced the Kremlin's determination to exploit such perceived weakness. Americans, for their part, accustomed to believing that a pact made in 1962 would still be honored in 1979, learned slowly that the Kremlin played by a different set of rules.

Clashing Dissent on the Soviet Naval Threat

The 1970s were marked by a wide variety of opinions on the Soviet naval threat. Depending on an analyst's political philosophy, depth of knowledge, and professional naval experience, his evaluation, more than likely, might be termed suspect by those who disagreed. For example, Congressman Les Aspin, a Democrat from Wisconsin and a former systems analyst in the Pentagon, played down the threat. Instead, he offered evidence from naval and defense studies as proof that U.S. naval strength was expanding relative to that of the Soviets. Aspin expressed satisfaction that "powerful allied forces" could "deter large-scale war." He asserted that if Soviet forces were powerful, Russia was also beset by economic and political setbacks. Therefore, Americans should avoid rhetorical overkill in estimating Russian strength. Rather, Washington should make measured responses and impress the Kremlin with U.S. resolve to meet its challenge.[44]

Aspin's optimistic generalizations did not coincide with the conclusions of Congressman Jack L. Kemp, a Republican from New York.[45] Kemp's argument, more detailed and authoritative than that of Aspin, gave evidence that the Soviet Navy's general purpose forces in the 1980s would reflect dramatic qualitative improvements. Furthermore, in numbers the Soviet fleet would total 1,389 to 462 for the U.S. Navy.

Kemp acknowledged that the impressive weaponry of Gorshkov's fleet could wreak enormous damage by a first strike against an enemy naval task force but he argued that the Soviet ability to sustain a war at sea was very limited. On the other hand, he recognized that in two respects the Russian Navy and its air arm represented a very real danger to the U.S. Navy and Marine Corps. First, in the event of an amphibious operation, particularly in the eastern Mediterranean, the U.S. forces would meet with determined opposition, a possibility discussed above. Second, the Soviet fleet posed a serious threat to allied ships sailing the traditional sea-lanes, those life-giving arteries that provided the United States with 68 of 71 vital raw materials.

Kemp condemned the administration's relatively meager shipbuilding program and called for an end to "the complacency which has so dominated the American government." Otherwise, Americans would learn, too late, that in the international political arena a "superior [Soviet] force is a powerful persuader."[46]

A Fleet Commander's Evaluation

A senior naval expert who brought to the debate his firsthand experience in dealing with Russian warships in the Mediterranean was Vice Admiral Gerald E. Miller, a former fleet commander in the Atlantic (1970–1971) and in the Mediterranean (1971–1973). Following his retirement in 1974 he emerged as an articulate, outspoken advocate of a stronger U.S. fleet.[47] Tall, athletic, and of commanding presence, Miller typified a growing disposition among retired military officers to speak out on defense issues, particularly the abilities of their respective services to carry out their assigned roles.

Forestalling attempts by critics to label his views parochial, Miller explained that such diverse observers as think-tank experts, munitions makers, the editor of *Janes Fighting Ships*, politicians, bureaucrats, and retired officers saw the Soviet naval threat through different lenses, a condition that produced a wide range of opinions. Think tanks, for example, were profit-oriented bodies that, rightly or wrongly, were open to the charge that their findings tended to produce predetermined conclusions. Similarly, lists of weapons, ships, and aircraft compiled by technical experts in assessing the threat were only as authoritative as the individual compiler.

Senior U.S. naval officers in the Pentagon who bore the responsibility for developing plans to counter the Soviet challenge at sea were not immune from bias, said Miller. As one who had held high positions in the Navy Department, no one knew better than he that a naval officer in presenting his version of the threat was often "constrained by the civil authority to whom he must be responsive." Thus his concept may be influenced, consciously or unconsciously, by his future career interests.

It also happened occasionally that an officer, though consciously candid, might be biased by his unique past experience, compelling him to see what he wished to see. In a wry afterthought, Miller added that the integrity of an officer (as perceived by others) "naturally improves after he retires."[48] Even the Kremlin's Admiral Gorshkov did not escape Miller, who suggested that Gorshkov may have slanted his views on Soviet sea power. Gorshkov, like his U.S. naval counterparts, was competing for budget funds with the Army and Air Force. Did he write to persuade his Kremlin bosses or to intimidate NATO leaders? Or did he truly believe that he had written the unadulterated truth? In short, said Miller, there were many interpretations of the Soviet naval threat. In evaluating the worth of an author's views, one would do well to examine the qualifications of the writer, his access to reliable intelligence data, and his susceptibility to outside pressures.

Given Miller's assumptions, an outside observer could not fail to sense that as a threat viewer few could challenge his credentials. In general terms, Miller gave the Soviet fleet high marks for its submarine force and worldwide command-and-control system. On the minus side he found shortcomings in the naval air arm, ASW, amphibious strength, and overseas bases. Confirming the conclusions of other experts, Miller expressed disquiet over the considerable number of Soviet cruisers, destroyers, and smaller warships. These ships were new, fast, and heavily armed with missiles. Some could launch missile salvos at surface targets. These missiles, in turn, could be homed in on their targets by long-range aircraft such as the Backfire B bomber. However, Miller found that Soviet ships suffered from a lack of reload missiles, a factor that would limit their endurance on combat missions.[49]

In focusing on a first-strike capability, Russian ship designers were forced to compromise among powerful engines (for speed), space for armament reloads, crew quarters, and electronic components. As a result, Miller regarded their ships' watertight integrity and hull strength as below U.S. standards. In other words, their ships were more likely to sink when damaged than their U.S. counterparts.

Admiral Miller, a carrier combat aviator, saw the relatively small Soviet carriers (even if equipped with VSTOL planes) as posing no threat at sea to U.S. surface ships since VSTOL aircraft were slow, relatively unmaneuverable, and limited in range. On the other hand, the editor of *Janes*, Captain J. E. Moore of the British Navy, noted that Soviet carriers could serve well in a task force deployed to support "wars of national liberation."[50] By their mere presence off Angola, Soviet warships had helped to shape events to the Kremlin's purpose.

Rating Soviet Leadership

Miller's assessment of the Soviet adversary ended with a suggestion to his colleagues not to underrate Russian naval leadership. Russian skippers collectively were fine seamen with extensive operational experience. In Admiral Gorshkov they had "probably the outstanding naval officer in modern times," a man who had obviously instilled pride in the naval service. Washington was aware that professional education of officers was given top priority in Moscow. For example, in 1979 no Soviet naval officer could command a second-rank ship (for example, a destroyer) unless he had completed a two-year war college course or a postgraduate course at a technical school, admittance to which was achieved by competitive examination.[51]

As for Soviet naval enlisted men, Miller believed that their training might be tainted by the Soviet trait of "following the rule book" too closely. Soviet sailors, if put to the test in combat, might not exhibit the needed initiative. Nevertheless, Soviet naval personnel in the Mediterranean appeared "highly disciplined" and of "superb appearance."

One Soviet ship captain at a Mediterranean anchorage startled Admiral Miller by his sense of humor. On the occasion of the death of longtime FBI director J. Edgar Hoover, the captain inquired by signal why the U.S. colors were at half-mast. When informed of the reason, the Russian skipper, in extending his sympathies, stated that he did so "although the Soviets had never enjoyed any of the same from Hoover."

Students of U.S. naval history will note that Miller did not commit the error of certain U.S. naval officers and American journalists of the 1930s when Japan was the Navy's potential enemy. At the time, the U.S. evaluation of the Japanese fighting prowess reflected a genial disdain for them as technical copycats whose ships and planes were second-rate imitations of British and American models. A favorite yarn in the U.S. Navy concerned a Japanese ship so top-heavy in design that it capsized after sliding down the ways.[52]

Captain W. D. Puleston, a respected U.S. naval intelligence expert, contributed to American feelings of superiority in a book published in early 1941.[53] In a final showdown, Puleston observed, the Japanese, aware of their economic, industrial, and military deficiences, should be convinced that they could never defeat the United States. Apparently, he did not envision that Japan might initiate a war on the assumption that it would end in a stalemate, leaving Japan with its spoils of victory in Asia. Secondly, Puleston erred when he assumed that the Japanese ruling clique always would act "rationally," that is, in accordance with Western norms of behavior. It is an error that Americans frequently make in dealing with people of a different culture.

Almost forty years later, Admiral Miller, in viewing the current Soviet adversary, concluded that the threat merited no doomsday approach, but neither should it be regarded as a figment of parochial imaginations. Miller believed that in the late 1970s the U.S. Navy could win a war fought in open-ocean areas. But if the naval war were waged closer to Russian home bases, the outcome would be far more uncertain. Soviet sea power wielded too much influence on world affairs to be taken lightly. The nation's security depended on the U.S. Navy's ability to meet it.

Radio Moscow and the U.S. Navy

Among the most vigilant monitors of U.S. naval fleet activities was the staff of Radio Moscow. As was evident from its worldwide broadcasts, not a movement of the Sixth or Seventh fleets went unobserved or uncriticized. A sampling of its news programs published by the U.S. Foreign Broadcast Information Service revealed the extent of Moscow's campaign against U.S. sea power and Soviet attempts to neutralize the Mediterranean and Indian Ocean.

On February 15, 1979, Radio Moscow let loose a blast that accused the United States, with NATO help, of planting military and naval bases "like poisonous mushrooms" on Mediterranean shores. On the other hand, it proclaimed, the Soviet Union had proposed that all submarines and surface warships with nuclear weapons be simultaneously withdrawn from the area. Such a move, the Soviet commentator declared, would make the Mediterranean into "a sea which links hands'' and would substantiate Soviet President Brezhnev's desire that it ''be a sea of peace, neighborliness, and cooperation.''

The Soviet propagandist's timing, whether by design or plain chance, coincided with the mullah-led revolution in Iran. The Middle Eastern oil supply for Europe, Japan, and the United States was in very real danger of being choked off as the thirty-year Israeli-Arab conflict continued to rage, with the United States in the unenviable position of referee. Clearly the chances were that the Sixth Fleet would be seen by some Mediterranean states in a less than favorable light. Understandably, the Soviet radio denounced the Sixth Fleet as a ''Mediterranean policeman'' attempting to transform certain nations into bridgeheads to defend imperialist interests in Europe, Africa, and the Middle East. It cited as examples Italy, Spain, Cyprus, and Greece, all of whose governments were being pressured by the NATO military. Presumably the Soviet squadron in the Mediterranean had only peaceful intentions in spite of Russian moves in Ethiopia and Yemen.

Radio Moscow broadcast equally acid comments on the U.S. Seventh Fleet in the Pacific, castigating the high command for conducting large-scale maneuvers, in company with Japanese warships, off Japan's Ryukyu Islands (the scene of the bloody battle of Okinawa in World War II). These warlike operations according to the Kremlin, threatened the stability of the Indian Ocean area as well as that of the nations of Southeast Asia. The announcer called on these countries to rid themselves of dependency on Washington and ''to liquidate U.S. war bases.''

The Russian commentator was enraged by the carrier *Constellation*'s swift passage toward the Indian Ocean during the Yemen crisis, labeling it an attempt to pressure patriotic revolutionists in Iran, India, and other countries. And he was wrathful that Singapore had permitted the United States to use its airports for reconnaissance flights, and he accused the United States of trying to persuade India to allow U.S. planes to use its airports in support of the U.S. ''stronghold on Diego Garcia Island.'' Finally, he warned Asian nations to demand of Washington that it end ''this game of playing with fire.''[54]

The Kremlin's angry concern with the global naval forces of the United States was historically well founded. Soviet naval strategists were aware of the well-published NATO strategy of bottling up the Soviet fleets in their restricted inland seas. The lack of open ports was a problem that had plagued the czarist regimes for centuries and still remained unsolved.

Radio Moscow's concentrated attacks on the U.S. Navy reflected Russia's age-old fear that its outlets to the seas (the Danish Straits, the Turkish Dardanelles, and the Japanese Tsushima and La Pérouse Straits) were controlled by foreign powers. It was very much to Moscow's advantage to use propaganda to expand Soviet naval influence by warning maritime allies and developing nations away from the West.

The Kremlin was quick to exploit other events that developed independently of

Soviet moves. The drift of Turkey's unsettled government away from NATO, the fall of the shah of Iran, the Egyptian-Israeli peace treaty that turned Saudi Arabia from a firm ally into a doubtful friend, all were examples of situations made to order for Radio Moscow's propaganda assaults on the U.S. Navy. Moreover, the Russians were cheered by the success of their campaign to persuade the United States not to use the neutron bomb. Victories such as this smashing propaganda triumph encouraged the Kremlin to launch similar attacks on the ubiquitous U.S. fleet.

Ten

THE SHIFT
TO THE INDIAN OCEAN

I think most of our people cannot understand that we
are actually at war. They need to hear shells. They are
not psychologically prepared for the concept that you
can have a war when you don't have actual fighting.

ADMIRAL HYMAN RICKOVER
addressing U.S. Senate Committee
on Defense Preparedness
January 6, 1958

Apprehension in Southeast Asia

NOTHING UNITES NATIONS like common danger. During 1978 and 1979, Vietnam's surge, with Soviet support, across Cambodia and Laos caused alarm in Thailand, the Philippines, and the rest of Southeast Asia. Mindful of the no longer discredited domino theory, these relatively weak nations looked in times of peril, as they had since World War II, for protection from Uncle Sam.

In the Philippines, where shortly before politicians had demanded that the U.S. Navy get out of its giant base at Subic, President Marcos told Americans in 1979, "We are your best friends in Asia." At the end of the Vietnam war, the Philippine and Thai governments had pressed the United States to end the SEATO pact because the stabilizing U.S. naval and military presence in the region was no longer necessary. But the horrors in Laos and Cambodia, together with the threat of war between China and Russia, brought a sharp shift in attitudes. Notably, Philippine Foreign Minister Carlos P. Romulo, an aging World War II veteran, pleaded that the United States "maintain its credibility as a Pacific power" in view of the Soviet military presence in Vietnam, including, presumably, Soviet naval use of Vietnamese ports.[1] Washington did not delay its reassuring response.

Vice-President Walter "Fritz" Mondale, a longtime champion of the good-example school of arms control and defense spending, brought renewed hope to Asian leaders by explaining the administration's new approach in defense policy during a trip to the Far East in September 1979. A former senator from Minnesota and a protégé of the late Hubert Humphrey, Mondale was assigned a White House office, which enabled him to confer several times a day with the president. Mondale's supporters considered him an astute and enlightened statesman; opponents saw him as an adept political street fighter who had overemphasized domestic programs to the detriment of long-range defense needs.[2] But all agreed that the president relied on his counsel.

In the course of a trip to Beijing (formerly Peking), Mondale arranged to visit the carrier *Midway* moored in Hong Kong harbor. There on the flight deck, attired in "scrambled eggs" bridge cap and jacket, the ebullient vice-president delivered a fiery speech to the ship's company.[3] Conscious of Southeast Asia's apprehension over the growing number of Soviet naval ships in the western Pacific, Mondale proclaimed that the Navy would protect the "vital" sea-lanes. He stressed that America's trade with Asia was crucial, and that Washington's new ties with China would contribute to world stability.

Some of Mondale's naval audience undoubtedly had been fired on less than five years before by weapons supplied to the North Vietnamese through China. Yet in 1979 the vice-president left the impression that China and the United States were quasi allies, as indeed they were.

Pointing to the growing might of the Seventh Fleet, Mondale announced that it would soon be strengthened by new missile-firing *Spruance* class destroyers powered by gas turbines. *Perry* class guided-missile frigates and *Los Angeles* class nuclear attack submarines soon would join the fleet. By January 1980 four of the six carriers in the Pacific would be equipped with powerful F-14 aircraft. And finally, the first Trident submarine would soon be operating in the Pacific.[4]

Observers remarked that the reinforcements listed by the spirited Mondale were essentially routine and had been generally known for some time. But coming from the vice-president this news was heartening to apprehensive Asians. Understandably, Mondale did not mention, perhaps through ignorance, the lack of logistic ships and amphibious vessels in the Seventh Fleet. Nor did he allude to the new emphasis on naval operations in the Indian Ocean that lay ahead for ships of the Seventh Fleet. But there was no question that the United States intended to remain a Pacific power.

The Navy in the Middle East

The Indian Ocean, the third largest in the world, covering 28 million square miles, links the Middle East with the shipping lanes to Western Europe, the

Americas, and Japan. Oceangoing ships may sail into or out of the Indian Ocean by way of the Cape of Good Hope, the Suez Canal and Red Sea, the Indonesian straits, and the area south of Australia. It is self-evident that these strategic bottlenecks, if controlled or threatened by enemy air or naval power, could be used to choke off Middle East oil to Japan and the West.[5]

During the years after World War II the Navy, with an eye on the area's gushing oil wells, continued to maintain a small, three-ship command in the Persian Gulf. Known as the Middle East Force and based at Bahrain, this tiny squadron posed no threat to Moscow. Nevertheless it was a political symbol of U.S. interest in the security of Iran and the Arab states as well as in the stream of oil tankers sailing the Arabian Sea and Indian Ocean.

Washington also counted on the military presence of British and French forces "east of Suez" to preserve stability in the region. British forces were positioned in places such as Oman, the Maldive Islands, Kenya, and Malagasy. The French, as well, had naval facilities at Djibouti, La Réunion, Diégo-Suarez, and Madagascar. Both London and Paris were determined to protect their substantial commercial investments in the Indian Ocean region as well as the oil lifelines on which Western Europe was so dependent.

In 1970, conscious of the potential for trouble and America's declining ability to respond to distant crises, a prominent military commentator observed that "U.S. forces, except for the Middle East Command, are conspicuous by their absence, and contingency planning is based—in the last analysis—on a 'couple of airborne divisions' to 'run the world.' "[6] Eight years later these pessimistic words were still valid. Writing in 1978 Defense Secretary Brown asserted with regard to a possible crisis in the Middle East that "the several Army divisions [such as the 82nd Airborne] Marine amphibious forces, and air wings that would not be immediately required for an initial defense of NATO should be adequate."[7]

A year later Brown phrased his assessment in less reassuring words:

> A conflict in the area of the Persian Gulf . . . occurring either prior to or simultaneously with a war in Europe, would obviously subject our [defense] posture to a most rigorous test. Presumably, if we could handle such a distant and difficult conflict, our forces would be adequate to deal with most of the other lesser contingencies that might arise.[8]

Brown made clear that he was not suggesting that U.S. naval forces would have to be used in every contingency. The United States, after all, had the Army and Air Force. But could the U.S. airborne forces meet, as Brown implied, the test of "sufficiency" in support of U.S. national strategy?[9] According to a Rand Corporation study, certain operational problems existed that the Pentagon strategists apparently chose to ignore.[10] For example, U.S. troop-carrying aircraft would have no air access over certain countries, unless of course, Washington chose to violate overflight restrictions.

Moreover, if U.S. planes were forced to fly around forbidden areas, some of these aircraft would not have the necessary range, while those that did would be forced to fly longer routes, thus increasing their time en route and generating aerial tanker demands.

The problem of getting troops to the scene paled into insignificance compared with the problem of supporting them, say, in the Persian Gulf. This area was within easy reach of Soviet air bases in southern Russia and after New Year's Day, 1980, in Afghanistan. Aside from the threat posed by Soviet air forces, the Navy in 1979 could count on no Persian Gulf port to furnish repair facilities for ships or to store heavy military equipment similar to the logistics bases provided by Japan in the Korean and Vietnam wars. Finally, to maintain a sizable number of troops in this potentially explosive area required an ocean pipeline of ships stretching some 10,000 miles from the United States. A U.S. naval task group commander had partially confirmed these melancholy conclusions while on a cruise to the Indian Ocean.

Logistic Problems in the Indian Ocean

U.S. naval officers were aware that intermittent strife in the Middle East would impose new burdens on the Navy, specifically in the Indian Ocean. As matters developed, logistic deficiencies cast doubt on the ability of the Navy to operate there for extended periods.

In October 1977 the carrier *Coral Sea,* with its escorts and an oiler, were detached from the Seventh Fleet under orders to cruise for four months in the Indian Ocean. Two years later a senior officer (who requested that his name be withheld) in the battle group, who had by then retired from active service, discussed its logistics problems with the author. In his view the need for a more rapid buildup of the U.S. naval base at Diego Garcia was painfully apparent. This British-owned island base leased to the United States in 1966 boasted a 12,000-foot airstrip and several warehouses, but a large pier had not yet been completed by the Seabees. Transfer of the small amount of dry stores (canned food, paper products, and the like) available there was accomplished by helicopters, a time-consuming process.

The ships encountered further obstacles when the Navy attempted to persuade the friendly governments of Malaysia, Australia, and Indonesia to relax their 72-hour prenotification requirement for U.S. aircraft logistic visits or overflights. Permission proved difficult and in some cases impossible to obtain.

The combination of highly complex equipment and hot, damp weather exacted penalties on the squadron. Because much of the electronic equipment was air-conditioned, a constant supply of Freon gas was required. When the ships ran out of Freon, many air-conditioning units, communication equipment, weapons launchers, and sensor equipment ceased functioning.

Much of the logistics trouble stemmed from the lack of support ships in the Pacific Fleet to replenish the battle group at sea regularly. As a less desirable alternative, the Navy turned to the Military Airlift Command operated by the Air Force. Large cargo planes loaded with needed stores and spare parts flew from Clark Air Force Base in Luzon to Malayan or Australian airfields adjacent to ports where the ships could anchor. Unfortunately, factors such as bad weather, international protocol (such as the 72-hour flight advisory rule), and the physical inability of aircraft to carry as much as a stores ship prevented the squadron from obtaining vitally needed spare parts. The situation, while serious, was not without its ludicrous moments. In one case the flagship's crew members stared unbelievingly as they received a year's supply of cleansing detergent by air, a classic example of Murphy's Law.[11]

On returning to the naval base at Subic Bay three-and-a-half months later, this officer concluded that unless a squadron in the Indian Ocean were supported by oilers, supply ships, and ammunition ships, its ability to remain combat effective would be questionable.

The distances are intimidating: from the Philippines to Singapore, some 1,200 miles; from Singapore to Diego Garcia, 1,800 miles; from Japan to Diego Garcia, 4,500 miles; from Diego Garcia to the Persian Gulf, 3,200 miles. To transit these vast distances required fuel. A naval task force steaming at 16 knots could cover almost 400 miles per day. Every four days (or 1,600 miles) prudence required that the ships be refueled. Naval veterans of World War II, Korea, and Vietnam expected without question that the underway replenishment (UNREP) ships would appear every fourth or fifth day. Any reduction of such support in the Indian Ocean and its damaging effect on ships' capabilities carried grave implications for the Navy's effectiveness in future operations at a time when the oil crisis was beginning to create a certain urgency in Washington.

Oil and the Free World's Survival

The Soviet Union's continued probes in the Middle East prompted a tougher attitude in Washington, particularly in the State Department where (to the wonderment of Pentagon officers) an official announced that "it is now widely perceived that military power is a legitimate tool in support of our economic interests."[12] Defense Secretary Harold Brown, in a two-fisted statement on February 25, 1979, declared that the oil flow from the Middle East was "a vital U.S. interest" and that the United States would take any action, including the use of military force, to protect it.[13] Secretary of Energy James Schlesinger (who had been defense

FIGURE 10
DISTANCE CHART OF INDIAN OCEAN

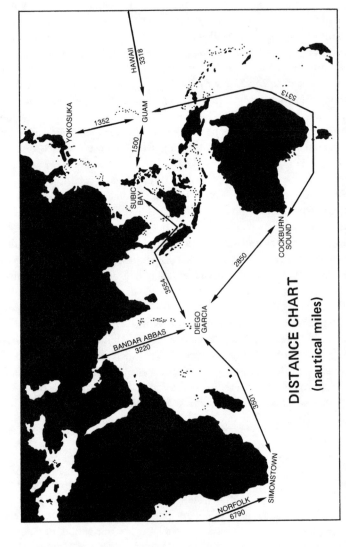

DISTANCE CHART
(nautical miles)

HAWAII
3318

YOKOSUKA

1352

GUAM

1500

5313

SUBIC
BAY

COCKBURN
SOUND

2850

3554

DIEGO
GARCIA

BANDAR ABBAS
3220

3501

SIMONSTOWN

NORFOLK
6790

The enormous distances involved in the U.S. naval operations in the Indian Ocean are evident here.

Source: Lt. Commander Kenneth R. McGruther, ''The Dilemma of the U.S. Pacific Fleet,'' *Naval Institute Proceedings,* June 1978. Reprinted with permission of Naval Institute.

secretary in the Ford administration) reaffirmed these fighting words, grimly asserting that the nation would protect its Persian Gulf interests even if it required the use of force or a military presence. So was the world put on notice that Washington would brook no interference with maritime oil deliveries from the Persian Gulf.

Despite the temporary Arab oil cutoff in 1973, the American people persisted in believing that the thin line of tankers from the Persian Gulf to North America would operate indefinitely. But in 1979 this vital artery suddenly became terrifyingly vulnerable to Soviet weaponry at a time when the Navy's range of operations in the Indian Ocean seemed marginal at best.

The disquieting facts were that the United States imported 3.2 million barrels a day from the Arab nations, one-third of which came from Saudi Arabia. Sixty percent of the world's seaborne oil was transported from the Persian Gulf through the narrow (26–60 miles wide) Hormuz Strait to the Arabian Sea and thence to the Indian Ocean. Hormuz Strait conceivably could be blocked by mines dropped by aircraft or even small fishing boats. Submarines lying in wait or fast missile-carrying craft lurking in the area could make any ship transit hazardous, prompting Schlesinger to identify the Persian Gulf as the most tempting target in the world. If the entrance to the gulf were blocked for a year, said Schlesinger, the result would devastate the free world's economy and wreck its alliances. The resulting chaos would degenerate into a wild scramble for oil.

The question was whether the American people and the Carter administration were prepared to abandon the post-Vietnam reluctance to back up fighting words with a big stick. The situation evoked thoughts of Theodore Roosevelt advising President Taft: never draw unless you are prepared to shoot, and never take a step in foreign policy unless you were sure that you could carry out your will by force.

The smoldering Middle East prompted the White House to remark through Defense Secretary Brown that the Navy might form a Fifth Fleet in the Indian Ocean.[14] Such an American naval presence presumably would discourage further Soviet-backed offensive thrusts by Cuban troops or other proxies. Nothing came of Brown's remark, which may have been uttered in part for its political impact on Moscow. Instead, the Seventh Fleet continued to detach ships for temporary assignment to the Indian Ocean, thus weakening its own forces in the western Pacific.

Moscow Denounces the Fifth Fleet

Predictably, Radio Moscow reacted angrily to the proposed formation of a Fifth Fleet. In an English-language broadcast in March 1979, its commentator hooted at U.S. explanations that the task force in the Indian Ocean was necessary to fill the gap in military plans caused by the loss of Iran, the chief U.S. ally in the Persian

Gulf. Dubbing the so-called Fifth Fleet a "Washington force" to support reactionary regimes and interfere in the internal affairs of sovereign states, he lashed out also at Chinese leaders for linking their strategic interests with those of Washington.

Baldly ignoring Soviet naval and military activities in the area, the Russian broadcaster damned the U.S. naval squadron as a "glaring contradiction with the spirit and letter of the UN resolution to transform the area into a zone of peace." As for the Soviet Union, he declared, "it stands for limiting and reducing military activity in the Indian Ocean."[15] Moscow's goal of neutralizing the Indian Ocean stemmed in part from the deadly threat to Russia posed by America's Poseidon or Trident missile nuclear submarines on patrol in the Indian Ocean. Plainly, it was to Moscow's advantage to join neutralist states bordering the Indian Ocean in condemning the U.S. Navy for its warlike moves that violated this "zone of peace."[16]

The Russians never publicized the steady growth since 1969 of the Soviet Indian Ocean fleet (by 1976 Soviet naval ship-days as observed by U.S. surveillance agencies totaled 7,300 compared with 1,100 for the U.S. Navy).[17] Put another way, the Soviet Navy averaged twenty ships per day in the area to three for the U.S. Navy. In addition, Soviet merchant ships furnished logistic support at ports or fleet anchorages at Socotra, Aden, the Mozambique Channel, and Indian ports such as Bombay and Visakhapatnam. Significantly, because of a dearth of ports or naval bases, the Soviet Indian Ocean force (like the U.S. battle groups) depended heavily on logistic support by ship. Reportedly, about half the Soviet force consisted of support vessels.[18]

As events turned out, the ironfisted Soviet invasion of Afghanistan abruptly stilled the voices of most neutral nations in Asia and Africa. Their shocked leaders suddenly sensed that nonaligned countries enjoyed no immunity in international power politics. The zone of peace notion died unnoticed and unmourned as a naval armada of some twenty U.S. warships took up patrol stations in the Indian Ocean.[19]

The Navy's Swing Strategy

Whether the Navy could support a Fifth Fleet in addition to its other missions turned on the validity of the one-and-a-half wars theory endorsed by the Pentagon since the Vietnam war. Harold Brown expressed current wisdom when he wrote in his 1979 *Annual Report* that U.S. interest in the Persian Gulf and Indian Ocean had understandably grown, but that overall it had become much more difficult than in the 1960s to imagine an Asian war simultaneously taking place with a major conflict in Europe. As Brown viewed the future, he apparently believed that U.S. naval forces, spread as thinly as they were, could assist in dealing with one major contingency (say, a Central European war) and one lesser crisis, as for example "in the vicinity of the Persian Gulf."[20]

Basic to Brown's thinking was the so-called swing strategy in which U.S. naval forces in the Pacific could be shuttled through the Panama Canal to the Atlantic in event of a NATO war or to the Indian Ocean and the Pacific in the event of a major Asian conflict. Such a strategy would work if the Navy possessed a reserve of ships in either ocean to meet emergencies elsewhere. But as Admiral Moorer pointed out, the Navy had major responsibilities on *both* sides of the world, a condition that did not permit the ships of one fleet to sail to the aid of another 10,000 miles away.[21] Therefore, it was futile to hope that a swing strategy could solve the basic problem of positioning too few ships in too many locations. Moreover, there was a danger that the Panama Canal locks (no longer exclusively guarded by U.S. forces) could be blocked by sabotage. Taking a more optimistic view, Brown, as the administration's spokesman, stoutly maintained that the Sixth and Seventh fleets constituted a "display of American military presence and resolve" that demonstrated "a continuing commitment to international peace."

The secretary was carefully avoiding any cheery optimism regarding U.S. military superiority. In emphasizing to the Congress that the United States had not fallen into an unacceptable military posture, he stressed that the gap between U.S. and Soviet defense expenditures could not continue to expand without a dangerous tilt in the relevant balances of power and a weakening of the overall U.S. deterrent.[22]

In a curiously worded warning, Brown declared: "The United States is certainly more ingenious and efficient than the Soviet Union. It [the United States] is not so much more ingenious and efficient that it can, without increased budgets, make up for increasing disparities between the two defense efforts."[23]

Observers noted that his convoluted double negatives raised doubts whether Brown meant that the gap in military spending must be reduced or that it must not be allowed to increase.[24] If the former, the proposed 1980 defense budget failed the test because it would not reduce the gap. In short, the gap had widened in the immediate past and, based upon forecasts, would continue to expand. But would public reaction to this obvious trend force the White House and the Congress to authorize larger defense budgets? Even as Brown was denying that the Soviets would attain strategic superiority in the early 1980s, he was concerned that Soviet perception of their superiority would lead them to "throw their weight around more."

Interestingly enough, in July 1979 the defense secretary foresaw possible trouble in Afghanistan that might affect future U.S. naval operations. Asked in a press interview if Soviet intervention there could follow if the Marxist regime in power was threatened by insurgents, Brown replied that the Soviets would "likely to be wise enough to avoid getting bogged down in that kind of situation. But one can't tell." He further observed that the Soviets were aware that "their military situation has improved a good deal during the last 10 or 15 years.'' Thus he prophetically remarked, ''they will press on the countries that geographically surround them.''[25]

Asked if there was any course open to the United States in the event of a crisis in the Persian Gulf, Brown answered that the United States needed to build up the ability to deploy Army and Marine Corps units very quickly to any area. He emphasized the need for more sealift (ships) and airlift (planes) for the defense of ''our friends'' near the Persian Gulf and U.S. ''vital interests'' there. No one could quarrel with Brown's reasoning, so far as it went. But naval officers noted that he apparently had more interest in a rapid deployment force and less concern for the logistic and amphibious vessels so essential to U.S. maritime operations in the Indian Ocean. Some six months later postmortem critics of Soviet moves declared that Washington's limited ability to respond to fast-breaking crises had not gone unobserved by the Kremlin's war planners.

In January 1980 Brown acknowledged that the Navy ''continued to face a serious underway replenishment (UNREP) and support ship, aging problem.'' At this time the average age of the 96 UNREP and support ships in the active fleet and fleet auxiliary (civilian-manned) forces was some 22 years. And 49 of the ships were older than 25 years, an age when many ships were no longer considered serviceable.

Not surprisingly, in view of continuous Indian Ocean operations, the Navy's most worrisome concern was a lack of fleet oilers. Brown announced that the Navy would purchase four oilers, two each in fiscal 1983 and 1984. Additionally, more fleet tenders were needed. Even though four destroyer tenders would be delivered within the next few years, a shortage of surface force tenders would occur in the mid-1980s. For the foreseeable future, Brown declared, the trend toward civilian-crewed UNREP ships could be expected to continue. He concluded that the United States needed to make ''major improvements in our defense program over and above those we have already programmed.'' Most important of all, he emphasized, was the need to increase the deployment, modernization, readiness, mobility, and sustainability of conventional (nonnuclear) forces. For the Navy, he made clear, a fleet of 550 ships by 1984 was essential.[26]

Battle Groups to the Arabian Sea

The experience of the *Coral Sea* and the worrisome conclusion that a lack of U.S. naval logistic support would affect extended ship operations in the Indian Ocean was borne out in 1979 when Iran erupted into revolution. The U.S. government, a longtime friend and arms supplier to Iran, reportedly had considered moves to steady the shah's faltering regime. According to rumors in Pentagon corridors, the question of sending a naval task force to the Persian Gulf as a stabilizing force had been discussed at a very high level. The proposal was abandoned when the Navy pointed out that it lacked adequate logistic ships as well as suitable shore bases in the Persian Gulf area.

Several months later trouble in the Middle East was touched off once more by Soviet-inspired attacks on North Yemen.[27] Immediately, the president directed (and later countermanded the order) the carrier *Constellation* to sail for the Arabian Sea. Naval officers familiar with the incident interpreted the cancellation as belated recognition by civilian strategists of the lack of logistic support ships. Shortly thereafter, the carrier and its escorts again were ordered to sail for the Yemen area. Critics charged with some truth that the operation was in essence a "cruise-past" and a "swing-around" with no extended patrol of the Yemen coast.

For the past thirty years the Navy's role in relatively short-lived incidents involving crisis management had obscured an equally important naval function, that of guarding sea-lanes thousands of miles from home. Since the end of World War II the fleet's mobility and credibility in crisis management had built up a mindset in Washington that paid scant attention to mobile logistic support. Over-

FIGURE 11

THE ARABIAN SEA

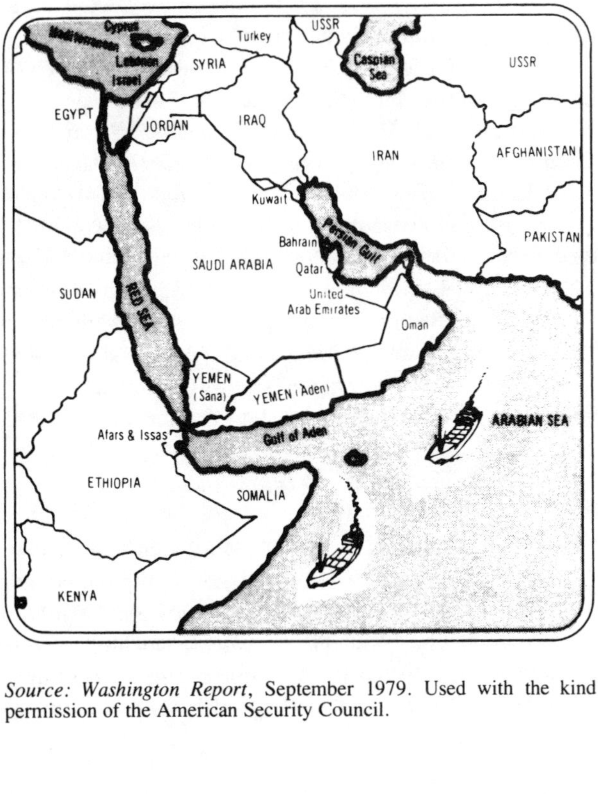

Source: Washington Report, September 1979. Used with the kind permission of the American Security Council.

looked by the Navy's civilian superiors was an appreciation that long-term U.S. strategy in three Asian wars had depended on this most essential element. If naval supply vessels were lacking, the Navy was limited in carrying out its missions.

In February 1979 Jimmy Carter was well into his third year as president when taut-jawed American television audiences watched the spectacle of the U.S. ambassador and one hundred of his staff at Tehran being paraded as hostages by fanatical anti-American supporters of the Ayatollah Khomeini.[28] Worse was yet to come. On November 4, 1979, militants again stormed the Embassy, captured some sixty Americans, and began a long, drawn-out campaign to force the United States into unacceptable concessions to free the prisoners.

In Afghanistan on February 14, 1979, the U.S. ambassador, Adolph Dubs, was kidnapped by Moslem terrorists in Kabul. That same day, he was gunned down by government security men, reportedly in an exchange of fire between the terrorists and the police. The latter was accompanied by Soviet advisors said to be KGB men. Late in November 1979, in yet a third attack on U.S. diplomatic personnel, Moslem mobs burned down the U.S. Embassy at Islamabad, Pakistan. Two U.S. servicemen, an army warrant officer and a Marine, were killed. Finally, came the Christmas week coup in Afghanistan, a Soviet move that opened up the grave possibility of a Soviet seizure of the Persian Gulf oil fields. In background briefings to the press, Carter's spokesmen said that the United States would have little choice but to oppose militarily any such Soviet expansionism.[29]

In swift succession the administration, in a series of get-tough actions, restricted trade with the Soviet Union and called for sanctions and censure from the United Nations. At the White House a somber President Carter declared that "the Soviet invasion of Afghanistan is the greatest threat to peace since the Second World War," thus raising the specter that the invasion would be "a stepping stone to their [the Soviets] possible control over much of the world's oil supply."[30] Administration hard-liners expressed satisfaction that the president had ceased to listen to State Department "romantics."[31] Other measures followed fast.

On January 14, 1980, Secretary of State Vance revealed that the president was considering announcement of "a framework for regional cooperation" in the Middle East and South Asia. Pentagon veterans observed that the new policy evoked memories of CENTO (Central Treaty Organization) and SEATO of the Eisenhower years [32] and the policy of "containment" first advanced by the State Department's George F. Kennan in 1947.

The upshot was the dispatch of two carrier battle groups to the Indian Ocean as a potential strike force. Next, Carter asked for and obtained authority from Britain to expand the naval base at Diego Garcia. At the same time a team of Defense Department representatives flew to the Middle East to negotiate, successfully, with Somalia, Oman, and Kenya on the use of ports and airfields. Simultaneously Defense Secretary Brown visited Beijing to explore "parallel aid" to Pakistan with his Chinese hosts. As President Carter swiftly modified U.S. foreign policy, it fell to the Navy to set up ship operations schedules for a permanent Indian Ocean force. The demands on the fleet inevitably would be severe.[33]

Following the Soviet refusal to evacuate its combat brigade in Cuba, the invasion of Afghanistan lent substance to the charge that the Kremlin had calculated its moves on the assumption that Washington would be forced to accept these *faits accomplis*. Because the invasion had an immediate impact on the future of the U.S. Navy, a discussion of the Kremlin's motives is in order. The temptation to swallow up Afghanistan was great. For one thing, an inept communist regime in Kabul was about to be toppled by nationalist insurgents. Rather than allow a staunchly Islamic anti-Soviet regime to take power, the Kremlin decided that, on balance, Russia should strike fast, establish a secure buffer zone, and quell Moslem activism in the process.[34]

Yet a third reason for the blitz appeared to stem from Russia's dwindling sources of domestic oil. Although the Soviet Union theoretically was self-sufficient in fossil fuels, nine-tenths of its resources lay buried in the windy steppes of Soviet Asia.[35] To drill, develop producing wells, and distribute the oil would require enormous outlays of money and technology difficult for the Soviets to obtain. Unavoidably, Moscow could tap its Asian oil riches only with the aid of foreign loans and equipment such as oil-drilling machinery from Texas.[36] Or it could use precious foreign currency to buy Middle Eastern oil. But the Kremlin planners had a tempting alternative: seize (or Finlandize) the Arab oil sheikdoms, gain control of the Persian Gulf, throttle the economy of the West and Japan, and thus attain political dominance over its oil-dependent adversaries. One may speculate that the relative ease of transporting Middle Eastern oil to European Russia (compared with the enormous task of transporting oil from Soviet Asia) probably gave added impetus to the Kremlin's decision to overwhelm its militarily weak neighbor.

Arab alarm over events in Afghanistan prompted a new appeasement policy in the Persian Gulf, according to one informed source. Allegedly intimidated by the Russian invasion, "both Saudi Arabia and Kuwait were willing to accommodate the Soviets by selling them oil," said the editor of the authoritative *MidEast Report* in New York in early March 1980.[37] The story went on to say that if the Saudis and Kuwaitis refused to sell oil to Moscow the situation would be "even tougher for the Persian Gulf oil producers." Significantly, the Soviet Union reportedly had curtailed oil exports to its Warsaw pact allies.

In analyzing the powerful incentives for Moscow to encroach on the Middle Eastern oil countries, Vice Admiral William J. Crowe, Jr., deputy chief of naval operations (plans, policy, and operations), and other observers concluded that by 1985 a gap would open between world oil demands and production. From that point on, they said, production would sag and ultimately cease. Many Western countries believed that national survival was in jeopardy and that Kremlin leaders presumably were convinced that they had ample reason to kill an already dying détente, risk world censure, and provoke economic sanctions by their decision to cross the Afghan border. Yet Moscow may not have foreseen that the invasion would rouse the U.S. public from its apathy and cause the administration and the Congress to reverse their policy of cutbacks in naval shipbuilding and weaponry. For the Navy, the struggle for sea control of the Arabian Sea and Persian Gulf had begun.

Eleven

AMERICA'S GREAT
TURNABOUT

The nation that cannot resist aggression is constantly
exposed to it. Its foreign policy is of necessity weak
and its negotiations conducted with disadvantage
because it is not in condition to enforce terms dictated
by its sense of right and justice.

PRESIDENT GROVER CLEVELAND
Annual Message, 1885

A Startling Switch in Public Opinion

THE SIZE AND STRENGTH of the Navy, dependent on U.S. public opinion,
suffer if the people are seized by apathy and a false sense of economy. For some
years Admiral Holloway, and his successor as CNO Admiral Hayward, identified
the big stumbling block in their goal of a Navy "second to none" as a lack of a
maritime constituency,[1] that is, an awareness by a majority of voters that their
future security and well-being to a large degree depended on the Navy. Holloway
and Hayward finally got that support, not through persuasive speeches and public
relations, effective to a degree though they were, but through the fateful impact of
totally unexpected international events.

The 96th Congress reconvened in January 1980, exhibiting a mood in startling
contrast to that of the year before, when its attention was fixed on reducing the
defense budget and cutting the federal deficit. Speaker Thomas P. O'Neill of the
House and Senate majority leader Robert C. Byrd freely predicted that the topic of
a stronger defense force would dominate the congressional agenda. Plainly, the
growing anxiety of the voters had turned the nation's defense policy around.

Sensitive to the ground swell of public sentiment, O'Neill, an old political pro
known as a champion more of social legislation than of defense programs,

declared that there was a "mood out there" in the country that the United States must be prepared for "conventional skirmishes," presumably including maritime confrontations. "The nation wants an uplifting of our defense, we can't stop World War III with what we have," asserted the now hawkish Speaker. O'Neill's assessment was confirmed by an Associated Press—NBC News poll that disclosed that in January 1980, 63 percent of those polled favored a higher defense budget and only 8 percent opposed it. [2]

Senator Byrd, having sampled voter sentiment in his home state of West Virginia, predicted that a "security-minded Congress" would vote for enlarged defense outlays because Afghanistan had "pushed other things into the background." [3] Many legislators suddenly talked of building more ships for the Navy, the B-1 bomber for the Air Force, and other defense projects that they had several times rejected.

Hard-liners quipped that if certain lawmakers had been alert, they would have realized that Afghanistan was not exactly the turning point in the U.S. attitude toward Moscow, but rather a milestone in Moscow's long-range and successful campaign to acquire international real estate. In any event, the new year opened the eyes of those in Washington who had concentrated on the uncertain benefits of SALT II to the detriment of U.S. sea power. Although not all Americans agreed, many believed that the Afghanistan coup had restored a sense of scale to those responsible for choosing priorities in U.S. national security.

As early as May 1979 Admiral Hayward had observed that because of events in Iran and elsewhere people were "beginning to understand what I have been trying to impress on them." Tactfully Hayward made plain that Washington decision makers finally had grasped the direct connection between U.S. naval security responsibilities for NATO Europe and for the stability of the Persian Gulf. [4] The Washington establishment had lagged behind the public in showing concern over declining defense forces. For example, in 1969 only 39 percent of the respondents to a Gallup poll believed that the public should give more support to defense spending. But by July 1977 this figure had risen to 67 percent, indicating a concern by the voters that was not reflected by the Carter administration or a majority of the Congress. [5]

Not all of Washington treated the issue of marginal military strength in the face of growing Soviet assertiveness lightly. Senator John Stennis, who had supported the Truman Doctrine as a newcomer to Capitol Hill in 1947, was conscious of the public's unease. Acknowledging the disagreeable truth in July 1978, Stennis lamented, "Reading the newspaper these days makes one increasingly anxious about Soviet intentions in the world . . . Without question the Soviets are devoting a larger proportion of their national wealth to defense needs than we are." [6] But a year and a half of valuable time sped by before the Congress opened its eyes and began a frantic effort to catch up with the Russians.

Noting the sudden change, one Capitol Hill staff member remarked, "You've heard of the military-industrial complex [of Eisenhower's day]. This is going to be

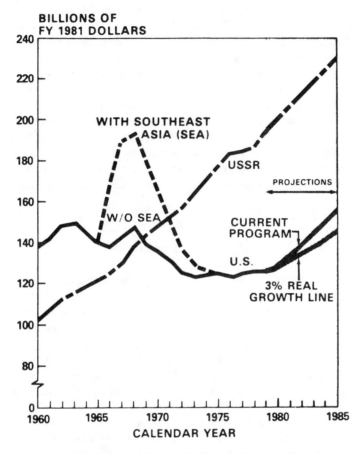

FIGURE 12

U.S. AND SOVIET DEFENSE PROGRAM TRENDS

1. U.S. OUTLAYS EXCLUDE RETIREMENT PAY, INCLUDE DEPARTMENT OF ENERGY AND COAST GUARD DEFENSE OUTLAYS

2. ESTIMATED SOVIET COSTS ARE BASED ON WHAT IT WOULD COST THE U.S. TO PRODUCE AND MAN THE SOVIET MILITARY FORCE AND OPERATE IT AS THE SOVIETS DO.

3. PROJECTIONS ARE BASED ON 3% ANNUAL REAL GROWTH FOR USSR, FOR US REAL GROWTH IN OUTLAYS AS PROJECTED BY FYDP.

The dotted line marked w/o SEA depicts U.S. defense outlays "without Southeast Asia" combat costs.

Source: Annual Report, Department of Defense, Fiscal Year 1981, January 26, 1980, p. 33.

the military-industrial Congress.''[7] The flippant words were on the mark. The *Detroit News* in an ''I told you so'' editorial snapped that ''precious years have been wasted by Washington dreamers who refused to believe what the Kremlin has been saying for six decades.'' The United States should establish forward bases in the Middle East and European governments should be pointedly encouraged to support such action, exhorted the *News*.[8]

How could the Congress act swiftly enough to ensure the safety of the oil-dependent West's so-called coronary artery? The list of essential actions was long and the issues were controversial: for example, rebuild the services to sustained, fighting competence; reinstate the draft; maintain a fleet with an embarked Marine landing force in the Indian Ocean; and build up bases in the Persian Gulf and Indian Ocean. Opposition to expending billions more for defense, bound to arise from proponents of more dollar-gobbling domestic programs, would have to be considered by nervous politicians anxious to avoid offending their constituencies in an election year.

Proposals for a Future Fleet

As the Navy entered the new cold war, its supporters campaigned with renewed vigor for a stronger fleet. Their ''want list'' could be described by the words, more and better: more nuclear aircraft carriers; more long-range carrier attack planes fitted with cruise missiles; complex interceptor aircraft to shoot down the Backfire bomber; improved antisubmarine systems for aircraft, surface ships, and submarines; more mine warfare ships and helicopters; more support ships such as the *Aegis* destroyer; more ships fitted with cruise missiles; more nuclear attack submarines; more long-range amphibious ships, more logistic support ships; and more repair ships and tenders.[9]

Admiral Hayward wanted more funds to develop missiles with greater ''stand-off'' capability. These weapons would allow U.S. ships and aircraft to destroy Soviet launch platforms (ships, planes, submarines) before they came within striking range of U.S. forces. Hayward further recommended that these stand-off weapons should be distributed among more U.S. ships and aircraft (as, for example, on board logistic support ships and amphibious vessels) but without diluting the power of the battle groups (carriers, cruisers, destroyers).

The need for more lethal missiles impelled Hayward to speak for increased research and development funds. Lack of money had limited innovation in weaponry since the Vietnam war, while the Soviets had forged ahead in developing new missiles. Equally critical, said Hayward, were inadequate arms stockpiles and a need for more sealift (cargo and troop ships) and the lack of a credible fighting posture.

Hayward's proposals appeared in May 1979 in the U.S. Naval Institute's

Proceedings. One may assume that his words were read with special interest by Kremlin officers planning contingency operations in Afghanistan. There was no doubt that the Navy could react fast, but could the Navy sustain fleet operations thousands of miles from its home bases?

The Navy was in the Indian Ocean to stay. At question was the cost of transferring ships from the Seventh Fleet in the western Pacific and the Sixth Fleet in the Mediterranean. Ironically, in 1978 Admiral Moorer had predicted in the *New York Times* that the Kremlin's global adventurism eventually would lead to this result. At the time he had urged that the nation accelerate its shipbuilding program toward a 650-ship Navy, including sixteen carriers.[10]

So acute was the need for more flattops that at the Pentagon, corridor rumor had it that the CNO had considered pulling the 30-year-old *Oriskany* out of mothballs.[11] If Washington showed little inclination toward more ships, the Kremlin had given the green light to Gorshkov's shipyards.

The Kremlin's Expanding Naval Program

In December 1979, Soviet naval shipbuilding entered an alarming new phase. On December 17, 1979, a *New York Times* story broke the news that the Soviets were creating a true carrier strike force, a report confirmed by Pentagon officials, who said that the Russians were constructing a giant nuclear carrier, the first of a series of four or five to follow. These ships, capable of handling fixed-wing jets, would represent a distinct advance over the less formidable *Kiev* class carriers with their VSTOL planes and helicopters. From the evidence, Admiral Gorshkov's planners clearly were determined to end the U.S. monopoly on carrier strike warfare. Those Washington critics who had scorned the *Nimitz* class as "turkeys" were silent.

There was still more jarring news. The Defense Department revealed that Russian shipyards were about to accelerate their output by constructing four new classes of nuclear cruisers. One class of ship would be a 30-knot battle cruiser fitted with heavy guns, apparently for shore bombardment in support of amphibious landings. Other classes of cruisers were designed for ASW, antiair warfare, and launching missiles.

Nor was Admiral Gorshkov neglecting his submarine force. In addition to the 42-knot titanium submarine under construction was a new type of submarine tender fitted to carry a supply of nuclear weapons. This intelligence, coming just a week before the Soviet assault on Afghanistan, spurred the Congress and the White House to move faster on defense programs.

At fleet headquarters in Pearl Harbor, Admiral Maurice Weisner, commander-in-chief of all Pacific forces, took a hard look at Russian naval expansion.[12] Speaking in late 1979 on the eve of his retirement from active service, the obviously concerned admiral recalled that in 1973 there was not a single Soviet missile submarine or attack submarine in the Pacific. But in 1979 both types were present in "substantial numbers." By 1978 some 64 modern Russian submarines and their essential support ships had sailed into the Pacific. Many of these boats were fitted with missiles. In addition, Admiral Gorshkov had positioned 64 major surface combatant ships in the Far East, plus support vessels.[13]

Tension between Russia and China accounted for some of the Soviets' new Pacific naval strength, but the bulk of the buildup was "clearly pointed at the line of oil tankers" sailing to and from the Persian Gulf, said Weisner. Looking at the prospects of a dwindling U.S. fleet, the hard-bitten admiral, a combat veteran of three wars, warned, "We've got to do one hell of a lot more for defense in increasing our armed forces levels." Obviously from his well-informed viewpoint the Pacific was taking on a distinctly Muscovite cast. Should the Kremlin perceive that the European nations and Japan would fail to show an unflinching resolve to defend the status quo, the Persian Gulf issue then would turn on the fortitude of the U.S. government and its people. These reasons caused the normally unruffled Weisner to become agitated over the growing Soviet might in the Far East.

Yet some civilian scholars of crisis management doubted that either side would be tempted to act rashly. In the past three decades, they argued, U.S. naval officers—and more recently, Soviet officers—had learned the so-called rules of the game.[14] In brief, both sides were aware that by biding their time in any potential showdown involving rival naval presences they would create an atmosphere conducive to a solution. On the other hand, others contended that a menacing U.S. naval presence in a sensitive region such as the Arabian Sea would increase tensions that might explode.

Naval officers who had served with the Sixth Fleet during the Yom Kippur war of 1973 anticipated that in the 1980s the Soviet Navy would continue to send anticarrier warfare ships such as missile-armed submarines, destroyers, and cruisers to counter the U.S. Indian Ocean forces. But many doubted that this display of naval might by itself would lead to an escalating confrontation ending in an O.K. Corral shoot-out. Doomsday prophecies aside, the United States (if aided by its allies) was prepared to defend the Persian Gulf.[15]

Basic U.S. Naval Fighting Strategy for the 1980s

As the U.S. public and the administration digested the idea that a bold new building program for the Navy would take some years to complete, the immediate question was: How could the fleet defeat the Soviets if war broke out in the interim? One answer derived from the Navy's general technical excellence and the endurance of the fleet in operations far from its home ports. Specifically, the

Navy's thin edge of superiority in conventional warfare lay in its carrier-borne aircraft and its twelve battle groups, which, with supporting ships, would take the war to the enemy far from U.S. shores. According to Admiral Hayward, the Navy would exploit the range of the fleet's offensive power, forcing the Soviet fleet to suffer the penalties imposed by geography. The maze of narrow straits through which Russian ships were forced to transit in breaking out to the open seas was the Achilles' heel of Russian sea power.

Although the U.S. fleet was structured for offensive action, it was too small in relation to the Soviet Navy to adopt a defensive posture or merely to react to Soviet moves, according to Hayward. Hence, by keeping the Soviets worried over their defensive weakness, the Navy "locks up Soviet naval forces in areas close to the USSR," said Hayward. As a result, the enemy fleet would be limited in its campaign against the sea lines of communication or in its attempts at offensive attacks, say, in the Middle East.

Next, Hayward continued, the Navy must ensure that enemy forces enjoy no sanctuaries, such as Korea and Vietnam. No longer could the Navy allow an adversary to attack U.S. ships with land-based planes (for example, Backfires) in the expectation that the United States would not strike its air bases.

Joining Admiral Zumwalt, who was a strong advocate of total integration of the U.S. and allied combat operations, Hayward proposed that the U.S. Navy should focus on offensive operations against the Soviets. Lacking offensive ships, NATO navies should concentrate on convoy escort, mine clearance, and port protection. And certain NATO governments should agree to their navies' fighting worldwide rather than being limited to protection of waters close to Europe.

As the spearhead of future allied naval thrusts against the enemy, the U.S. Navy would count on having maximum capabilities built into its ships. There was no room for cheap and less lethal compromises, warned Hayward, who believed that marginal, cost-effective ships were predisposed to end up as seagoing coffins. American naval combat strategy was based on commanders' taking calculated risks. That is to say, they would choose combat situations in which the scale of potential battle damage was favorable to the U.S. side.[16] This principle of favorable attrition ratios offered the U.S. Navy the only suitable prospect of progressively defeating the Soviet fleet at sea. To do otherwise, reasoned Hayward, even if a U.S. commander accepted a one-for-one ship attrition ratio, would be a strategy for defeat.

Finally, Hayward put his finger on a factor that had received little attention from the average citizen. He suggested the possibility that at the end of a war with the Soviets, the presence of "residual" naval forces at sea might determine the final settlement. In the face of such a terrifying prospect, it was better that these ships be U.S. nuclear submarines and surface warships, capable of cruising in waters where their presence would be unknown to the opponent. In any peace settlement, the Soviets would be potential cheaters; in any truce, residual U.S. naval forces would serve as enforcers of the settlement. A surviving mobile fleet, including nuclear missile submarines, would serve as insurance during an uneasy postwar period.

Zumwalt's Imaginative Concepts

Admiral Zumwalt, an inventive thinker, urged that the Navy perfect its satellite reconnaissance; electronic countermeasures against enemy weaponry, radar, and communications; and acoustic sensors so that enemy target information could be collected, correlated, and disseminated generally to U.S. naval ships and aircraft. Implicit in Zumwalt's suggestion was the need for billions of additional dollars for research and development of these space age devices.[17]

Zumwalt feared that in a short, conventional war the Soviet Navy could overcome the U.S. Navy through powerful missile attacks launched from air, surface, submarine, and land platforms. He reasoned that the United States could not match this devastating capability, nor had the Pentagon developed a reliable defense against it.

No matter what the threat, Zumwalt observed, U.S. surface ships must operate in dispersed formations to confuse the enemy. Large carriers should be positioned in less threatened areas until sea control was attained.

Convinced of the need for many small sea control ships of 7,000 to 10,000 tons equipped to carry a few VSTOL planes, Zumwalt continued to press for the "right mix" in his High-Low concept. A sea control ship could launch a VSTOL targeting aircraft to fly above the fleet and send over-the-horizon targeting data to missile-armed ships below, he argued. Then sea control task groups could gain control of a specified area, thus allowing large carriers to sail into the region and deliver air strikes against enemy targets.

As for submarines, the most survivable of U.S. warships, Zumwalt proposed that the attack submarine, with its antiship missiles ready for use, be used in an antisubmarine screen around U.S. battle groups.

Other innovative systems that required research and development were fast patrol boats with antiship missiles and long-range naval patrol planes, possibly a jet similar to the Soviet Backfire. The objective, Zumwalt proposed, was to achieve a variety of weaponry so that a sea control force could use the tactics required "to prepare the way for the large power-projection carriers."

Finally, he urged the development of the surface effect ship (SES) in the 3,000 to 5,000 ton range. Next to the VSTOL, he considered this program the most important development for the surface navy. With its very high speed, he envisioned the perfected SES as an ideal ASW ship, with the added feature of a landing deck for handling aircraft. The Soviets were fighting a protracted conflict with intelligence and increasing success, a contest that confronted the U.S. Navy with its greatest challenge, he concluded.

The Navy's Manpower Dilemma

Any comparison of the fighting abilities of the U.S. and Russian fleets must include an assessment of the quality of their personnel. For the U.S. Navy the outlook was mixed. If Admiral Hayward could boast that "the quality of our people represents one of our major advantages over the Soviets," he was also worried about problems of recruiting and retention of both officers and enlisted personnel. [18] In basic terms, could the Navy continue to operate a force of twelve carrier battle groups at a tempo that in the 1980s was bound to tax already overworked ships and men?

The reasons people left the service were traceable in part to long overseas cruises and arduous maintenance schedules when the ships returned home. In the trauma of the post-Vietnam years, the Nixon administration, in terminating the hated military draft, had opted for an all-volunteer force. The Pentagon, perhaps unwillingly, accepted the change, reasoning that an elevated pay scale would attract enough recruits.

Unfortunately, this inducement was not enough. Lieutenant commanders and lieutenants were resigning in droves, leaving critical gaps in the vital head-of-department and division-officer billets on board ships and in air squadrons. There was a severe shortage of physicians in the Navy and Marine Corps. And equally grave, many petty officers in the technical ratings were lured to industrial jobs by high salaries. Because most women in the Navy were assigned to coveted shore billets, men were kept at sea for longer periods, thus aggravating the apparently insoluble retention problem. Obviously, the notion of an all volunteer force was open to question.

During his tenure as navy secretary, W. Graham Claytor had worried that the all-volunteer force concept was not providing a broad mix of new recruits. Unfortunately, the high pay scale in the early 1970s attracted many poorly educated young people who could not qualify for the Navy's technical schools. Claytor referred to the requirement that "quality" (read educational) standards in personnel be maintained in order to produce a more efficient operational force and fewer disciplinary problems. Yet adherence to such essential standards led to shortages of qualified people. Although the admirals could take pride in the efficient performance of their ship crews, the service did not retain enough of them.

How critical was the retention problem? In a memorandum to Defense Secretary Harold Brown, Admiral Hayward spelled out the specifics. The Navy needed 20,000 petty officers. In 1979 the service retained only 45 percent (instead of the

60 percent desired) of enlisted people who had completed two four-year enlistments. The retention rate of nuclear-trained submarine officers was expected to fall below 40 percent in 1980, of surface ship officers to 31 percent, and of naval aviators to 28 percent.[19] What had accelerated this exodus of trained personnel that, Hayward warned, jeopardized the Navy's fighting ability? The paramount reason was that, even with periodic pay raises, "the large net loss in purchasing power which military people have experienced since 1972" was driving Navy men into civilian life. Only Congress could solve this problem, possibly by a combination of more pay and conscription.

So desperate was the personnel picture that Admiral Hayward declared his willingness to give up shipbuilding money to help the Navy retain its people. If personnel shortages persisted, he warned, certain ships and aircraft squadrons might be decommissioned, further eroding the Navy's effectiveness.

Acknowledging the evidence that the military manpower problem was grave, a reluctant President Carter took a tentative step toward a return to military conscription. In his 1980 State of the Union speech he announced steps toward a peacetime draft registration (not conscription) of draft-age youths, but only time would tell whether campus opposition to draft registration would be taken seriously by the public.[20] Many thought these relatively few young demonstrators shouting "Hell no, we won't go" and "Peace plus draft equals war" were out of step with the vast majority of the American people.

Commenting on the president's State of the Union address, Senator Jake Garn proposed that the administration press for more funds for the Reserve forces rather than adopt the draft. Naval officers were aware that the 87,000-man Naval Reserve, while sufficient in numbers, lacked support funds for training. They pointed out that a Reserve organization remained effective only if it maintained its naval skills, and under 1979 conditions, the Reserve was deteriorating. Senator Sam Nunn spoke for many in the Pentagon by stating flatly that the all-volunteer force was not working and that the time had come for draft registration.[21]

Perhaps an army general summed up the perilous personnel situation best when he commented that the country could draft an armed force, or pay for it, or drift along while its effectiveness declined ever faster.

Launching the Carter Doctrine

On the evening of January 23, 1980, while Soviet troops were consolidating their grip on Afghanistan, President Carter delivered the State of the Union address before the assembled Congress and a nationwide television audience. Looking drawn, but speaking firmly, the mild-mannered president announced an historic change in U.S. foreign policy. Its impact on the Navy was bound to be lasting. Fully aware of surging popular anger, Carter proclaimed that the Indian Ocean and

Persian Gulf were off limits for any future Soviet takeovers of these waters: ''An attempt by any force to gain control of the Persian Gulf region will be regarded as an assault on the vital interests of the United States of America. And such an assault will be repelled by use of any means necessary, including military force.'' In short, he warned Moscow that the United States had claimed a distant sea as an area of special responsibility and that the United States would fight to defend that vital interest.

The Carter Doctrine, as it was labeled by the press, involved basic national security. In taking this action, the president, in a sense, was following the path of James Monroe who in 1823 warned European powers to keep clear of the Caribbean and South Atlantic if they harbored aggressive, antirevoluntiary intent toward the Americas. Monroe's objectives were to guard U.S. economic interests and to preserve stability in a specified region. But Monroe's small navy was incapable of fending off Spain and other European empires.

In 1980 the U.S. Navy by itself would be hard pressed to hold the Soviet Navy at bay in the Indian Ocean. Accordingly, President Carter looked to Britain, France and other NATO nations, to Australia and New Zealand, and to small Middle Eastern and African countries to provide political support, naval forces, and military bases for enforcement of the Carter Doctrine. Defense Secretary Brown acknowledged as much before the Senate Armed Services Committee, stating that if the Russians tried to take control of the Persian Gulf region, the United States would count on help from allies and friends in the Middle East and elsewhere.[22]

A second historic parallel to the Carter Doctrine was the Truman Doctrine of 1947 in which the spunky Missourian took a hard line toward the Soviet Union by rushing warships and military aid to Greece and Turkey. Like Truman, who had watched the Russians swallow the nations of Eastern Europe after the allied victory over Germany, Carter realized, as did most Americans, that the Kremlin had finally gone one step too far.

Although the president's speech was short on specific actions, even as he spoke 25 U.S. warships were on patrol in the Arabian Sea. Together with the 24-ship Soviet naval squadron, they constituted one of the greatest fleet concentrations ever seen in the region. The continued level of each naval force would depend on the effectiveness of its combat reserves and logistic pipelines.

Recognizing the difficulties of going it alone in the Indian Ocean, the president in his message obliquely asked U.S. allies and friends to share the burden. The United States, he said, was prepared to share with them ''a cooperative security framework'' to enhance ''the independence, security, and prosperity of all.'' The major theme of his words was clear. The Persian Gulf and Indian Ocean were menaced. The U.S. naval ships were on station. But ''the grave threat to the movement of oil demanded the participation of those who relied on oil from the Middle East and who were concerned with global peace.''

Carter's veiled hints to NATO nations reflected counsel that Admiral Moorer had publicized over eighteen months before.[23] However, ignoring charges that the president learned the facts of international life slowly, his supporters praised him for having taken firm steps to stem further Soviet expansion.

Choices for the Future

Faced with the prospect of higher taxes to pay for the gaps in the nation's defense readiness, how would the U.S. people react? In the 1970s the Soviets routinely expended from 11 to 15 percent of their gross national product on national defense. By way of contrast, in 1979 Americans allocated a tiny slice of their total economic output—just over 4.5 percent—to national defense. Surprisingly, the national outlays from 1957 to 1965 had averaged 8.6 percent of the gross national product. According to economist Paul W. McCracken, the U.S. economy had demonstrated before that it could carry the load imposed by an expanded defense program and continue to function well.

Over the next decade the American taxpayer would accept a steep rise in taxes needed to pay for billions in defense, said McCracken. "We can afford whatever is necessary for our external security because, quite simply, we cannot afford not to do so," he said. With the thought in mind that events have not dealt kindly with nations that ignored their defense needs, he cautioned that the Soviet economic system (run by a relatively small elite) would continue to nudge itself inexorably

FIGURE 13

THE FEDERAL BUDGET DOLLAR

Fiscal Year 1981 Estimate

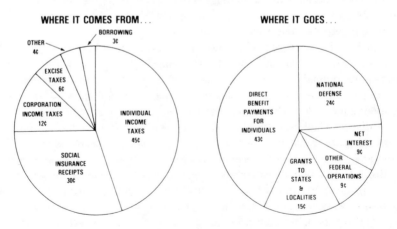

Source: Department of Defense.

toward expending more resources on defense. Aside from geopolitical considerations, what better reason was needed for the Kremlin to annex "the next country," asked McCracken.[24]

Apparently the Congress agreed with McCracken. Defense outlays jumped from $123.5 billion in fiscal year 1980 to about $143 in fiscal year 1981. The proposed 1981 budget for new spending authority soared to $157 billion, a 5.7 percent increase over that of 1980. The *Wall Street Journal,* which generally took a hawkish line, went further and urged that the annual defense budget be increased by 20 percent, or $30 billion, to be concentrated on procurement of armaments.[25]

The outcry for more defense funds was welcome news at the Navy Department where war plans officers prayed for more carriers to lighten the load on the twelve available. Moreover, senior naval air officers fretted that they could not obtain enough planes from the production lines to replace aircraft operational losses.

Few people knew that all of the Navy's twelve carrier air wings were badly under strength. There was a serious shortage of the EA6B, an electronic countermeasures plane that could "spook" the deadly accurate Soviet SAMs. Another deficiency existed in F-14 fighters armed with the Phoenix missiles, the Navy's primary counterweapon to the Soviet Backfire aircraft armed with antiship missiles.

These incredible shortcomings were magnified when carrier aircraft were recalled for repair and modernization. In other words, the Navy lacked sufficient reserve aircraft to replace those in extended overhaul. Put another way, if each aircraft wing were brought completely up to strength, there would be enough planes for only nine carriers.[26] Another shocking report alleged that the Navy would require $9 billion just to bring its ammunition stocks back to authorized levels.[27] Some wondered if the $15.3 billion defense increase would be enough to restore all the services to their proper strength. Clearly, playing catch-up with the Soviet Navy would be a long and expensive undertaking.

Would patriotic Americans be tranquilized (again) into somnolence if smiling Soviets launched a "peace offensive" that might appeal to those weary of cold war and high taxes? Americans, an ingenuous and generally friendly people, find it difficult to comprehend that the Soviets can and do practice deceit and deception in dealing with the West. They want to believe that if one treats his neighbor fairly by observing the Golden Rule, the neighbor will reciprocate. Periodically they have been disabused of this notion, including even President Theodore Roosevelt. Some 75 years ago he told a British friend, "I like the Russian people but abhor the Russian system of government and I cannot trust the word of those at the head."

Since World War II Americans have learned that Roosevelt's words are still valid. In the 1980s many would affirm that a strong United States required a first-class Navy under the leadership of a resolute commander-in-chief and that the cost of this national insurance would have to be borne by the people if the nation were to remain a free republic.

The Endless Rivalry

During the years of the cold war, American puzzlement about why a durable peace could not be concluded with Moscow derived from ignorance of (or a refusal to recognize) the words of Lenin, which the Soviets, in some form or other, had been proclaiming for over six decades. The confrontation began in 1917 when the revolutionary Kerensky government was overthrown by a Bolshevik minority whose ideological successors, as represented by Stalin, Khrushchev, and Brezhnev, continued the fight.

Many in the United States still clung to the belief that if Americans tried hard enough, the Soviets would sense eventually that détente or linkage or arms control pacts would promote peaceful coexistence in a nuclear-threatened world. Those who believed that the Soviets could be persuaded to accept such mutually beneficial ''accommodation'' were supported by others who perversely professed that preparedness for war was the surest way for the shooting to start.

For too long the optimistic assumption that U.S. differences with Russia ultimately would be settled caused the electorate, the Congress, and successive administrations to ignore the declining power of the Navy. But other factors also contributed to the shrinking of U.S. sea power: the nibbling away of a once indomitable armada could be traced to the so-called nitpicking, also known as micro-management, of Navy programs by certain members of Congress; the Navy's much-publicized litigation with defense contractors; the collective tendency of voters and politicians to put off costly arms appropriations; and, most important, the notion that conventional naval forces never would be deployed in a major conflict.

Paralysis by Analysis

The Navy's difficulties were made more onerous by civilian analysts in the government who chipped away at naval proposals for shipbuilding, armament, and even aviation flight training to the point where planning was paralyzed by continuous studies. Individually the pecks may have been minor; collectively they compromised the Navy's fighting strength.

Misplaced zeal to find cheaper solutions within limited budgets for future combat situations blinded these civilian analysts to the big questions, such as the Soviet Navy's missile capability, the overall lack of U.S. warships, and the manpower drain that had to be reversed if the Navy were not to lay up ships and air squadrons for lack of crews. The faulty logic of those experts who squeezed their solutions into a framework based on economy-driven assumptions dangerously stifled the structure of the Navy. As Admiral Gorshkov continued openly to build powerful ships for the future, it was plain that by the same token the U.S. Navy of the late twentieth century would need high-performance—and costly—ships to oppose a technologically advanced adversary who had outspent the United States by $100 billion in defense funds in the 1970s.

Only when the American people understood that time was short and demanded that naval buildup plans be protected from the Pentagon's maze-like methods for selecting arms programs, could the Navy move swiftly to construct the 650-ship fleet so essential to raise the global reach of a one-and-a-half-ocean Navy to a three-ocean force.

A Tardy Acknowledgment of Enlightened Self-Interest

It is an ill wind that blows no one any good, and so it proved for the U.S. armed forces after the Soviet invasion of Afghanistan. Suddenly growing numbers of American voters were shocked that for too long they had ignored the state of the nation's conventional fighting forces. Once again the United States was aroused to action when confronted with a real threat to the nation's safety.

Since World War I Americans have taken it for granted that whatever the nature of the peril the United States could meet a challenge in sufficient time to win the war. The public forgets that in the initial years of World Wars I and II, the allied nations engaged the enemy, holding him back for months while the United States belatedly built ships and planes and trained soldiers, sailors, and airmen before mounting offensive operations. No informed person would deny that in a future conflict the country could no longer count on a similar period of grace. No longer could the nation neglect its state of combat preparedness on the assumption that its industries could be mobilized to speed up production of armaments while thousands of draftees were being trained for combat. The Soviets are bound by none of the handicaps to instant mobilization that the United States voluntarily assumes and that have contributed to the growing imbalance of Soviet and U.S. forces.

This sudden perception of the critical shortcomings in defense prompted political finger-pointing by both Republicans and Democrats about the responsibility for the weaknesses. Defense Secretary Brown implied that Congress, by reason of its cuts in past defense budgets, bore much of the responsibility.[28] He also suggested that defense policymakers knew all along that more defense spending was necessary. Declared Brown, "Public perceptions of our [defense] needs have begun to catch up with the facts" and that "a new consensus is forming around the President's leadership." The truth was that many citizens had sensed sooner than cost-conscious Pentagon experts that the Navy was on a downhill slide and that time was not on the side of the United States.[29]

Many Americans understood by 1980 that reduced U.S. naval strength may have encouraged Arab OPEC nations to impose successive oil price rises. Foreign attacks on U.S. embassies suggested that until the United States shed its image not only of flagging power but also of prolonged caution and indecision in its diplomacy, Third World nations would continue to seize U.S. diplomats, burn chancelleries, and scorn official protests.

Many Americans, in both public and private life, failed to see that, despite the debates and peacekeeping actions of the United Nations, there always would be a need for strong task forces to back up U.S. diplomatic actions. The concept was simple: without a strong U.S. Navy, the Soviets and Third World nations would be tempted to take actions that would would have been ''unthinkable'' in the past when American naval power was clearly visible. Yet in the post-Vietnam years certain U.S. policymakers deluded themselves that a powerful fleet was not essential for the future.

In March 1980, as Task Force 70 cruised in the Arabian Sea (dubbed Camel Station by American sailors), the Navy found itself at a historic crossroads. Either it would retain its slim edge of superiority over the Soviet fleet, or it would be known in history more for its pre – Vietnam War triumphs than for its future. Such was the unpalatable choice facing Americans in an era of double-digit inflation and growing unemployment.

FIGURE 14

CURRENT U.S./USSR MARITIME BALANCE

U.S.	FACTOR	SOVIET UNION
• OPEN ACCESS TO OCEANS	GEOGRAPHY	• CONSTRAINED ACCESS TO OCEANS
• LONG DISTANCES TO ALLIES		• SHORT DISTANCES TO ALLIES
• SEA CONTROL/POWER PROJECTION	MISSIONS	• SEA DENIAL/PERIPHERAL SEA CONTROL
		• LAND BASED NAVAL AIR FORCE
• FEW LARGE SHIPS	OFFENSIVE	• MANY SMALLER SHIPS
• SEA BASED AVIATION	CAPABILITY	• ANTI-SHIP MISSILE SYSTEM
• ATTACK SUBMARINES		• ATTACK SUBMARINES
• AMPHIBIOUS FORCES		
• MARGINAL ANTI-AIR WARFARE CAPABILITY	DEFENSIVE CAPABILITY	• MARGINAL ANTI-AIR WARFARE CAPABILITY
		• INADEQUATE ANTI-SUBMARINE WARFARE
• ANTI-SUBMARINE WARFARE		INADEQUATE SEA-BASED AIR
• AIR COVER		
• EXCELLENT UNDERWAY REPLENISHMENT	SUSTAINED OPERATIONS	• LIMITED UNDERWAY REPLENISHMENT
• WORLD WIDE BASE STRUCTURE		• LIMITED OVERSEAS BASE SYSTEM
• MAJOR ADVANTAGE-- OFFENSIVE AND DEFENSIVE TECHNOLOGY	TECHNOLOGY	• ANTI-SHIP MISSILES AND SURFACE OCEAN SURVEILLANCE
• EXTENSIVE EXERCISES	EXPERIENCE	• LIMITED AT-SEA TIME
• VOLUNTEER FORCE		• MANNING BY CONSCRIPTS
• WARTIME EXPERIENCE		

Source: Department of Defense.

Portents for the Future

The hard fact was that under the then existing restrictions of the Navy's current five-year plan, it could not attain its modest goal of a 550-ship fleet. Under current plans the decommissioning of its worn-out vessels would continue at almost the same rate as newly built ships joined the operating forces.

In addition to a shrinking combat fleet, the Navy of the future seemed bound to suffer from an absence of "surge" capability in the nation's shipyards, steel mills, and aerospace industries. None of these was equipped to gear up for vastly increased production in the event of a national emergency. Moreover, the corrosive effect of abnormal inflation wrecked any substantive predictions for future defense spending, especially when one considered the long lead time for building a ship—as much as seven years—from concept to fleet operations.

By 1980 the American people had frittered away valuable time; if the Navy continued to build ships at the 1980 rate, then its combat force of ships would decline from 442 to 285 ships by the year 2000. If the Navy wished to maintain the same size fleet during the next twenty years, as in 1980, it would have to add to its building plan three ships per year, *every year*, starting in 1980 and continuing through 1996. If this target were to be met, money, long-range planning, and most of all, public support were required at once. Yet chances for a sharp increase in shipbuilding funds were not bright. In the administration's 1981 budget, the Defense Department was scheduled to receive but 24 percent, but the newly formed Department of Health and Human Services would get an impressive 36 percent.[30]

Upon the American people rested the decision to build up the Navy in the face of charges that such a program penalized the poor, the elderly, and the handicapped. Yet the alternative—risking the Navy's capability to ensure access to vital overseas resources and to defend the equally vulnerable sea-lanes—was to undercut America's ability to survive as a nation. Those who suspected that the United States lacked the collective discipline to meet a national emergency forgot that in the past Americans have usually met crises resolutely. In the future, there was every reason to believe that they would do so—if informed of the disturbing facts.

In 1980 countless Americans finally shook off the delusions of the past decades. Those who chose to believe that the United States could not stay the course in making up for lost time forgot that it was still a nation with seemingly limitless potential. Its people, once they sense danger, have traditionally met crises with a staunch fixity of purpose. The danger in 1980 was symbolized by Soviet sea power, a questionable U.S. policy of nuclear parity, and American dependency on Arab oil. A modernized and larger U.S. Navy, supported and maintained by an aroused and united public, would help to restore to the United States the security and the international prestige befitting its standing as a superpower.

Appendix A

COMDR. JAMES B. STOCKDALE'S
TALK TO HIS PILOTS
ON BOARD THE *ORISKANY*
EN ROUTE TO VIETNAM
APRIL 29, 1965

Having reviewed for you the terrain of Vietnam, the enemy's order of battle, the rules of engagement, and to some extent the modern history of the conflict and the evolution of America's strategy, I think I owe you in addition a straight from the shoulder discussion of pilots' mental attitudes and orientation in "limited war" circumstances. I saw the need for this last summer aboard *Ticonderoga*—after the start of the war had caught us by surprise and we had gone through those first, exciting days pretty much on adrenaline. In the lull that followed, as we prepared for a next round, I could sense that those fine young men who had measured up so well in the sudden reality of flak and burning targets wanted to talk and get their resources and value systems lined up for the long haul. Like most of you, they were well read, sensitive, sometimes skeptical—those educated in the American liberal tradition to think for themselves—those who are often our most productive citizens—and just as often, our best soldiers. They realized that bombing heavily defended targets is serious business and no game—that it is logically impossible, in the violence of a fight, to commit oneself, as an individual, only in some proportion of his total drive and combative instinct. It has to be all or nothing; dog eat dog over the target. I think they were asking themselves, as you might—Where do I as a person, a person of awareness, refinement and education, fit into this "limited war," "measured response" concept?

I want to level with you right now, so you can think it over here in mid-Pacific and not kid yourself into imagining "stark realizations" in the Gulf of Tonkin. Once you go "feet dry" over the beach, there can be nothing limited about your commitment. "Limited war" means to us that our target list has limits, our ordnance loadout has limits, our rules of engagement have limits, but that does *not* mean that there is anything "limited" about our personal obligations as fighting men to carry out assigned missions with all we've got. If you think it is possible for a man, in the heat of battle, to apply something less that total *personal* commitment—equated perhaps to your idea of the proportion of *national* potential being applied—you are wrong. It's contrary to human nature. So also is the idea I was alarmed to find suggested to me by a military friend in a letter recently: that the prisoner of war's Code of Conduct is some sort of a "total war" document. You can't go half way on that, either. The Code of Conduct was not written for "total wars" or "limited wars," it was written for *all* wars, and let it be understood that it applies with full force to *this* Air Wing— in *this* war.

What I am saying is that national commitment and personal commitment are two different things. All is not relative. You classical scholars know that even the celebrated "free thinker" Socrates was devoted to ridiculing the Sophist idea that one can avoid black and white choices in arriving at personal commitments; one sooner or later comes to a fork in the road. As Harvard's philosophy great, Alfred North Whitehead, said: "I can't bring half an umbrella to work when the weatherman predicts a 50% chance of rain." We are all at that fork in the road this week. Think it over. If you find yourself rationalizing about moving your bomb release altitude up a thousand feet from where your strike leader briefs it, or adding a few hundred pounds fuel to your over target bingo because "the Navy needs you for greater things," or you must save the airplane for some "great war" of the future, you're in the wrong outfit. You owe it to yourself to have a talk with your skipper or me. It's better for both you and your shipmates that you face up to your fork in the road here at 140° East rather than later, 2,000 miles west of here, on the line.

Let us all face our prospects squarely. We've got to be prepared to obey the rules and contribute without reservation. If political or religious conviction helps you do this, so much the better, but you're still going to be expected to press on with or without these comforting thoughts, simply because this uniform commits us to a military ethic—the ethic of personal pride and excellence that alone has supported some of the greatest fighting men in history. Don't require Hollywood answers to "What are we fighting for?" We're here to fight because it's in the interest of the United States that we do so. This may not be the most dramatic way to explain it, but it has the advantage of being absolutely correct.

I hope I haven't made this too somber. I merely want to let you all know first of all where this Wing stands on Duty, Honor and Country. Secondly, I want to warn you all of excessive caution. A philosopher has warned us, that of all forms of caution, caution in love is the most fatal to true happiness. In the same way I believe that "caution in war" can have a deleterious effect on your future self-respect, and in that sense, surely your future happiness. When that Fox Flag is two-blocked in the Gulf, you'll be an actor in a drama that you'll replay in your mind's eye for the rest of your life. Level with yourself now. Do your duty.

Appendix B

TRENDS IN DEFENSE SPENDING AND NAVAL FORCES

TABLE B-1
DEPARTMENT OF THE NAVY BUDGET
FISCAL YEARS 1979–1981
FINANCIAL CHRONOLOGY OF TOTAL OBLIGATIONAL AUTHORITY[a]
(In Billions of Dollars)

	1979	1980	1981	Change 1980–81
Current dollars (January 1980)	41.8	46.1	50.3	+4.2
Constant dollars (fiscal 1981)	48.7	49.7	50.3	+0.6

Source: U.S., Department of Defense, Annual Report, Fiscal Year 1981 (January 1980).
[a]The authority granted to the Navy to obligate funds now for the production of materiel, such as ships, to be delivered in future years.

TABLE B-2
DEPARTMENT OF DEFENSE BUDGET
FISCAL YEARS 1979–1981
(In Billions of Dollars)

Current dollars (January 1980)	Actual 1979	Estimate 1980	Estimate 1981	Increase 1980–81
Total obligational authority	124.8	139.3	158.7	19.4
Constant fiscal 1981 dollars				
Total obligational authority	146.4	150.7	158.7	8.1

Source: U.S., Department of Defense, Annual Report, Fiscal Year 1981 (January 1980).

TABLE B-3
DEPARTMENT OF THE NAVY
GENERAL PURPOSE FORCES HIGHLIGHTS
FISCAL YEARS 1964–1981

	1964	1968	1979	1980	1981
Naval Forces					
Active fleet	803	875	388	395	418
Carriers	24	23	13	13	12[a]
Other ships	82	49	10	7	7
Reserve ships	62	54	53	53	42
Fleet auxiliary force ships	–	1	19	22	22
Marine Corps Divisions					
Active	3	4	3	3	3
Reserve	1	1	1	1	1
Marine Corps Air Wings					
Active	3	3	3	3	3
Reserve	1	1	1	1	1

Source: U.S., Department of Defense, *Annual Report, Fiscal Year 1981* (January 1980).
[a]The 27-year-old carrier *Saratoga* was scheduled for an extended refit and modernization beginning October 1980, reducing the number of active carriers to twelve.

TABLE B-4
NAVAL AND MARINE CORPS
CONVENTIONAL FORCES, 1964–1980

	30 June 1964	30 June 1968	30 Sept. 1978	30 Sept. 1979	30 Sept. 1980
Attack and ASW carriers	24	23	13	13	13
Nuclear attack subs	19	33	70	72	75
Other warships	363	385	166	170	181
Amphibious warships	133	157	64	65	63
Naval attack air wings	15	15	12	12	12
Marine Corps divisions	3	4	3	3	3
Marine Corps attack airwings	3	3	3	3	3

Source: Office of the Secretary of Defense

TABLE B-5
THE ANEMIC NAVAL AIR ARM

Fiscal Year	Total Operating A/C[a]	Total A/C Bought	VF/VA Bought[a]
1973	5,590	279	254
1974	5,179	302	177
1975	4,915	211	98
1976	4,931	263	94
1977	4,698	214	99
1978	4,512	160	74
1979	4,476	131	75
1980	4,586	103	39

Source: Admiral Thomas H. Moorer, *Wings of Gold*, Summer 1979, p. 5. Courtesy of Association of Naval Aviation.

[a]A/C: aircraft; VF: fighter plane; VA: attack plane.

These shrinking figures do not show that 49 percent of the Navy's planes were more than ten years old.

TABLE B-6
ACTIVE DUTY AND RESERVE (PAID STATUS) NAVAL AND
MARINE CORPS PERSONNEL
(End of Fiscal Year, in Thousands)

	1964	1968	1972	1976	1978	1979	1980
Navy	667	765	588	525	530	524	528
Marine Corps	190	307	198	192	191	190	189
Naval Reserve	123	124	124	97	83	87	49
Marine Corps Reserve	46	47	41	30	33	34	34

Source: Office of the Secretary of Defense.

Notes

Chapter One

1. Quoted in Paolo Coletta, "James Vincent Forrestal," in Paolo Coletta, ed., *The American Secretaries of the Navy* (Annapolis: Naval Institute Press, 1980).

2. In 1948 a poll by the American Institute of Public Opinion found that of its respondents, 63 percent wanted a bigger navy, 74 percent a bigger air force, and 61 percent a bigger army. In another poll 73 percent thought that the United States was being "too soft" in its policy toward Russia. (*Public Opinion Quarterly*, Summer 1948, pp. 349, 354.)

3. Edward N. Luttwak, *The Political Uses of Sea Power* (Baltimore: Johns Hopkins University Press, 1974), p. 3.

4. E. B. Potter, *Nimitz* (Annapolis: Naval Institute Press, 1976), p. 402.

5. For a critical analysis of unification, see Vice Admiral Edwin B. Hooper, *The Navy Department: Evolution and Fragmentation* (Washington, D.C.: Naval Historical Foundation, 1978).

6. For an account, see Potter, *Nimitz*, pp. 407−8.

7. In April 1942 then Lieutenant Colonel Doolittle had become a national hero by leading sixteen B-26 bombers on a dramatic raid on Tokyo. Paradoxically, these Army Air Forces planes had taken off from the carrier *Hornet* while the ships and their escorts were some six hundred miles from Japan. If the damage inflicted by Doolittle's gallant flyers was not overly impressive, their daring feat gave a tremendous boost to American morale during the dark days following Pearl Harbor. The raid was originally conceived by Admiral King and Captain Francis S. Low, USN, in January 1942 as a retaliation for Pearl Harbor. For an account of the raid, see Samuel E. Morison, *The History of United States Naval Operations in World War II*, vol. 3, *The Rising Sun in The Pacific, 1931−April 1942* (Boston: Little, Brown, 1950), pp. 389−98.

8. Vincent Davis, "The Politics of Innovation: Patterns in Navy Cases," in John E. Endicott and Roy W. Stafford, Jr., eds., *American Defense Policy*, 4th ed. (Baltimore: Johns Hopkins University Press, 1977), pp. 390−97.

9. See Robert E. Osgood, *Limited War: The Challenge to American Security* (Chicago: University of Chicago Press, 1957), chap. 7.

10. For an account of Radford's arguments, see Stephen Jurika, Jr., ed., *From Pearl Harbor to Vietnam: The Memoirs of Admiral Arthur W. Radford* (Stanford: Hoover Institution Press, 1980), chaps. 13−15.

11. For the text of this letter, see Robert D. Heinl, *Soldiers of the Sea* (Annapolis: U.S. Naval Institute, 1963), p. 527.

12. Potter, *Nimitz*, p. 446.

13. Osgood, *Limited War*, p. 153.

14. Malcolm W. Cagle and Frank A. Manson, *The Sea War in Korea* (Annapolis: Naval Institute Press, 1957), chap. 1; and Nikita Khrushchev, *Khrushchev Remembers*, tr. and ed. by Strobe Talbot (Boston: Little, Brown, 1974), p. 368.

Chapter Two

1. *The New Columbia Encyclopedia*, 4th ed. (New York: Columbia University Press, 1975), p. 1498.

2. *Washington Post*, February 12, 1956.·

3. Malcolm W. Cagle and Frank A. Manson, *The Sea War in Korea* (Annapolis: Naval Institute Press, 1957), p. 471.

4. Based on conversations between pilots and the author on board a carrier off Korea in the weeks before the armistice was signed on July 27, 1953, after two years of stop-and-go negotiations.

5. Cagle and Manson, *The Sea War in Korea*, p. vii.

6. Ibid., p. vi.

7. Radford also wore a second hat as commander-in-chief, Pacific Fleet. An Annapolis graduate (1916) and a naval aviator, Radford had commanded carrier task groups in World War II. In the late 1940s he had served as vice-chief of naval operations.

8. Dean Acheson, "Crisis in Asia: An Examination of U.S. Policy," *Department of State Bulletin* 22 (Jan. 23, 1950): 111–18.

9. Edwin B. Hooper, Dean C. Allard, and Oscar P. Fitzgerald, *The United States Navy and the Vietnam Conflict*, vol. 1 (Washington, D.C.: Government Printing Office, 1976), p. 173.

10. Ibid., p. 247, citing messages CNO 192323Z and CNO 202023Z, both of March 1954.

11. Stephen Jurika, Jr., ed., *From Pearl Harbor to Vietnam: The Memoirs of Admiral Arthur W. Radford* (Stanford: Hoover Institution Press, 1980), p. 398.

12. Ibid., p. 406.

13. Melvin Gurtov, *The First Vietnam Crisis* (New York: Columbia University Press, 1967), p. 188.

14. Eight nations signed the SEATO pact on September 8, 1954: the United States, Great Britain, France, Australia, New Zealand, the Philippines, Thailand, and Pakistan. The organization merely provided a forum for members to consult on defense measures if a crisis arose. Following the victory of the North Vietnamese in Indochina, the members agreed on September 24, 1975, to phase out the alliance "in view of changing circumstances."

15. A Gallup poll for June 5, 1953, noted that among those questioned, 56 percent were in favor of sending arms, 28 percent were opposed, and 16 percent had no opinion. But by a ratio of ten to one, respondents on September 18, 1955, opposed sending ground troops. Admiral Radford, in his oral history (Princeton University), said, "I was not ready to support the French at Dien Bien Phu or anywhere else unless we could make proper military arrangements with them. Our negotiations fell down because the British wouldn't play . . .

But if the British had gone along, I still think we would have had considerable trouble with the French.'' (See Leonard Mosley, *Dulles* [London, 1978], p. 358.)

16. Com 7th Flt., Report, FY1955, p. 11, U.S. Naval Operational Archives; cited in Hooper, Allard, and Fitzgerald, *The United States Navy and the Vietnam Conflict,* p. 267.

17. An attack plane designated AD.

18. Formosa (''beautiful'') was originally named by the Portuguese. Its Chinese name is Taiwan.

19. *U.S. Statutes at Large,* lix, 7 (resolution signed January 29, 1955).

20. The Seventh Fleet comprised some one hundred ships including four carriers. The U.S. Air Force moved 60 F-86 fighters from Okinawa and the Philippines to Taiwan during the Tachen operation.

21. For a detailed account see Hooper, Allard, and Fitzgerald, *The United States Navy and the Vietnam Conflict,* pp. 348−50.

22. The author was executive officer of Admiral Pride's flagship, the cruiser *Helena,* at the time.

23. *Time,* February 7, 1955, p. 11.

24. Hooper, Allard, and Fitzgerald, *The United States Navy and the Vietnam Conflict,* p. 313, citing Defense Department study.

25. Memo, Admiral Duncan to Admiral Radford, ser 00034P33, May 26, 1954; ibid., p. 268.

26. ''Special Message to the Congress Transmitting Reorganization Plan 6 of 1953 Concerning the Department of Defense,'' April 30, 1953, in *Dwight D. Eisenhower: 1953,* Public Papers of the Presidents of the United States (Washington, D.C.: Government Printing Office, 1960), p. 225.

27. I have borrowed freely from Vice Admiral Edwin B. Hooper's cogent analysis, *The Navy Department: Evolution and Fragmentation* (Washington, D.C.: Naval Historical Foundation, 1978).

28. *Report of the Committee on Organization of the Department of the Navy* (Washington, D.C.: Government Printing Office, 1961), p. 69. This report is known as the Franke Report.

29. Three members were retired or serving officers of the Army or Air Force.

30. Rockefeller Brothers Fund Special Studies Project, Panel II, *International Security: The Military Aspect,* America at Mid-Century Series (New York: Doubleday and Co., 1958), p. 27.

31. Hooper, *The Navy Department,* pp. 31−35. For a synthesis of the issue of organizational changes in the Pentagon, see John E. Endicott and Roy W. Stafford, Jr., eds., *American Defense Policy,* 4th ed. (Baltimore, Johns Hopkins University Press, 1977), especially chap. 6; and Davis B. Bobrow, ed., *Components of Defense Policy* (Chicago: Rand McNally and Co., 1965).

32. Hooper, *The Navy Department,* p. 39, describes how Admiral Claude V. Ricketts, the vice-chief of naval operations, summed up the Navy's fears in 1962.

33. Richard G. Hewlett and Francis Duncan, *Nuclear Navy* (Chicago: University of Chicago Press, 1974), p. 308, citing Admiral Burke's Memorandum for the Record, December 25, 1955.

34. Ibid., p. 309.

35. For firsthand accounts by the skippers of these record-breaking submarines, see

William R. Anderson, with Clay Blair, Jr., *Nautilus 90 North* (Cleveland: World Publishing Co., 1959); James F. Calvert, *Surface at the Pole: The Extraordinary Voyages of the USS Skate* (New York: McGraw-Hill, 1960); and Edward L. Beach, *Around the World Submerged: The Voyage of the Triton* (New York: McGraw-Hill, 1960).

Chapter Three

1. Theodore Sorensen, *Kennedy* (New York: Harper and Row, 1965), pp. 269—70.

2. Arthur M. Schlesinger, Jr., *A Thousand Days* (Boston: Houghton Mifflin Co., 1965), pp. 312—15.

3. For a discussion, see Lieutenant Commander K. R. McGruther, USN, "Conceptual Strategies for Naval Planning," manuscript (Newport, R.I.: U.S. Naval War College, 1974). pp. 2—3.

4. See William W. Kaufmann, *The McNamara Strategy* (New York: Harper and Row, 1964), for an analysis of McNamara's impact on the military.

5. The Naval War College library holds copies of early pamphlets on "the estimate of the situation" written in the 1930s.

6. Alain C. Enthoven and F. Wayne Smith, *How Much Is Enough?* (New York: Harper and Row, 1971), pp. 89—90.

7. Frederick H. Hartmann, "The Game of Strategy: The Cost-Cutter's Guide," manuscript (Newport, R.I.: U.S. Naval War College, 1976), pp. 272—74.

8. Letter to author, July 5, 1979.

9. Admiral Burke informed the author that in his opinion, Eisenhower's concept of the plan to aid Free Cubans never approached the scale of the actual operation (Letter to author, September 25, 1979).

10. "The Reminiscences of Admiral Robert Lee Dennison, U.S. Navy (Retired)," unpublished oral history, U.S. Naval Institute, Annapolis, 1975, pp. 332—33, 352, 366—67.

11. Ibid., p. 366.

12. In December 1962, 1,113 prisoners were ransomed for $53 million in food and medicines. The previous April, 60 wounded prisoners were released for $2.9 million in cash. (*Facts on File*, 1962, pp. 458—59.)

13. "Recollections of Admiral Arleigh A. Burke, USN (Ret.)," unpublished oral history, U.S. Naval Institute, Annapolis, 1973, pp. 4—216—4—218 (hereafter, "Burke Recollections").

14. Ibid., p. 3—175. See also "Official Inside Story of the Cuba Invasion," *U.S. News and World Report*, August 13, 1979, pp. 79—83. Admiral Burke is quoted as saying, when asked if the Joint Chiefs had approved the operation, "Technically no. Morally, they did."

15. Letter from Admiral Burke to author, June 23, 1979.

16. "Burke Recollections," p. 4—218. For two notable books, see Mario Lazo, *Dagger in the Heart: American Foreign Policy Failures in Cuba* (New York: Twin Circle Publishing Co., 1968); and Peter Wyden, *Bay of Pigs: The Untold Story* (New York: Simon and Schuster, 1979).

17. Letter to author, April 16, 1979.

18. Schlesinger, *A Thousand Days*, p. 290, referring to Allen W. Dulles, CIA director, and Richard Bissell, manager of the Bay of Pigs operation.

19. Arthur Krock, *In the Nation, 1932—1966* (New York: McGraw-Hill, 1967), pp. 321—25.

20. Paradoxically, during the postmortem of the debacle, McNamara, who later made something of a record for his direct participation in combat operations, observed: "A military operation should never be conducted except under a military man" (see *U.S. News and World Report*, August 13, 1979, p. 82).

21. For example, Elie Abel, *The Missile Crisis* (Philadelphia: J. B. Lippincott, 1966). David Detzer, *The Brink* (New York, 1979), is the most recent publication.

22. Detzer, *The Brink*, pp. 138, 154.

23. Ibid., p. 212; and Abel, see *The Missile Crisis*, p. 154—55.

24. U.S., Congress, House, Armed Services Committee, *Hearings on Military Posture*, 88th Cong., 1st sess., January 30, 1963, p. 897.

25. Vasily Kuznetsov to John J. McCloy, *Newsweek*, June 12, 1978, p. 31.

26. Norman Polmar, *Soviet Naval Power, Challenge for the 1970's* (New York: Crane, Russak, 1974), chap. 4. Polmar cites the Suez crisis of 1956 as the beginning of Soviet realization that they must acquire strategic and conventional naval forces superior to those of the U.S. Navy.

27. AGTR: a ship designation meaning Auxiliary, Technical, Research.

28. "The Record of the Court of Inquiry into Attack on USS *Liberty* (AGTR5)," pp. 161—72, on file at U.S. Naval Historical Center, Washington, D.C.

29. Captain Yaakov Nitzan, Israeli Navy, in a letter to *Naval Institute Proceedings*, November 1978, p. 111. For a description of the Israeli attack, see Richard K. Smith, "The Violation of the *Liberty*," *Naval Institute Proceedings*, June 1978, pp. 63—70.

30. See Vice Admiral Edwin B. Hooper, *The Navy Department: Evolution and Fragmentation* (Washington, D.C.: Naval Historical Foundation, 1978), p. 41. See also James Ennes, *Assault on the Liberty* (New York: Random House, 1980).

31. Letter to editor, *Washington Post*, July 6, 1967; also quoted in Hooper, *The Navy Department*, p. 54.

32. Jonathan Trumbull Howe, *Multicrises, Sea Power and Global Politics in the Missile Age* (Cambridge, Mass.: M.I.T. Press, 1971), pp. 102—4. See also Phil G. Goulding, *Confirm or Deny* (New York: Harper and Row, 1970), p. 97. Goulding was assistant defense secretary for public affairs during McNamara's tenure. Goulding's admiration for McNamara as a dedicated, diligent, and brilliant manager is apparent in this account of Pentagon public relations.

33. U.S., Congress, House, Armed Services Committee, *Report on the Activities of the House Committee on the Armed Services*, HASC no. 91—35, 91st Cong., 1st sess., 1969, p. 5109.

34. Admiral Hooper was the commander of the Service Force, Pacific Fleet, based at Pearl Harbor. Admiral Hooper strongly implies that field commanders lacked authority to take any action regarding the *Pueblo* without first checking with Washington, a time-consuming process at best. See also Trevor Armbrister, *A Matter of Accountability* (New York: Coward-McCann, 1970), for a well-researched account of the *Pueblo* affair.

35. Letter to author, July 5, 1979.

Chapter Four

1. U.S., Department of Defense, *United States and Vietnam Relations, 1945–1967*, IV, B-2, "The Advisory Buildup," Part Two (Washington, D.C.: Government Printing Office, 1977), p. 18.

2. State of the Union message to Congress, January 9, 1958, in *Dwight D. Eisenhower: 1959*, Public Papers of the Presidents of the United States (Washington, D.C.: Government Printing Office, 1960), p. 6.

3. Robert E. Osgood, *Limited War: The Challenge to American Strategy* (Chicago: University of Chicago Press, 1957), deals with the question of how the United States could foster its interests (including containment) abroad without risking a nuclear war.

4. For example, see Admiral U. S. G. Sharp, *Strategy for Defeat: Vietnam in Retrospect* (San Rafael, Calif.: Presidio Press, 1978), p. 2.

5. See James S. Roherty, *Decisions of Robert S. McNamara* (Coral Gables, Fla.: University of Miami Press, 1970), for an assessment of McNamara's Pentagon years.

6. General William C. Westmoreland, "Vietnam in Perspective," *The Retired Officer*, October 1978, p. 22.

7. See Sharp, *Strategy for Defeat*, for repeated examples.

8. Clark G. Reynolds, *Command of the Sea: The History and Strategy of Maritime Empires* (New York: William Morrow and Co., 1974), pp. 583–84.

9. Letter to author, December 18, 1972. Paul Ignatius served in various Pentagon posts from 1961 to 1968. A management expert, he specialized in logistics. See Paul B. Ryan, biographical sketch of Ignatius, in Paolo Coletta, ed., *American Secretaries of the Navy* (Annapolis: Naval Institute Press, 1980).

10. U.S., Congress, House, Committee on the Armed Services, *The Changing Strategic Naval Balance, USSR vs. U.S.A.*, 90th Cong. 2d sess., December 1968, pp. 21–25. See also *Armed Forces Journal*, August 31, 1968, p. 13, and *Armed Forces Management*, October 1968, pp. 55–60.

11. Sharp, *Strategy for Defeat*, p. 86.

12. A Texan metaphor for victory.

13. "Reminiscences of Hanson Weightman Baldwin," manuscript, (Annapolis: U.S. Naval Institute, 1976), p. 709.

14. Ibid., pp. 695, 704.

15. Ibid., pp. 701, 704. Baldwin traveled to Germany, Korea, Japan, and Taiwan and found that U.S. forces in Vietnam had "eaten into the stockpiles of equipment at all these places." The capability of U.S. forces abroad to carry out their missions was inevitably eroded.

16. Ibid., p. 700.

17. Ibid., pp. 703–4.

18. Scott Blakey, *Prisoner at War: The Survival of Commander Richard A. Stratton* (New York: Doubleday, Anchor Press, 1978), p. 6.

19. Letter to author, July 5, 1979.

20. Copy provided by Vice Admiral Stockdale to the author and used with permission. The original script used in his talk is held by Admiral Stockdale.

21. Two-block Fox: an old naval signal in which the Fox (F) flag is hoisted (two-

blocked) to the top of its halyard, thereby announcing that the ship is engaged in flight operations.

22. Admiral Stockdale later served as commander of a carrier group before becoming president of the Naval War College in 1977.

23. Admiral Cousins' words are quoted in Malcolm W. Cagle, "Task Force 77 in Action Off Vietnam," *Naval Institute Proceedings*, Naval Review Issue, May 1972, p. 108.

24. Ibid., pp. 66—109.

25. Conversation with author, August 21, 1979. See also Cagle, "Task Force 77," p. 109.

26. Cagle, "Task Force 77"; Captain Wayne P. Hughes, USN, "Vietnam: Winnable War?" *Naval Institute Proceedings*, July 1977, pp. 60—65, provides a trenchant comment on the strategy of the war and why senior, serving officers muted their voices even though opposed to the administration's strategy.

27. For Sharp's recollections of the war, see *Strategy for Defeat*.

28. In a lecture at the Naval War College, March 29, 1972.

29. Baldwin, "Reminiscences," pp. 706, 708—10.

30. U.S., Department of Defense, *United States and Vietnam Relations, 1945—1967*, IV, C. 3 (Washington, D.C.: Government Printing Office, 1971), pp. 136—40. (Memorandum for the president, "Evaluation of the Program of Bombing North Vietnam," July 30, 1965).

31. Sharp spelled out his plan in a dispatch to the JCS in February 1967. See *Strategy for Defeat*, pp. 141—43.

32. U.S., Congress, Senate, Committee on the Armed Services, Preparedness Investigating Subcommittee, Hearings: *Air War Against North Vietnam*, 90th Cong., 1st sess., 1967, parts 1—5.

33. Admiral Sharp, lecture at the Naval War College, March 29, 1972.

34. Preparedness Investigating Subcommittee, *Air War Against North Vietnam*, p. 294.

35. Ibid., p. 441.

36. The report was printed in full in the *New York Times*, September 1, 1967, p. 10.

37. *New York Times*, September 2, 1967, pp. 1, 9.

38. The panel's comments may also be found in Department of Defense, *United States and Vietnam Relations, 1945—1967*, IV C. 7b, pp. 90—101.

39. *New York Times*, September 1, 1967, p. 30.

40. David Halberstam, *The Best and the Brightest* (New York: Random House, 1972), pp. 488—90.

41. Ibid., p. 644.

42. In 1978, McNamara addressed an audience at the Stanford Business School on the missions of the World Bank. During the question period, McNamara declined to answer any questions about his role in the war on the grounds that as an appointed government official, such comment would be inappropriate.

43. Halberstam, *The Best and the Brightest*, p. 490. Admiral McDonald was CNO from 1963 to 1967. Admiral Thomas Moorer, his relief, served from 1967 to 1970 before being appointed chairman of the JCS.

44. Sharp, *Strategy for Defeat*, p. 268.

45. For an admirable essay on the ethical question of whether government officials and service officers should have criticized crucial decisions by their superiors during the Vietnam war, see Commander Roy L. Beavers, USN (Ret.), "An Absence of Accountability," *Naval Institute Proceedings,* January 1976, pp. 18–23.

46. Letter to author, July 5, 1979.

Chapter Five

1. Zumwalt, from Tulare, California, was a member of the class of 1943 at Annapolis and stood 33 in a class of 616.

2. Elmo R. Zumwalt, Jr., *On Watch* (New York: New York Times Book Co., Quadrangle, 1976), pp. 36–39, describes the evolution of Vietnamization.

3. Interview with David Packard, October 6, 1972. Packard was chosen by Laird as his deputy secretary of defense. A world-renowned industrialist, Packard contributed to the de-emphasis of centralized control in the Pentagon. See also *Armed Forces Journal,* April 12, 1969, p. 31.

4. Henry Kissinger, *The White House Years* (Boston: Little, Brown, 1979), p. 201.

5. Chafee was secretary from January 1969 to April 1972. He resigned to run (unsuccessfully) for the Senate from Rhode Island. In 1976 he ran again for the Senate and won.

6. Always known as a persuasive speaker, Zumwalt won two gold watches in oratory as a midshipman.

7. Zumwalt, *On Watch,* p. 34.

8. Vice Admiral Gerald E. Miller, USN (Ret.), "High-Low," *Naval Institute Proceedings,* December 1976, p. 81.

9. Zumwalt, *On Watch,* pp. 46–47.

10. See ibid., pp. 182–96, for Zumwalt's chapter, "Mickey Mouse, Elimination of."

11. Navy Secretary Chafee's "Memorandum to Flag and General Officers," June 5, 1970.

12. U.S., Congress, House, Special Subcommittee on Disciplinary Problems in the U.S. Navy, *Hearings,* HASC no. 93–13, 92nd Cong., 2d sess., October 1973. Zumwalt states that the chairman of the Armed Services Committee, Congressman Edward Hébert of Louisiana, initiated the probe because he preferred to maintain the Navy's traditional policies toward minorities (*On Watch,* pp. 245, 251).

13. Zumwalt, *On Watch,* p. 259. See also Paul B. Ryan, "USS *Constellation* Flareup: Was It Mutiny?" *Naval Institute Proceedings,* January 1976, pp. 46–53.

14. Conversation with Admiral Carney, May 21, 1979; and his letter to author, January 9, 1980. Letter from Admiral Burke, January 20, 1980.

15. Vincent Davis, "The Politics of Innovation: Patterns in Navy Cases," in John E. Endicott and Roy W. Stafford, Jr., eds., *American Defense Policy,* 4th ed. (Baltimore: Johns Hopkins University Press, 1977), pp. 390–97.

16. Interview with newsman from *Fresno* (Calif.) *Bee,* quoted in "Admiral Zumwalt Regrets Only Some Lack of Caution," Associated Press dispatch, May 22, 1974.

17. *U.S. News and World Report,* November 26, 1979, p. 24, reported that U.S. officials were aware that the Soviets at Cienfuegos had built a structure of the kind that in the Soviet domain was used to house missiles in firing position.

18. The understanding held that the Soviet Union, in exchange for a lifting of the U.S. blockade, would not introduce major offensive weapons into Cuba. By extension one could assume that the introduction of Soviet combat troops (not "advisors") would be opposed by the United States as a violation of the pact.

19. Zumwalt, *On Watch*, p. 279.

20. Ibid., pp. 279–82.

21. Ibid., p. 280.

22. Interview, May 21, 1979.

23. The riots took place on May 3–5, 1971. A combined force of 9,000 police and federal troops was required to restore order.

24. Zumwalt, *On Watch*, pp. 290–91.

25. See Jack Spence, "Naval Armaments in the Indian Ocean," in George H. Quester, ed., *Sea Power in the 1970s* (New York: Dunellen Publishing Co., 1975), pp. 117–58, for an assessment of Soviet naval strategy. Angola concluded a twenty-year friendship treaty with Moscow on October 8, 1974, evidence of the Kremlin's search for global naval bases. See Avigdor Haselkorn, *The Evolution of Soviet Security Strategy* (New York: Crane, Russak, 1978), p. 26, citing *Pravda*, October 9, 1976.

26. For a lucid discussion, see Admiral Stansfield Turner, "The Naval Balance: Not Just a Numbers Game," *Foreign Affairs*, January 1977, pp. 339–54.

27. For this comparison a major ship is one over 250 feet long. I am indebted to Professor Lawrence J. Korb's "The Erosion of American Naval Preeminence, 1962–1978" in Kenneth J. Hagan, ed., *Peace and War: Interpretations of American Naval History, 1775–1978* (Westport, Conn.: Greenwood, 1978), from which I have drawn liberally.

28. Zumwalt, *On Watch*, p. 421.

29. Ibid., pp. 339–40.

30. Ibid., pp. 59–84.

31. John T. Hayward, "Comment and Discussion: High-Low," *Naval Institute Proceedings*, August 1976, pp. 71–72. Admiral Hayward was a former president of the Naval War College and a combat naval aviator.

32. Gerald E. Miller, "High-Low," *Naval Institute Proceedings*, December 1976, pp. 79–85.

33. From 1969 to 1979 spending for national defense rose 44 percent compared with 359 percent for community and regional development; 335 percent for education, training, employment, and social services; 319 percent for health; and 332 percent for income security. "Budget Sham," (*Wall Street Journal*, September 10, 1979, p. 22).

34. In a display of Soviet support of the Arab nations, fourteen Soviet naval vessels anchored at Port Said and Alexandria after the shooting ceased (see Hannes Adomeit, *Soviet Risk-Taking and Crisis Behaviour*, Adelphi Papers, no. 101 [London: International Institute for Strategic Studies, 1973], p. 14).

35. Admiral Isaac Kidd, "View from the Bridge of the Sixth Fleet Flagship," *Naval Institute Proceedings*, February 1972, p. 19.

36. Zumwalt, *On Watch*, pp. 300–301.

37. Kissinger, *White House Years*, p. 926.

38. Zumwalt, *On Watch*, p. 435, quoting a report by the Sixth Fleet commander, Vice Admiral Daniel Murphy.

39. Ibid., p. 434.

40. Ibid., p.436.

41. Ibid., pp. 432–44. Zumwalt believed that Kissinger "almost certainly" was responsible for the refusals of permission.

42. Ibid., pp. 447–49.

43. Diego Garcia is a small atoll situated in the center of the Indian Ocean. After the British government leased the 14-mile long island to the United States in 1966, the U.S. Navy in 1971 built an 8,000-foot runway on it. By 1973 Diego Garcia served as a global communication station. The Navy planned to extend the runway to 12,000 feet, build a fuel oil farm, and construct a harbor for deep-draft ships. For a discussion on Diego Garcia as a political issue, see Tan Su-cheng, *The Expansion of Soviet Sea Power and the Security of Asia* (Taipei: Asia and the World Forum, 1977), pp. 66–68.

44. Zumwalt, *On Watch*, pp. xiv-xv, 319–21, 390–91, is highly critical of the Nixon-Kissinger determination to obtain the SALT I treaty.

45. *The Foreign Policy of the Soviet Union* (Moscow, 1975). The quotation of Gromyko appears in Robert Conquest's "The Rules of the Game: Why the West is Down and the East is Up," in James E. Dornan, ed., *United States National Security Policy in the Decade Ahead* (New York: Crane, Russak, 1978), p. 100.

46. Conquest, "The Rules of the Game," p. 101.

47. Zumwalt, *On Watch*, p. 332.

48. Brent Scowcroft, letter to *Wall Street Journal,* January 28, 1980, p. 17. Scowcroft was deputy director, National Security Council, during the Ford administration.

Chapter Six

1. In the Navy, he was known as James Earl Carter, Jr. The Annapolis yearbook described him as one who would be remembered for his willingness to help his classmates with academic problems. Carter stood 59th in a class of 820. Because of the need for officers, the 1947 class was graduated in 1946.

2. Statement by Defense Secretary James Schlesinger in a letter to Senator McClellan of the Appropriations Committee, published October 24, 1975. See *Facts on File*, 1975, p. 801.

3. Arthur J. Alexander, Abraham S. Becker, and William E. Hoehn, Jr., "The Significance of Divergent U.S.-U.S.S.R. Military Expenditures," U.S. Air Force study prepared by the RAND Corp., N-1000-AF, February 1979, p. 22.

4. *Aviation Week*, February 19, 1979, p. 14.

5. For example, in "Apes on a Treadmill," *Foreign Policy*, Spring 1975, pp. 12–29, Paul C. Warnke, who was active in the SALT II negotiations during the Carter administration and before that as assistant secretary of defense for international affairs in the Johnson administration, wrote: "As its only living superpower model, our words and actions are admirably calculated to inspire the Soviet Union to spend its substance on military manpower and weaponry." Warnke argued, wrongly as it turned out, that the Soviets would follow the U.S. lead on arms reduction.

6. *New York Times*, June 10, 1977, p. 5.

7. *Time*, April 24, 1978, p. 20.

8. *New York Times*, February 21, 1979.

9. The outer ring of offices reserved for senior officials.

10. "Statement of Defense Secretary Brown Before the Budget Committees of the House and Senate," February 21, 1979, p. 1, available from Secretary Brown's office.

11. Ibid., p. 13.

12. Alexander, Becker, and Hoehn, "U.S.-U.S.S.R. Military Expenditure," pp. vi-viii.

13. Quoted in George Will's column, *Newsweek*, June 25, 1979, p. 104.

14. "West's Superiority, Even If True, Is It Decisive?" *Wall Street Journal*, October 5, 1978, p. 20.

15. Adelman noted that the myth of economic and technological power turned traditional ideologies on their heads: "Here are the Communist Soviets embracing Adam Smith's notion that 'defence is of much more importance than opulence' and the capitalist Americans touting Marx's thesis that economics directs the flow and tempo of history's march."

16. Robert Conquest, "The Role of the Intellectual in International Misunderstanding," *Encounter*, August 1978, pp. 29—42.

17. "The Navy Under Attack," *Time*, May 8, 1978, p. 14.

18. Enthoven was assistant secretary of defense for systems analysis under Robert S. McNamara.

19. Quoted in *Time*, May 8, 1978, p. 15.

20. U.S., Congress, House, Committee on the Merchant Marine, and Fisheries, Subcommittee on the Merchant Marine, 95th Cong., 2d sess., 1978, *Merchant Marine Misc.*, part 3, serial 9552, pp. 141—145.

21. The three elements of the U.S. Triad were the strategic submarines, the strategic air force and the land-based Minuteman missile system. The Carter administration temporarily shelved the MX missile in 1978 because of the SALT II negotiations then in progress. In late 1979 events in Central America, Cuba, and the Middle East prompted the administration to reactivate the MX.

22. The USS *Ohio*, the first Trident boat, was launched at Groton, Conn., on April 7, 1979.

23. *Wall Street Journal*, June 25, 1979, p. 1, quoting a study by Amitai Etzioni of Columbia University.

24. Ibid.

25. General Sir John Winthrop Hackett in his 1962 Lee Knowles Lectures, U.S. Naval War College.

26. Statement on February 9, 1978, available from chief of information, Navy Department.

27. Rostow in his foreword to Lewis W. Walt, *The Eleventh Hour* (Ottawa, Ill.: Caroline House Publishers, 1979).

28. Admiral Thomas B. Hayward, CNO, stated this theme in remarks quoted in *Shipmate* (Naval Academy Alumni Journal), June 1979, p. 14.

29. Quoted in *Time*, April 7, 1961, p. 20.

30. *Who's Who in American Politics, 1973—1974*. (New York, 1973), s.v.

31. U.S., Congress, House, Committee on Armed Services, *Report: Department of Defense Appropriations Act, 1979*, Report no. 95—1118, 95th Cong., 2d sess., May 6, 1978, views of Congressman Dellums, pp. 130—32.

32. For examples of Nunn's views, see *New York Times*, January 14, 1979, p. 6; May 1, 1979, p. 5; June 19, 1979, p. 14.

33. In a speech at the U.S. Naval Academy, Annapolis, March 22, 1979, available from Senator Moynihan's office.

34. Poll released March 15, 1979, by the Committee on the Present Danger, Washington, D.C.

35. *New York Times,* February 21, 1979, p. A4.

36. Ibid., May 23, 1977, p. 1.

37. Lord Acton, 1834–1902, said, "Power tends to corrupt and absolute power corrupts absolutely."

38. Statement before the Budget Committee of the House, February 21, 1979, p. 10, copy available from Department of Defense.

Chapter Seven

1. This became strikingly clear when the nuclear carrier *Kitty Hawk* was dispatched to the Indian Ocean in November 1979 from Subic Bay in the Philippines.

2. Part of the drastic cutback in carrier strength between 1965 and 1975 from 25 to 13 can be traced to the phase-out of nine ASW carriers and their air squadrons.

3. His father, Admiral James L. Holloway, Jr., was in command of naval forces at the landing of U.S. Marines in Lebanon in 1958.

4. The Subcommittee on Defense, House Committee on Appropriations, July 20, 1976, copy available from chief of information, Navy Department.

5. U.S., Congress, Congressional Budget Office, "Planning U.S. General Purpose Forces: The Navy," December 1976, (hereafter, CBO Study).

6. U.S., Congress, House, Committee on Armed Services, *"U.S. Navy Analysis of Congressional Budget Office Budget Issue Paper, General Purpose Forces: Navy,* 95th Cong., 1st sess., January 12, 1977. I have drawn on this analysis in presenting the Navy's rebuttal.

7. Holloway acknowledged that occasionally there had been disagreement on a "specific platform" (i.e., ships or aircraft serving as a platform for combat equipment) or program. "These were reasonable differences among responsible men as to how to achieve the best cost effective mix within a balanced force."

8. "General purpose" encompasses all U.S. naval forces except the strategic nuclear submarines.

9. CBO Study, pp. 23–24.

10. Michael Krepon, "A Navy to Match National Purposes," *Foreign Affairs,* January 1977, pp. 355–67. At the time Krepon was legislative assistant to Congressman Floyd V. Hicks, Democrat of Washington.

11. The Hampton Roads tests are described in Clarke Van Vleet, Lee M. Pearson, and Adrian O. Van Wyen, *United States Naval Aviation, 1910–1970* (Washington, D.C.: Government Printing Office, 1970), pp. 47–48.

12. Clark G. Reynolds, *Command of the Sea: The History and Strategy of Maritime Empires* (New York: William Morrow and Co., 1974), p. 484.

13. *Report of the Secretary of the Navy* (Washington, D.C.: 1921), p. 7.

14. Samuel E. Morison, *The History of United States Naval Operations in World War II*, vol. 1, *The Battle of the Atlantic* (Boston: Little, Brown, 1947) pp. vii, xi. Morison was commissioned as a lieutenant commander in World War II after Roosevelt assigned him the task of preparing a naval history of the conflict. Morison eventually attained the rank of rear admiral, USNR.

15. Ibid., pp. xxxix, xliii.

16. Reynolds, *Command of the Sea*, pp. 440−42, 483−85. Battleships were sunk in World War II, but only when they lacked a combat air patrol flying cover. Control of the air was essential for the security of any surface fleet in wartime.

17. For a description of post−World War I naval strategic doctrine, see Reynolds, *Command of the Sea*, pp. 483−500.

18. The F-14 could track as many as 24 targets simultaneously. It could launch and guide six Phoenix missiles to targets over fifty miles distant. In addition, it carried Sidewinder missiles. The F-14 resulted from the bitter F-111/TFX aircraft controversy of the McNamara era in the Defense Department. As air force secretary at the time, Harold Brown was a leading proponent of the F-111 for use by the Air Force and the Navy.

19. The application of naval and air power overseas to meet a challenge at a level of force appropriate to the task is the essence of power projection.

20. Sea control is the use of naval and air power to keep open a specified sea area for military and commercial sea traffic against a challenge by the enemy.

21. For a summary of a study on a sea-based air platform cost/benefit study, see Center for Naval Analysis, "Annual Report, 1977," pp. 14−17.

22. The VSTOL aircraft, still in its infancy, offered hope that it might replace conventional carrier jets during the 1980s.

23. John Kenneth Galbraith expounds on this theme in his *The Nature of Mass Poverty* (Cambridge, Mass.: Harvard University Press, 1979), pp. 35−42, 321.

24. Battle group is the term that replaced the World War II−originated "task group."

25. *Report of Secretary of Defense Harold Brown to the Congress on the FY1980 Budget, Jan. 25, 1979* (Washington, D.C.: Government Printing Office, 1979), p. 16, *Sea Power*, March 1979, p. 44.

26. Quoted in *Time*, May 8, 1978, p. 19. Hart, a "liberal" Democrat, opposed the nuclear carrier but favored smaller flattops.

27. Speech before National Aviation Club and Aero Club, Washington, D.C., September 28, 1978. See *Shipmate* (U.S. Naval Academy Alumni Journal), December 1978, p. 9.

28. A similar situation occurred in 1952 when General Eisenhower became president. U.S. Army officers understandably were overjoyed at the prospect of future fat budgets for the Army.

29. "CVN Veto Sustained but Repercussions Continue," *Sea Power*, October 1978, pp. 16−18.

30. The steady reduction of U.S. overseas bases penalized the U.S. Navy in the sense that its "movable bases," the carriers and their air groups, were called on to display a U.S. presence in various foreign areas where previously the U.S. flag had flown ashore. The U.S. evacuation from Taiwan followed a ten-year pattern in which America's overseas bases dropped from 105 in 1969 to some forty a decade later. The loss of the U.S. port complex (which cost $525 million) at Camranh Bay, Vietnam, became particularly painful when in

1978 the Soviet Pacific fleet made use of it. Such a development was not surprising, considering the status of Vietnam as a client state of the USSR. Paradoxically, in August 1980 the United States, in order to protect its Mideast oil supply, arranged with Somalia to take over the former Soviet airbase and port facilities at Berbera on the Gulf of Aden. The Soviets had been evicted in 1977 after they threw their support to Ethiopia, Somalia's enemy.

Chapter Eight

1. Jayne, then 33 years old, was a graduate of the Air Force Academy and a former Air Force fighter pilot. In 1969 he earned a Ph.D. in political science at MIT. Before his assignment as the ranking defense specialist in the Office of Management and Budget, he was on the staff of the National Security Council.

2. *New York Times,* March 29, 1978, p. 18.

3. Ibid., April 15, 1978, p. 9.

4. Ibid., March 28, 1978, p. 10.

5. Ibid.

6. U.S., Congress, House, Committee on Armed Services, *Report: Department of Defense Appropriations Authorization Act, 1979,* Report no. 95–1118. 95th Cong., 2d sess., May 6, 1978 (hereafter, Price Report).

7. SOSUS: the acronym for sonar surveillance system, a system of undersea cables employed by the Navy in the North Atlantic and elsewhere to detect the presence of enemy submarines and other vessels.

8. Price Report, pp. 21–22.

9. Ibid., p. 23.

10. The Department of Health, Education and Welfare suffered a series of scandals involving graft and theft in the 1970s.

11. Price Report. McDonald's views are on pp. 143–46.

12. Churchill, *The Gathering Storm,* vol. 1, *The Second World War* (Boston, 1948), p. 190, quoted by Breckenridge in Price Report, p. 147. For Breckenridge's complete remarks, see pp. 147–53.

13. W. T. Lee, "Intelligence: Some Issues of Performance," in Francis P. Hoeber and William Schneider, Jr., eds., *Arms, Men, and Military Budgets: Issues for Fiscal Year 1978* (New York: Crane, Russak, 1977), p. 289.

14. Although the Backfire (or TU-22M) was not counted against Soviet limits in SALT II, 200 B-52 USAF bombers laid up in reserve were counted against U.S. weapons limits. Estimates of the amount of time needed to place the B-52s in flyable condition ranged up to a year.

15. *New York Times,* June 24, 1978, p. 22.

16. May 1979, copy available from Bureau of Public Affairs, State Department.

17. Woolsey was a Stanford-trained lawyer who served with distinction as under secretary for three years.

18. Newport, R.I., March 28, 1978, copy available from chief of information, Navy Department.

19. For the year 2000, indicative of the span of the study. An unclassified summary of Sea Plan 2000 was provided the author.

Chapter Nine

1. For a thought-provoking discussion of Gorshkov's bureaucratic victories in the Byzantine environment of the Kremlin, see Lieutenant Commander Kenneth R. McGruther, *The Evolving Soviet Navy* (Washington, D.C.: Government Printing Office, 1978), pp. 75–82.

2. The Soviets first tested shipboard missiles in 1955. On October 4, 1957, they launched *Sputnik* into global orbit, thus spurring the United States to step up its own aerospace program. (See McGruther, *The Evolving Soviet Navy*, p. 18.)

3. Commander Robert W. Herrick, *Soviet Naval Strategy* (Annapolis: U.S. Naval Institute, 1968), pp. 68–69.

4. U.S., Navy Department, *Understanding Soviet Naval Developments* (Washington, D.C.: Government Printing Office, 1978), p. 4.

5. Nikita Khrushchev, *Khrushchev Remembers*, tr. and ed. Strobe Talbott (Boston: Little, Brown, 1974), pp. 30–33.

6. Herrick, *Soviet Naval Strategy*, p. 73.

7. As students of naval history will recognize, Rear Admiral Mahan's writings on sea power at the turn of the century aroused worldwide attention. His most famous work is *The Influence of Sea Power upon History, 1660–1783*, (Boston, 1890).

8. Published by the Naval Institute Press, Annapolis. The original Russian version was published in Moscow in 1976.

9. S. G. Gorshkov, *The Sea Power of the State* (Annapolis: Naval Institute Press, 1979), p. 221.

10. Ibid., p. 217.

11. Ibid., p. 221.

12. John J. Herzog, "Perspectives on Soviet-Naval Development: A Navy to Match National Purposes," in Paul J. Murphy, ed., *Naval Power and Soviet Policy*, Studies in Communist Affairs, vol. 2 (Washington, D.C.: Government Printing Office, 1978), p. 51.

13. Ibid., p. 55.

14. Beginning in the 1970s, the 41 *Polaris* boats were fitted with a new long-range missile. Upon conversion they were termed *Poseidon* boats.

15. For an assessment of the Soviet fleet, see Admiral Stansfield Turner, "The Naval Balance: Not Just a Numbers Game," *Foreign Affairs*, January 1977, pp. 339–54.

16. Siegfried Breyer and Norman Polmar, *Guide to the Soviet Navy* (Annapolis: U.S. Naval Institute, 1977), pp. 115–17. The keels of these two ships were laid in 1963 and 1964, respectively.

17. Herzog, "Perspectives on Soviet Naval Development," p. 50.

18. The Soviets classified the *Kiev* class an ASW type, presumably as a means of evading the restrictions of the Montreux Convention of 1936, which forbids the use of aircraft by warships in transiting the Dardanelles. The Bosporus and Dardanelles, the straits connecting the Black Sea with the Mediterranean, are of immense strategic value to the Soviet Navy.

19. Statement of Rear Admiral Sumner Shapiro to Sea Power Subcommittee of the House Armed Services Committee, February 14, 1979, copy provided by the Navy Department.

20. On March 15, 1979, Charles Corddry, the defense correspondent for the *Baltimore*

Sun, reported that Washington had learned of a 60,000-ton Soviet naval ship under construction near Archangel. There was a strong possibility that the ship was a nuclear-powered carrier.

21. Herzog, "Perspectives on Soviet Naval Development," pp. 43—44.

22. The Soviet Union and India signed a twenty-year treaty of friendship on August 9, 1971. (This move came shortly after President Nixon had arranged for his surprising visit to Peking, in February 1972). Both nations found common ground in their fear of the Chinese menace.

23. James D. Theberge, *The Soviet Presence in Latin America* (New York: Crane, Russak, 1974). p. 68; and Michael MccGwire, ed., *Soviet Naval Development: Capability and Context* (New York: Praeger, 1973), pp. 397—99.

24. The deputy chief of the Soviet naval staff visited Cuba in November 1969, presumably to inspect possible naval base facilities.

25. Henry Kissinger, *The White House Years* (Boston: Little, Brown, 1979), pp. 635—52, gives a detailed account.

26. Hannes Adomeit, *Soviet Risk-Taking and Crisis Behaviour,* Adelphi Papers, no. 101 (London: International Institute for Strategic Studies, 1973), pp. 14—15.

27. Testimony before a congressional panel, February 22, 1979. Copy available from the chief of information, Navy Department.

28. Interestingly, Soviet warships, which were assigned to the operation for the Cuban-assisted takeover of Angola by Communists, anchored in Guinean ports for a week before the operation began. Apparently Moscow was testing U.S. reaction. When no overt U.S. opposition appeared likely, the operation proceeded according to plan.

29. U.S., Navy Department, *Understanding Soviet Naval Developments,* (Washington, D.C., 1978), pp. 22—23.

30. Norman Polmar, *The Ships and Aircraft of the U.S. Fleet,* 11th ed., (Annapolis: Naval Institute Press, 1978).

31. Address at Naval War College, Newport, R.I., May 17, 1979. Hayward's theme was that the U.S. Navy must stay ahead of the Soviets if it was to remain capable of carrying out its assigned tasks.

32. In July 1903 the U.S. government concluded a treaty with Cuba that in essence gave the naval base to the United States in perpetuity.

33. *San Francisco Examiner,* September 9, 1979, p. 1.

34. *Newsweek,* February 19, 1979, p. 19.

35. *Washington Post,* May 9, 1979, p. 22

36. *U.S. News and World Report,* May 9, 1979, p. 22.

37. *Time,* October 22, 1979, p. 46.

38. *San Francisco Chronicle,* October 18, 1979, p. 17. The Atlantic Fleet schedules an annual amphibious exercise in the Caribbean for the fleet's Marine forces, usually on Puerto Rican shores.

39. President Carter's speech, October 1, 1979, available from the Department of State's Bureau of Public Affairs.

40. *U.S. News and World Report,* October 15, 1979, p. 24.

41. "Troubled Waters," *Time,* October 22, 1979, p. 45.

42. *U.S. News and World Report,* October 15, 1979, p. 24, contains remarks by Nunn and Zorinsky.

43. Ibid.

44. Les Aspin, "Putting Soviet Power in Perspective," *AEI Defense Review* 2, no. 3 (1978): 2–14.

45. Jack L. Kemp, "The Soviet Threat," *AEI Defense Review* 2, no. 3 (1978): 15–36.

46. Ibid., p. 15, quoting Winston Churchill, 1942.

47. See Gerald E. Miller, "An Evaluation of the Soviet Navy," in Grayson Kirk and Nils H. Wessell, eds., *The Soviet Threat: Myths and Realities* (New York: Academy of Political Science, 1978), pp. 47–56.

48. Ibid., p. 48.

49. Soviet cruise missiles weighed too much to be carried as reloads by some ships because of the heavy fuel load necessary for long range (see Kemp, "The Soviet Threat," p. 32).

50. *Janes Fighting Ships*, 1978–1979, p. 129.

51. Vice Admiral James B. Stockdale, "Taking Stock," *Naval War College Review*, July/August 1979, p. 3.

52. For an account of the U.S. attitude toward Japan before Pearl Harbor, see Paul B. Ryan, "How Young We Were," *Naval Institute Proceedings*, December 1968, pp. 27–36.

53. W. D. Puleston, *The Armed Forces of the Pacific* (New Haven, Conn.: Yale University Press, 1941).

54. Foreign Broadcast Information Service, *Daily Report—Soviet Union* 3, no. 003, pp. A-3–A-4.

Chapter Ten

1. *Baltimore Sun*, August 15, 1979, quoted in the American Enterprise Institute *News Digest*, August 16, 1979.

2. *Aviation Week and Space Technology*, May 14, 1979, p. 16.

3. *San Francisco Chronicle*, September 3, 1979, p. 9.

4. The first *Trident*, the USS *Ohio*, was scheduled for delivery by the shipbuilder in November 1980. The basic *Trident* construction rate in 1980 was three ships every two years. On January 31, 1980, the CNO announced that two of the oldest *Polaris* submarines were awaiting inactivation. Two days before, Defense Secretary Brown had informed the Congress that the ten oldest *Polaris* boats would be retired (five in fiscal year 1980 and five in 1981). The remaining 31 *Poseidon* submarines were converted to carry more lethal missiles, thus permitting them to operate in much larger patrol areas and increasing their survivability.

5. For a professional naval analysis of the Indian Ocean as a strategic area, see Commander Alan F. Masters, USN, "A U.S. Strategy for the Indian Ocean Area in the 1970s" (Ph.D. diss., U.S. Naval War College and George Washington University, 1972).

6. Hanson W. Baldwin, *Strategy for Tomorrow* (New York: Harper and Row, 1970), p. 227.

7. U.S., Department of Defense, *Annual Report, Fiscal Year 1979*, p. 92.

8. U.S., Department of Defense, *Annual Report, Fiscal Year 1980*, p. 99.

9. Ibid.

10. P. M. Dadant, "Shrinking International Airspace as a Problem for Future Air Movements," (Santa Monica, Calif.: Rand Corp., 1978), p. v; cited by Vice Admiral

William J. Crowe, USN, "The Persian Gulf: Central or Peripheral to United States Strategy," *Naval Institute Proceedings,* May 1978, p. 209.

11. "If something can go wrong, then some person, inadvertently, will find a way to cause it to go wrong." In this case, it was suspected that a careless computer programmer was at fault.

12. *Wall Street Journal,* March 26, 1979, p. 1.

13. Richard J. Levine, "The Outlook," *Wall Street Journal,* March 26, 1979, p. 1.

14. See *New York Times,* March 1, 1979, p. 14; March 9, 1979, p. 5; March 14, 1979, p. 10.

15. On December 16, 1971, the U.N. General Assembly adopted a "Declaration of the Indian Ocean as a Zone of Peace." The USSR and the United States abstained. Congressional opposition to expansion of U.S. naval facilities at Diego Garcia was apparent in 1975—1976 when the question of allocating $13.8 million was frozen until April 1976.

16. Foreign Broadcast Information Service, *Daily Report—Soviet Union,* 3, no. 052, pp. F-12—F-13, J-6—J-7.

17. U.S., Navy Department, *Understanding Soviet Naval Developments* (Washington, D.C., 1978), p. 14.

18. Tan Su-cheng, *The Expansion of Soviet Sea Power and the Security of Asia* (Taipei: Asia and the World Forum, 1977), pp. 59—63.

19. In January 1980 the press reported a force that varied from 20 to 24 ships, including two carriers. As for the zone of peace, after the Afghanistan invasion the Carter administration dropped diplomatic talks with Moscow on a proposal to limit naval ships and bases in the Indian Ocean (*U.S. News and World Report,* January 28, 1980, p. 26).

20. U.S., Department of Defense, *Annual Report, Fiscal Year 1980,* p. 98, p. 100.

21. *Wings of Gold* (quarterly journal of the Association of Naval Aviation), Winter 1979, pp. 13—15.

22. U.S., Department of Defense, *Annual Report, Fiscal Year 1980,* p. 17.

23. Ibid.

24. Arthur J. Alexander, Abraham S. Becker, and William J. Hoehn, Jr., "The Significance of Divergent U.S.-U.S.S.R. Military Expenditures," U.S. Air Force study prepared by the RAND Corp., February 1979, pp. 55—56.

25. "U.S. Power and Mideast Oil," *U.S. News and World Report,* July 30, 1979, pp. 27—29.

26. U.S., Department of Defense, *Annual Report, Fiscal Year 1981,* pp. 9—10, 169, 183—85.

27. Press reports revealed that Soviet planes had airlifted some three thousand Cuban troops and 350 Soviet advisors to South Yemen for a war by proxy similar to those engineered in Angola and Ethiopia.

28. Militants stormed the Embassy in Iran on February 14, 1979. Nineteen U.S. Marine guards fought with tear gas and shotguns for an hour before surrendering to the mob. The Americans were released after two hours, and two days later Washington recognized the revolutionary regime.

29. Jack Nelson and Robert C. Toth, "Doomsday Talk in Washington," *San Francisco Chronicle,* January 19, 1980, pp. 1, 8.

30. Ibid.

31. *Newsweek,* January 21, 1980, p. 22.

32. The Central Treaty Organization, comprising Turkey, Iran, Pakistan, and Britain, with the United States bound to each member by bilateral pacts, was set up in 1959 as a wall against communist aggression. The South East Treaty Organization included the United States, Britain, France, Australia, New Zealand, the Philippines, Thailand, and Pakistan. Established in 1954, it called on its members to ''consult immediately'' in time of crisis.

33. The two carrier groups and the Navy's Middle East Force totaled some twenty ships and over 16,000 officers and men. The Seventh Fleet's normal strength (from which the two battle groups were drawn) averaged only 22,000 men in normal times. (*U.S. News and World Report,* December 31, 1979, p. 47.) Brown's visit to China had been planned for some weeks and was not a result of the Afghanistan crisis.

34. Moslems in the Soviet Union comprised some 40 percent of the population. In 1979 there was no evidence that this segment of the Soviet population might rise up against their Kremlin masters in a jihad.

35. Vice Admiral William J. Crowe, USN, ''The Persian Gulf: Central or Peripheral to United States Strategy,'' *Naval Institute Proceedings,* May 1978, p. 202.

36. In 1975, Moscow owed $46 billion to foreign lenders (Vice Admiral W. J. Crowe in a speech at the Naval War College, March 29, 1978).

37. United Press International dispatch, March 4, 1980.

Chapter Eleven

1. A phrase used by Hayward in a speech at Dallas, Texas, April 19, 1979.

2. The result of this poll of 1,595 adults was published in the *Stanford Daily,* January 23, 1980, p. 10. Of the remaining respondents, 21 percent advocated keeping the current level and 8 percent ''did not know.''

3. *San Francisco Chronicle,* January 23, 1980, p. 12.

4. Admiral Thomas B. Hayward, ''The Future of U.S. Sea Power,'' *Naval Institute Proceedings,* May 1979, p. 67.

5. Survey published in *Public Opinion,* March/April 1978, p. 14.

6. *New York Times,* July 12, 1978.

7. *San Francisco Examiner,* January 27, 1980, p. 10A.

8. *Detroit News,* January 13, 1980. Coincidentally, a Pentagon spokesman had been negotiating for in-and-out ship and aircraft operations with the governments of Oman, Somalia, and Kenya.

9. Vice Admiral Gerald E. Miller, ''Tomorrow's Navy,'' *Wings of Gold,* Winter 1979.

10. Thomas H. Moorer, ''Countering Soviet Global Aims,'' *New York Times,* June 8, 1978, p. 27.

11. *U.S. News and World Report,* March 17, 1980, p. 6.

12. Robert C. Miller, ''Retiring Pacific Commander Warns Soviet Buildup Is Threat,'' *Houston Post,* December 2, 1979; reprinted in American Enterprise Institute *News Digest,* December 11, 1979.

13. Paul H. Nitze, Leonard Sullivan, Jr., and Atlantic Council Working Group, *Securing the Seas: The Soviet Naval Challenge and Western Alliance Options,* Atlantic Council Policy Study (Boulder, Colo.: Westview Press, 1979), pp. 97, 102.

14. For a discussion of the Soviet "learning experience" in gunboat or coercive diplomacy, see Bradford Dismukes and James M. McConnell, eds., *Soviet Naval Diplomacy* (New York: Pergamon Press, 1979), particularly chap. 8, "The Rules of the Game," by James M. McConnell.

15. On January 29, 1980, President Carter told journalists at the White House, "I don't think it would be accurate for me to claim that at this time or in the future we expect to have enough military strength and enough military presence there [in the Persian Gulf] to defend the region unilaterally" (*San Francisco Chronicle*, February 1, 1980, p. 19).

16. According to Hayward, just before the Battle of Midway, Admiral Chester Nimitz, the commander-in-chief of the Pacific Fleet, enjoined the U.S. fleet commander, Admiral Raymond Spruance, to observe this principle. Spruance, although outnumbered, proceeded to win this most critical battle of the war, a turning point in the Pacific campaign.

17. Zumwalt's proposals appear in his article, "Total Force," *Naval Institute Proceedings*, May 1979, pp. 88–107.

18. *All Hands* (Navy Department), March 1979, pp. 4–5.

19. Quoted in *Pittsburgh Press*, January 17, 1980; reprinted in American Enterprise Institute's *News Digest*, January 23, 1980.

20. *New York Times*, January 24, 1980, pp. 1, 14.

21. Senators Garn and Nunn appeared on a CBS-TV program on January 24, 1980.

22. *San Francisco Chronicle*, February 1, 1980, p. 19.

23. See Moorer, "Countering Soviet Global Aims."

24. Paul W. McCracken, "National Defense Is Affordable," *Wall Street Journal*, January 28, 1980, p. 16.

25. Editorial, *Wall Street Journal*, January 17, 1980.

26. This information came from a very high source in the Navy Department.

27. George F. Will, "Running out of Choices," *Newsweek*, February 4, 1980, p. 90.

28. U.S. Department of Defense, *Annual Report, Fiscal Year 1981*, p. 3.

29. For a startling refutation of President Carter's recommended defense budget by the Joint Chiefs of Staff before a congressional panel, see Richard Halloran, "Joint Chiefs Dissent on Carter-Brown Military Budget," *New York Times*, May 30, 1980, p. D14. Admiral James D. Watkins, the Navy's vice-chief of naval operations, representing Admiral Thomas B. Hayward, testified that the administration's desired budget was insufficient to support the Navy's three-ocean fleet. General Robert Barrow, commandant of the Marine Corps, when queried if the budget was "adequate" as announced by the president (who also claimed that "it's approved by the Joint Chiefs of Staff"), replied bluntly: "In a word, no." (See "Guns vs. Butter: Carter Wants Both," *U.S. News and World Report*, June 9, 1980, p. 11; and *Wall Street Journal*, May 28, 1980, p. 24, and June 2, 1980, p. 22.)

30. On June 12, 1980 the Congress voted approval of a military spending figure for fiscal year 1981 of $153.7 billion. But it reduced future defense outlays by $800 million. This latter amount would be allotted to domestic social programs.

Selected Bibliography

General Works

Abel, Elie. *The Missile Crisis*. Philadelphia: J. B. Lippincott, 1966.

Armbrister, Trevor. *A Matter of Accountability*. New York: Coward-McCann, 1970.

Baldwin, Hanson W. *Strategy for Tomorrow*. New York: Harper and Row, 1970.

Blakey, Scott. *Prisoner at War: The Survival of Commander Richard A. Stratton*. New York: Doubleday, Anchor Press, 1978.

Cagle, Malcolm W., and Frank A. Manson. *The Sea War in Korea*. Annapolis: Naval Institute Press, 1957.

Detzer, David. *The Brink*. New York: Crowell, 1979.

Enthoven, Alain C., and F. Wayne Smith. *How Much Is Enough?* New York: Harper and Row, 1971.

Gorshkov, Sergei G. *Red Star Rising at Sea*. Translated by Theodore A. Neely, Jr.; edited by Herbert Preston. Annapolis: Naval Institute Press, 1974.

———. *The Sea Power of the State*. Annapolis: Naval Institute Press, 1979.

Goulding, Phil G. *Confirm or Deny*. New York: Harper and Row, 1970.

Halberstam, David. *The Best and the Brightest*. New York: Random House, 1972.

Hooper, Edwin B., Dean C. Allard, and Oscar P. Fitzgerald. *The United States Navy and the Vietnam Conflict*. Vol. 1. Washington, D.C.: Government Printing Office, 1976.

Howe, Jonathan Trumbull. *Multicrises, Sea Power and Global Politics in the Missile Age*. Cambridge, Mass.: M.I.T. Press, 1971.

Jurika, Stephen, Jr., ed. *From Pearl Harbor to Vietnam: The Memoirs of Admiral Arthur W. Radford*. Stanford: Hoover Institution Press, 1980.

Kaufmann, William W. *The McNamara Strategy*. New York: Harper and Row, 1964.

Khrushchev, Nikita. *Khrushchev Remembers*. Translated and edited by Strobe Talbot. Boston: Little, Brown, 1974.

Kissinger, Henry. *The White House Years*. Boston: Little, Brown, 1979.

Krock, Arthur. *In the Nation, 1932–1966*. New York: McGraw-Hill, 1967.

Lazo, Mario. *Dagger in the Heart: American Foreign Policy Failures in Cuba*. New York: Twin Circle Publishing Co., 1968.

Luttwak, Edward N. *The Political Uses of Sea Power*. Baltimore: Johns Hopkins University Press, 1974.

Millis, Walter, ed., with the collaboration of E. S. Duffield. *The Forrestal Diaries*. New York: Viking Press, 1951.

Morison, Samuel E. *The History of United States Naval Operations in World War II*, vol. 1, *The Battle of the Atlantic*; vol. 3, *The Rising Sun in the Pacific, 1931–April 1942*. Boston: Little, Brown, 1947, 1950.

Mosley, Leonard. *Dulles*. London: Hodder and Stoughton, 1978.

Nathan, James A., and James K. Oliver. *The Future of United States Naval Power*. Bloomington: Indiana University Press, 1979.

Nitze, Paul H., Leonard Sullivan, Jr., and Atlantic Council Working Group. *Securing the Seas: The Soviet Naval Challenge and Western Alliance Options*. Atlantic Council Policy Study. Boulder, Colo.: Westview Press, 1979.

Potter, E. B. *Nimitz*. Annapolis: Naval Institute Press, 1976.

Puleston, W. D. *The Armed Forces of the Pacific*. New Haven, Conn.: Yale University Press, 1941.

Reynolds, Clark G. *Command of the Sea: The History and Strategy of Maritime Empires*. New York: William Morrow and Co., 1974.

Roherty, James S. *Decisions of Robert S. McNamara*. Coral Gables, Fla.: University of Miami Press, 1970.

Schlesinger, Arthur M., Jr. *A Thousand Days*. Boston: Houghton Mifflin Co., 1965.

Sharp, U. S. Grant. *Strategy for Defeat: Vietnam in Retrospect*. San Rafael, Calif.: Presidio Press, 1978.

Singer, J. D., and Melvin Small. *The Wages of War*. New York: Wiley, 1972.

Sorensen, Theodore. *Kennedy*. New York: Harper and Row, 1965.

Wyden, Peter. *Bay of Pigs: The Untold Story*. New York: Simon and Schuster, 1979.

Zumwalt, Elmo R., Jr. *On Watch*. New York: New York Times Book Co., Quadrangle, 1976.

Monographs and Special Studies

Adomeit, Hannes. *Soviet Risk-Taking and Crisis Behaviour*. Adelphi Papers, no. 101. London: International Institute for Strategic Studies, 1973.

Bagley, Worth H. *Sea Power and Western Security: The Next Decade*. Adelphi Papers, no. 139. London: International Institute for Strategic Studies, 1977.

Breyer, Siegfried, and Norman Polmar. *Guide to the Soviet Navy*. Annapolis: U.S. Naval Institute, 1977.

Coletta, Paolo, ed. *The American Secretaries of the Navy*. Annapolis: Naval Institute Press, 1980.

Dismukes, Bradford, and James M. McConnell, eds. *Soviet Naval Diplomacy*. New York: Pergamon Press, 1979.

Dornan, James E., ed. *United States National Security Policy in the Decade Ahead*. New York: Crane, Russak, 1978.

Haselkorn, Avigdor. *The Evolution of Soviet Security Strategy*. New York: Crane, Russak, 1978.

Herrick, Robert W. *Soviet Naval Strategy*. Annapolis: U.S. Naval Institute, 1968.

Hoeber, Francis P., and William Schneider, Jr. *Arms, Men and Military Budgets: Issues for Fiscal Year 1977*. New York: Crane, Russak, 1976.

Hooper, Edwin B. *The Navy Department: Evolution and Fragmentation*. Washington, D.C.: Naval Historical Foundation, 1978.

MccGwire, Michael, ed. *Soviet Naval Developments: Capability and Context*. New York: Praeger, 1973.

McGruther, Kenneth R. *The Evolving Soviet Navy*. Washington, D.C.: Government Printing Office, 1978.

Murphy, Paul J., ed. *Naval Power in Soviet Policy*. Washington, D.C.: Government Printing Office, 1978.

Osgood, Robert E. *Limited War: The Challenge to American Security*. Chicago: University of Chicago Press, 1957.

Pechman, Joseph A., ed. *Setting National Priorities: The 1979 Budget*. Washington, D.C.: Brookings Institution, 1978.

———. *Setting National Priorities: The 1980 Budget*. Washington, D.C.: Brookings Institution, 1979.

Polmar, Norman. *The Ships and Aircraft of the U.S. Fleet*, 11th ed. Annapolis: Naval Institute Press, 1978.

———. *Soviet Naval Power, Challenge for the 1970's*. New York: Crane, Russak, 1974.

Quester, George H., ed. *Sea Power in the 1970s*. New York: Dunellen Publishing Co., 1975.

Schneider, William, and Francis P. Hoeber, eds. *Arms, Men, and Military Budgets: Issues for Fiscal Year 1977*. New York: Crane, Russak, 1976.

Schratz, Paul R., ed. *Evolution of the American Military Establishment Since World War II*. Lexington, Va.: George C. Marshall Research Foundation, 1978.

Tan, Su-cheng. *The Expansion of Soviet Sea Power and the Security of Asia*. Taipei: Asia and the World Forum, 1977.

Theberge, James D. *The Soviet Presence in Latin America*. New York: Crane, Russak, 1974.

U.S., Department of Defense. *United States and Vietnam Relations, 1945 – 1967*. Washington, D.C.: Government Printing Office, 1971.

———. Navy Department. *Keeping the Peace*. Washington, D.C.: Government Printing Office, 1966.

———. ———. *Understanding Soviet Naval Developments*. Washington, D.C.: Government Printing Office, 1978.

Van Vleet, Clarke, Lee M. Pearson, and Adrian O. Van Wyen. *United States Naval Aviation, 1910 – 1970*. Washington, D.C.: Government Printing Office, 1970.

Articles

Adelman, Kenneth L. "West's Superiority, Even If True, Is It Secure?" *Wall Street Journal*, October 5, 1978, p. 20.

Aspin, Les. "Putting Soviet Power in Perspective." *AEI Defense Review* 2, no. 3 (1978): 2 – 14.

Beaver, Roy L. "An Absence of Accountability." *Naval Institute Proceedings*, January 1976, pp. 18 – 23.

Cagle, Malcolm W. "Task Force 77 in Action Off Vietnam." *Naval Institute Proceedings*, May 1972, pp. 66 – 109.

Conquest, Robert. "The Rules of the Game: Why the West Is Down and the East Is Up." In James E. Dornin, ed., *United States National Security in the Decade Ahead*. New York: Crane, Russak, 1978, pp. 99–120.

Crowe, William J. "The Persian Gulf: Central or Peripheral to United States Strategy." *Naval Institute Proceedings*, May 1978, pp. 184–209.

Hayward, John T. "Comment and Discussion: High-Low." *Naval Institute Proceedings*, August 1976, pp. 71–72.

Hayward, Thomas B. "The Future of U.S. Sea Power." *Naval Institute Proceedings*, May 1979, pp. 66–71.

Herzog, John J. "Perspectives on Soviet Naval Development: A Navy to Match National Purposes." In Paul J. Murphy, ed., *Naval Power and Soviet Policy*. Studies in Communist Affairs, vol. 2. Washington, D.C.: U.S. Air Force, 1978, pp. 37–55.

Hughes, Wayne P. "Vietnam: Winnable War?" *Naval Institute Proceedings*, July 1977, pp. 60–65.

Kemp, Jack L. "The Soviet Threat." *AEI Defense Review* 2, no. 3 (1978): 15–36.

Kidd, Isaac. "View from the Bridge of the Sixth Fleet Flagship." *Naval Institute Proceedings*, February 1972, pp. 18–29.

Korb, Lawrence J. "The Defense Budget and Detente." *Naval War College Review*, Summer 1975, pp. 19–27.

———. "The Erosion of American Naval Preeminence, 1962–1978." In Kenneth J. Hagan, ed., *Peace and War: Interpretations of American Naval History*. Westport, Conn.: Greenwood, 1978, pp. 327–45.

Krepon, Michael. "A Navy to Match National Purposes." *Foreign Affairs*, January 1977, pp. 355–67.

McConnell, James M. "The Rules of the Game." In Bradford Dismukes and James M. McConnell, eds., *Soviet Naval Diplomacy*. New York: Pergamon Press, 1979, pp. 240–80.

McCracken, Paul W. "National Defense Is Affordable," *Wall Street Journal*, January 28, 1980, p. 16.

Miller, Gerald E. "An Evaluation of the Soviet Navy." In Grayson Kirk and Nils H. Wessell, eds., *The Soviet Threat: Myths and Realities*. New York: Academy of Political Science, 1978, pp. 47–56.

———. "High-Low." *Naval Institute Proceedings*, December 1976, pp. 79–85.

———. "Tomorrow's Navy." *Wings of Gold*, Winter 1979, pp. 13–15.

Moorer, Thomas H. "Countering Soviet Global Arms." *New York Times*, June 8, 1978, p. 27.

Ryan, Paul B. "How Young We Were." *Naval Institute Proceedings*, December 1968, pp. 27–36.

———. "USS *Constellation* Flareup: Was It Mutiny?" *Naval Institute Proceedings*, January 1976, pp. 46–53.

Spence, Jack. "Naval Armaments in the Indian Ocean." In George H. Quester, ed., *Sea Power in the 1970s*. New York: Kennikat, 1975, pp. 117–57.

Stockdale, James B. "Taking Stock." *Naval War College Review*, July/August 1979, pp. 1–3.

Turner, Stansfield. "The Naval Balance: Not Just a Numbers Game." *Foreign Affairs*, January 1977, pp. 339–54.

Warnke, Paul C. "Apes on a Treadmill." *Foreign Policy,* Spring 1975, pp. 12–29.

Westmoreland, William C. "Vietnam in Perspective." *The Retired Officer,* October 1978, p. 22.

Zumwalt, Elmo R., Jr. "Total Force." *Naval Institute Proceedings,* May 1979, pp. 88–107.

Government Documents

Alexander, Arthur J., Abraham S. Becker, and William E. Hoehn, Jr. "The Significance of Divergent U.S.-U.S.S.R. Military Expenditures." U.S. Air Force study prepared by the RAND Corp., N-1000-AF, February 1979.

Center for Naval Analysis. "Annual Report, 1977."

U.S., Congress, Congressional Budget Office. "Planning U.S. General Purpose Forces: The Navy." December 1976.

————, ————, House, Committee on Armed Services. *Report: The Changing Strategic Naval Balance, USSR vs. U.S.A.* 90th Cong., 2d sess., December 1968.

————, ————, ————, ————. *Report: Department of Defense Appropriations Act, 1979.* Report no. 95–1118. 95th Cong., 2d sess., May 6, 1978.

————, ————, ————, ————. *U.S. Navy Analysis of Congressional Budget Office Issue Paper, General Purpose Forces: Navy.* 95th Cong., 1st sess., January 12, 1977.

————, ————, ————, Committee on the Merchant Marine and Fisheries, Subcommittee on the Merchant Marine. *Merchant Marine Misc.,* Part 3. 95th Cong., 2d sess., September 20, 1978.

————, ————, Senate, Committee on the Armed Services, Preparedness Investigating Subcommittee. *Hearings: Air War Against North Vietnam.* 90th Cong., 1st sess., August 9, 10, 16, 25, 1967.

Index

About the Author

Captain Paul B. Ryan, USN (Ret.) was educated at the U.S. Naval Academy, Stanford University (A.M., International Relations), and San Jose State University (M.A., History). He is now a Research Fellow at the Hoover Institution on War, Revolution and Peace at Stanford University. His naval career includes World War II submarine combat patrols, three sea-commands in Asian and Mediterranean waters, two tours in the Pentagon, and duty as Naval Attache in pre-Castro Cuba and, later, Canada. He is the author of *The Panama Canal Controversy* (Hoover Press, 1977) and coauthor with Thomas A. Bailey of *The Lusitania Disaster* and *Hitler vs. Roosevelt: The Undeclared Naval War*.

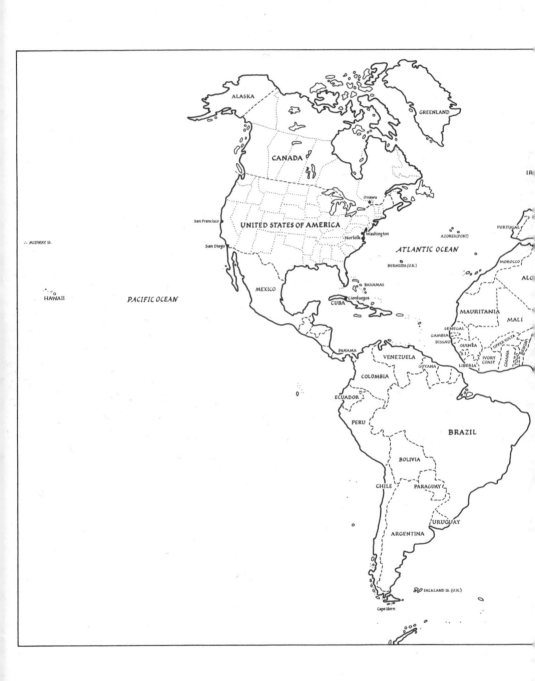